COLOUR ENCYCLOPEDIA
OF MUSICAL INSTRUMENTS

Colour Encyclopedia

of Musical Instruments

by Alexander Buchner

Translated by Simon Pellar, B. A.

HAMLYN

London · New York · Sydney · Toronto

LIST OF INSTITUTIONS AND COLLECTIONS

Amsterdam, Collection of J. Kunst 304 Ankara, Archeological Museum 26 Antwerp, Musée Royal des Beaux-Arts Plaatsnijderstraat 2, 81—82 Bagdad, Iraq Museum 25 Berlin, Staatliches Institut für Musikforschung, Musikinstrumenten Sammlung 89, 116 Staatliche Museen, Vorderasiatische Abteilung 24 Brno, Moravské Muzeum 12, 13 Nová radnice 223—224 Brunswick, Herzog Anton Ulrich Museum 126 Brussels, Musée instrumental du Conservatoire Royal de Musique 166, 167 Budapest, Magyar Nemzeti Múzeum 104, 171 Nemzeti képtár 129 Cairo, Egyptian Museum 30 Cambridge, St. John College 60 Colmar, Musée d'Unterlinden 112 Copenhagen, Nationalmuseet 14—16 Darien, Mechanical Music Center 392 Florence, Accademia 87 Frederiksborg, Det Nationalhistoriske Museum 95 Fuldatal, Mechanisches Musik Museum 396 The Haag, Haags Gemeentemuseum 113—114 Heidelberg, Universitätsbibliothek 71 Koburg, Gymnasium Casimirianum 83 Křivoklát, Zámecká knihovna 59 Leningrad, Institut teatra, muzyki i kinematografii 10, 108, 130, 140, 146—147, 149, 150, 164, 178, 185, 232, 266, 269, 336, 337, 349, 350, 355, 356, 358, 403 Litoměřice, Okresní archív 99 London, British Museum 22, 45, Private Collection 152—153, Horniman Museum 106, 120, 132—133, 144—145, 162, 163, 166, National Gallery 1, Royal Academy 188, W. E. Hill & Sons 176—177 Madrid, El Escorial 61—64, Museo del Prado 117 Markneukirchen, Musikinstrumenten-Museum 131, 137, 157, 193, 195, 201, 205, 209, 216, 260, 280, 292, 301, 361, 362, 376, 377, 389, 390 Milano, Museo degli Strumenti Musicali, Castello Sforzesco 107, 118—119 Modene, Galleria e Museo Estense 181—182 Moscow, Muzej imeni A. S. Pushkina 49, 158, Gossudarstvennyj tsentralnyj muzej muzykalnoj kultury imeni M. I. Glinki 194, 254, 261, 262, 281, 290, 291, 296, 308, 354 Munich, Antikensammlungen 37, Bayerisches Museum 90, Müncher Stadtmuseum, Musikinstrumentensammlung 218, Staatliche Bibliothek 53—54 Naples, Biblioteca Nazionale 70, Museo Nazionale 40, 41, 46, 50, 51, 52 New Delhi, National Collection 246 New York, Metropolitan Museum of Art 103, 122, 136, 217, 230 North Carolina, Museum of Art 121 Olomouc, Universitní knihovna 85 Oxford, Ashmolean Museum 35, 124—125 Paris, Bibliothèque Nationale 56, Musée Instrumental du Conservatoire 148, 170, 172, Musée National du Louvre 20, 21, 27, 159 Péruggia, Museo Archeologico 42 Prague, Hradní poklad 57, Kapitulní knihovna 73, Muzeum hl. města Prahy 210, Národní galerie 109, Národní muzeum — Historické muzeum 9, 19, 36, Knihovna Národního muzea 58, 74, Muzeum české hudby 127—128, 139, 142—143, 154—155, 160, 161, 168—169, 173, 174, 175, 179, 183—184, 189—192, 391, 393, Náprstkovo Muzeum 247, 250—253, 268, 272—274, 278, 279, 293, 297, 303, 306, 318—320, Národní technické muzeum 384, Uměleckoprůmyslové muzeum 134, 135, Univerzitní knihovna 75—80, 88, Private Collection 96, 202, 385—387 Rotterdam, Museum Voorland en Volkenkunde 305 Utrecht, Museum van Speeldoos tot Pierement 397 Versailles, Musée National de Versailles et des Trianons 165 Vienna, Kunsthistorisches Museum 86, 92, 93, 97—98, 101—102, 105, 110, 111, 115, 123, 151, 156, 394—395 Wroclaw, Biblioteka Uniwersytecka 65—68 Wuppertal, Museum Mechanischer Musikinstrumente 398

LIST OF PHOTOGRAPHERS AND OWNERS OF THE PHOTOGRAPHS

ACME, Woodford 407 Agence Hoa-Qui, Paris 321, 324 Antikensammlungen, Munich 37 Archeological Museum, Ankara 26 Arizona Highways 317 Ashmolean Museum, Oxford 124—125 Association for International Cultural Relations, Tokyo 284—289, 294 Bachet Frères, Paris 404, 405 Bärenreiter-Verlag, Kassel 188 Bayerisches Nationalmuseum, Munich 90 Biblioteca Nazionale, Naples 70 Bibliothèque Nationale, Paris 56 Biblioteka Uniwersytecka, Wroclaw 65—68 Bonnaud L., Limoges 330 Brandt A. 95 British Museum, London 22, 45 Brückner, Koburg 83 Büchner A. 9, 10, 12, 13, 16—19, 23, 28, 29, 32, 34, 35, 36, 39, 41—44, 47, 49, 55, 58, 59, 61—64, 71, 74—80, 84, 85, 88, 94, 96, 99, 100, 106, 108, 109, 111, 120, 127, 128, 130—135, 139, 140, 142—147, 149, 150, 157, 158, 160, 161, 162, 164, 166—169, 173—180, 183—185, 187, 189—192, 194—199, 202, 204, 206—214, 220, 221, 225, 226, 229, 231, 232, 239, 241, 246, 247, 250—254, 261, 262, 265—270, 272—283, 290—293, 296—298, 300, 302, 303, 308, 309, 310, 312, 313, 318—320, 322, 327, 329, 335—338, 342, 346—351, 354—360, 362—366, 368, 372—377, 379, 380, 382, 385—387, 389, 390, 396, 399, 400, 403, 406 Československé hudební nástroje, Hradec Králové 235 Cooper A. G., London 152, 153 Dabac T., Zagreb 367 Daedalus Magazine, Dialogue vol.3 413 Danielou A., Berlin 295, 299 Edgerton H. E., New York 392 Egyptian Museum, Cairo 30 Ehm J., Prague 384, 391, 393 Galleria e Museo Estense, Modena 181, 182 Groth I. Kimball 307 Guillemin G., Limoges 381 Hanzelka J.—Zikmund M., Prague 311, 314, 316 Herschtritt L., Paris 323 Herzog Anton Ulrich Museum, Brunswick 126 Holics G., Budapest 104, 171, 215 Holman F., Hradec Králové 4, 219, 222, 228, 233, 234, 236—238, 240, 243, 401, 402 Honty T., Prague 57, 306, 371 Hýsek J. E., Prague 141, 223, 224 Illek J—Paul A., Prague 69 IPS, New York 410—412 Jairazbhoy N. A., London 248, 249, 255 Jisl L., Prague 258 Jonsborg K., Oslo 341, 345 Kroh A., Zakopane 353 Kubica V., Prague 328, 331, 333, 339, 340 Kunsthistorisches Museum, Vienna 86, 101, 102, 110, 115, 123, 151, 156, 394, 395 Leach J., London 271, 332, 344, 378 Machulka B., Prague 326 Mellema R. L., Amsterdam 304 Meyer, Vienna 92, 93, 97, 98, 105, 111 Michaud R., Paris 325 Müller E., Kassel 51, 112, 138, 388 Münchner Stadtmuseum, Munich 218 Musée des Instruments Musicaux, Brussels 33, 48 Musée National du Louvre, Paris 20, 21, 27 Musée Royal des Beaux-Arts, Plaatsnijdersstraat 2-B-2000, Antwerp 81—82 Museo degli Strumenti Musicali, Castello Sforzesco, Milano 107, 118, 119 Museo del Prado, Madrid 117 Museo Nazionale, Naples 40, 46, 50, 52 Museum of Art, North Carolina 121 Museum Voorland en Volkenkunde, Rotterdam 305 Musikinstrumente und Kulturwaren, Plauen 242 Nationalmuseet, Copenhagen 14, 15 National Gallery, London 1 National Museum, Athens 38 Nemzeti képtár, Budapest 129 Neruda J., Prague 154, 155, 343 Oorthuys C., Amsterdam 383 Photographs Services, Metropolitan Museum of Art, New York 103, 122, 136, 217, 230 Press Information Bureau, New Delhi 244, 245, 256, 257 Publimages, Paris 148, 170, 172 Rapid, Prague 200, 203 Reinhard K., Berlin 334 Rieger-Kloss, Krnov 227 Sammlung Haags Gemeentemuseum, The Hague 113, 114 Saurin-Sorani, Wuppertal 398 Scala, Florence 87 Seidel G., Leipzig 408, 409 Service de documentation photographique de la Réunion des Musées Nationaux, Paris 159, 165 Sobieski M., Warsau 352 Šolc V., Prague 314 Staatliche Museen, Vorderasiatische Abteilung, Berlin 24 Staatliche Bibliothek, Munich 53, 54 Staatliches Institut für Musikforschung, Musikinstrumenten Sammlung, Berlin 89 Steinkopf W. 116 Stephan S. Adorf 137, 193, 201, 205, 216, 260, 301, 361 St. John College, Cambridge 60 Státní ústav památkové péče, Prague 72, 73 Szabó T., Bratislava 369, 370 Tass, Moscow 259, 263, 264 Vaniš—Sís, Prague 284

Designed and produced by Artia for
The Hamlyn Publishing Group Limited
London · New York · Sydney · Toronto
Astronaut House, Feltham, Middlesex, England

© Copyright Artia, Prague 1980
Text by Alexander Buchner
Translated by Simon Pellar
Drawings by Ivan Kafka
Graphic design by František Prokeš
ISBN 0 600 36421 6

Printed in Czechoslovakia by Svoboda
2/13/02/51-06

CONTENTS

INTRODUCTION 7
Musical Instruments and Their Makers 9
The Sound Generation of Musical Instruments 9
The Classification of Musical Instruments 14

I. THE DEVELOPMENT OF MUSICAL INSTRUMENTS FROM 18
PREHISTORY TO THE PRESENT
Prehistory 18
The Ancient Age 29
Mesopotamia 29
Egypt 36
Judaea 40
Greece 43
Italy 49
The Middle Ages 58
The New Age 81
Renaissance 81
The Baroque and Classical Eras 113
Instruments of the Modern Orchestra 142

II. NATIONAL AND FOLK MUSIC INSTRUMENTS 198
Asia 198
India and Pakistan 198
Mongolia and Soviet Central Asia 207
China, Japan and Korea 213
Southeast Asia 235
The Indonesian Archipelago and Oceania 240
America 246
Latin America 246
North America 255
Africa 257
Arabia 265
Europe 275
Scandinavia 275
The European U.S.S.R. 280
Central Europe 291
Southeastern and Southern Europe 302
Western Europe 308

III. MECHANICAL MUSICAL INSTRUMENTS 312

IV. ELECTRIC AND ELECTRONIC MUSICAL INSTRUMENTS 327

Tuning and Notation of the most common European Musical Instruments 341
Glossary of Terms 344
Important World Collections of Musical Instruments 345
Selected Bibliography 346
Index of Names 347
Index of Topics 349

1 Flutes and a viola da gamba
Robert Tournières (1667 – 1752): *Court Chamber Musicians.*
The two sitting flautists represent Jean and Jacques Hotteterre of the famous family of wind instrument
players and makers, oil, Paris, ca. 1705. The National Gallery, London

INTRODUCTION

MUSICAL INSTRUMENTS AND THEIR MAKERS

Music accompanies us from the cradle to the grave. Apart from the human voice, it is only musical instruments that can express our hopes, aspirations and faith, our joys and sorrows, by means of tones.

The development of music and musical instruments has always been deeply affected by society's level of cultural development and standard of living. Moreover, the musical culture of isolated societies has only very slowly reached the higher stages of development, whereas cultural life and music has developed much more intensively in those places where different civilizations came together to complement, and at the same time conflict with, each other, sometimes creating the right conditions for a new and qualitatively higher level of musical development.

To follow the development of musical instruments is to set out upon a fascinating path of man's ingenuity, which has wound its way gradually up to the extremely complex and intricate electronic instruments of today. But the story of musical instruments is at the same time an exciting voyage through the changing seas of aesthetic feeling and taste. Throughout all ages and cultures the ideal of beauty of perceived sound has undergone great changes, and musical instruments came into favour only to lose it again later. Instruments whose sound at some time was accorded beautiful were produced in many variations and great care was paid to their appearance. Often such instruments achieved so high a level of design or decoration that they can be regarded as genuine works of art. Indeed, such exquisite instruments have always inspired the interest and enthusiasm of musicians, instrument makers, artists, and collectors.

Decoration sometimes predominated over function. Instruments were made of rare woods,

2 18th century musical instrument manufacture
French period engraving

7

3 View of the brass instrument and drum workshop of František Václav Červený in Hradec Králové, Czechoslovakia
Steel engraving, 1889

ivory, and precious metals, adorned with gems, mother-of-pearl, lazulite and other types of material. Even in this, musical instruments were subject to changes of taste so that they became artefacts attesting objectively to changes of style. However, like all artefacts, musical instruments reached perfection only when they were no longer regarded merely as decorative objects or as things used for the production of sound, in other words when beauty and function reached an equilibrium.

To determine when the earliest musical instruments were invented and to trace their later development is not an easy task. The brittle materials of which they were usually made have only rarely been preserved, and the oldest extant musical instruments in the average museum collection hail from the eighteenth century. Earlier instruments have survived only exceptionally and then simply when they were made of age-resistant material. The student of early musical instruments is therefore totally dependent on rare archaeological discoveries or literary or pictorial sources. With archaeological findings and pieces of sculpture, the fact has to be always kept in mind that the fragile parts of the work—and therefore most probably certain significant sections of the instrument—will usually be the most damaged and that even the restorer will sometimes be unable to determine their original shape. Similar caution has to be exerted when dealing with written records and documents since these only rarely give anything more than the name of the instrument, mostly omitting details concerning its appearance or construction.

Therefore the most invaluable source material for early musical instruments are two-dimensional works of art. The author of a written document may have been content with only the name of the instrument but an illustrator is bound to present its image. A drawing or painting,

8

then, may often capture details totally disregarded in a written text. However, caution is the rule here too because not every instrument will have been presented true to life. And it is precisely these sometimes shaky foundations—part guesswork, conjecture and deduction—which form the basis of the organologist's work when tracing the outline, construction, function and tuning of an ancient instrument. Naturally, for the tracing of the development of the classical instruments the researcher has at his or her disposal a host of source material, be it the work of other researchers, visual works of art or the preserved instruments.

While some information on ancient musical instruments can be obtained from literary sources and preserved artefacts, little is generally known about the instrument makers. Historians of music have not so far paid much attention to the history of instrument making so that scattered snippets of information must be searched for painstakingly in source materials relating to the crafts and guilds.

For a long time musicians mostly made their instruments themselves. The change came during the Renaissance, which was characterized by an increased interest in art collecting. Since musical instruments were ranked among works of art, especially when made of rare woods, exquisitely carved or decorated with ivory, gems or horn, they began to be collected, too. In the course of the sixteenth century centres of manufacture were established in Nuremberg (brass, automatophones); Bologna and Venice (lutes); Cremona (violins); Antwerp (keyboard chordophones), and so on. Still later the manufacture of musical instruments extended throughout Europe—in Paris, Füssen, Vienna and Mittenwald to name but a few—and in the 1850's modern industrial methods were finally applied to the means of production.

THE SOUND GENERATION OF MUSICAL INSTRUMENTS

The key to the understanding of the principle on which musical instruments are constructed and of how their sound character is obtained lies in our grasping the fundamental physical phenomena governing the generation of sound. These are the subject of *acoustics* (from the Greek *akuein*—to hear). The term originally covered the science of hearing, i.e. hearing perception, but in a broader sense of the word it also deals with the object of the hearing process, i.e. sounds and tones, and is therefore concerned with musical instruments.

Every musical instrument has a vibrating component, a *vibrator* whose function is to generate

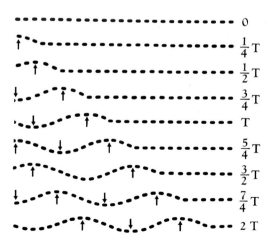

Circular wave generation

9

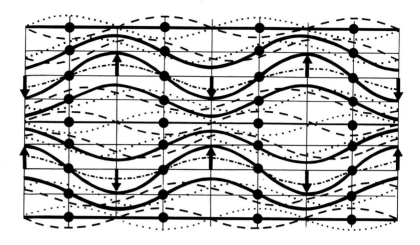

sound waves, and a generating component, or a *generator* whose function is to make the vibrator vibrate. If the sound waves generated by the vibrator lack sufficient amplitude, an amplifying part or *amplifier* will be also added.

The most important part of any musical instrument is the vibrating component or components. These are either solid or elastic bodies and when excited (or oscillated) they vibrate with their entire mass for a shorter or longer time. The body may be variously shaped — in bars, tubes, straight or curved plates, for instance — and of various materials, like stone, glass, metal or wood. Vibrators can be freely suspended: if they are fixed at one point, they deflect in various directions; if fixed at two points, they are free to deflect in one direction only. Vibrators can also be supported, but the supports should be designed to come in contact with the smallest possible area of the vibrator body. These vibrator types are the so-called self-sounding instruments or *idiophones*. Sometimes the vibrator is partially fixed and only part of its mass is left free to vibrate. Such instruments are called semi-self-souding, or *hemiidiophones*.

In air-sounding instruments, or *aerophones,* the function of the vibrator is performed by air enclosed within the tube walls of the instrument and made elastic due to compression.

Non-solid stable bodies can also vibrate. They become elastic due to artificial longitudinal or surface tensioning as in strings and membranes. In order to make the sound audible these

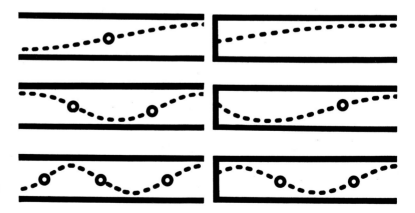

Air column vibrating in open (unstopped) and stopped pipes

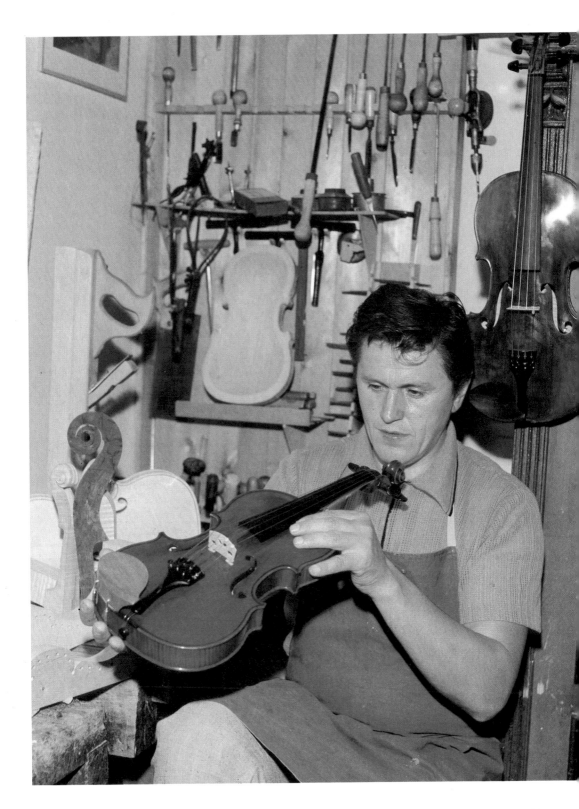

4 Modern violin shop, Czechoslovakia

instruments require an amplifier. Instruments of this type are called *chordophones* and *membranophones*.

The generator which causes the vibrator to oscillate may be a hammer, spring, pneumatic or electromagnetic action, or a stick, bow, or tuning fork, or the fingers and lips of the player. However, a vibrator can be oscillated basically in five ways. A single strike will lend the vibrator energy through impact, and it will vibrate freely until the vibration becomes attenuated. Repeated strikes give the vibrator energy through uninterrupted impulses, which generate undecaying vibrations. Plucking deflects the vibrator from its balanced state and quickly releases it again, generating a free vibration which will eventually decay. When the vibrator is subjected to friction, i.e. when it is repeatedly plucked and freed again, undecaying vibration will again be generated. The fifth method is caused by an internal variable force transmitting its vibration to a vibrator which will not oscillate on its own.

If the surface of the vibrator is too small and therefore incapable of producing sufficient sound energy (as in the case of strings and membranes), a great variety of amplifiers can be used, the amplifier having similar properties to the vibrator, plus a greater surface area to radiate sound energy. In such a case the oscillation of the vibrator is transmitted into the amplifier, which lends it sufficient energy. Amplifiers come in various shapes, such as cases, boxes, vessels, tubes, and so on. Sometimes energy can be increased by adding an artificial extension to the vibrator's surface area. The body of a large surface area attached to the vibrator is called a diffusor (from the Latin *diffundere* = to spread out).

If the amplifier is to function properly, it must amplify—if possible without distortion—any

5 Classification of stringed instruments after J. Lehmann

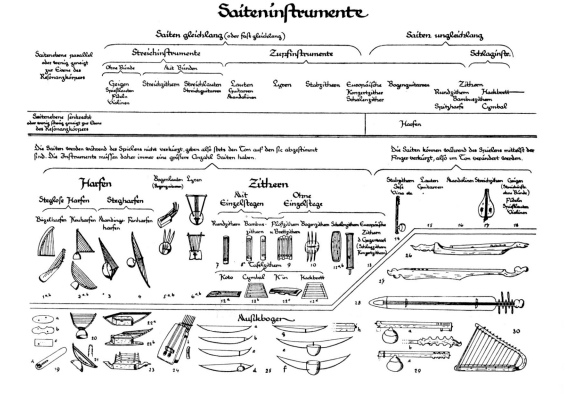

frequency of oscillation. Therefore such bodies are used as amplifiers, whose shape and dimensions will not allow the body to oscillate on its own, or whose oscillation is either above or below the limit of vibration of the vibrator proper. In some cases when the vibrator is tuned to a certain frequency range, the amplifier vibration frequency is kept within the same limits and is finely coordinated with the vibrator vibrations. The amplifier then amplifies the vibrator frequencies with its own vibration (e.g. reed pipes, tuning fork) and is called a *resonator*.

From the physical and technical point of view musical instruments are classified according to the vibrator and generator type. Any further subclassification can follow according to amplifier types and other technical and acoustic aspects. The classification represented by the table below covers only some instruments from European music and does not always respect the commonly used classification systems since it is based on the acoustic properties of the vibrator, generator and amplifier.

	VIBRATOR	GENERATOR	AMPLIFIER	INSTRUMENT
idiophones	horizontal bars	beaters	—	xylophone, glockenspiel
			resonators	vibraphone
		hammer action		celesta
	suspended bars	beater	—	triangle, tubular bells
		concussion	—	cymbals
	suspended plates	beater	—	gong, tam-tam
hemi-idioph.	bars fixed on one end	air stream	resonators	reed pipes — organ, harmonium, accordion
aerophones	air column	air stream hitting the edge of a side hole	—	side-blown (cross) flutes
		air stream hitting a fipple in the head	—	recorders
		reed	—	clarinets, saxophones
		double reed	— —	oboes, bassoons
		player's lips taut on the mouth-piece	—	trumpets, trombones, horns, tubas
chordophones	strings	plectrum	resonator body	mandoline, guitar, banjo,
		fingers		harp
		hammer action	resonator case	piano, upright piano
		plucking action		harpsichord
		beaters		dulcimer, cimbalom
membranoph.	single membrane	beaters	kettle	tympani
		hands	hollow cylinder	timbales, bongoes
			barrel	congas
			frame	tambourine
	two membranes	beater	hollow cylinder	bass drum
		beaters		side drum, snare drum

THE CLASSIFICATION OF MUSICAL INSTRUMENTS

Musical instruments are those objects man uses to produce the sounds necessary for music making. However, music is not composed of any haphazard noise but of sounds especially selected and precisely organized. The sounds produced by musical instruments have definite duration, volume, timbre and tone pitch. Although musical instruments naturally do exist independently of man, the latter sometimes becomes an integral part of them, or rather man and his instrument form an integral whole. As an air stream produced by bellows is required to sound bagpipes or organs, so human breath is required to sound other wind instruments. In the case of mouthpiece instruments parts of the body are used, i.e. the lungs (which is also true of most wind instruments) and the lips enclosed by the edges of the mouthpiece so that due to the *embouchure,* the lips act as a sound-generating spring. Objects made originally for totally different purposes can often be transformed into musical instruments. Consequently, it is difficult to decide what a musical instrument is. From a traditional definition which stated that 'a musical instrument is that instrument which produces a voice, we have arrived at the present definition that musical instruments are purposely constructed and modified sound-producing instruments intended for making music and which, due to their acoustic properties, can objectively contribute to the musical artistic effect since their acoustic characteristics correspond to the standards of the musical culture of the ethnic group and historical period in question.

The ancient nations were the first to attempt to systemize musical instruments. For instance, the ancient Chinese theorists divide musical instruments according to the material used in their construction, while the ancient Indian treatise *Natya Shastra* (6th century B.C.) classifies musical instruments according to the physical properties of the primary sounded matter. Medieval Europe did not pay any great attention to organology and the simple systemization into stringed *(tensibilia),* wind *(inflatibilia)* and percussion *(percussibilia)* instruments as created by the French musicologist Johannes de Muris (died after 1351) was not developed any further.

6—7 Classification of ancient Egyptian harps after H. Hickmann

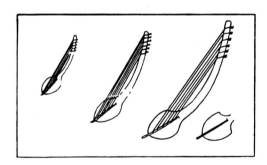
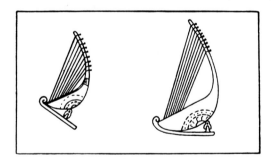
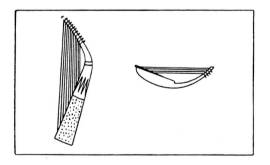

One of the few exceptions is the work of Hieronymus de Moravia (ca. 1250) called *Tractatus de musica* which—apart from some old-fashioned parts stemming from the period conventions—offered important evidence on the tuning of medieval viols. Medieval organology culminated in the second volume of a treatise, *Syntagma musicum,* called *De organographia.* This is a historical document of great importance written by Michael Praetorius (1571–1621).

The pioneer of modern scientific musical instrument systemization was François Auguste Gevaert of Belgium whose *Traité d'instrumentation* (1863) divides musical instruments into stringed, wind, membrane and autophonic families. The instruments of the first two categories are further subdivided according to the manner of sounding, so that the strings are subgrouped into scraped, plucked and percussion instruments, while the winds are composed of flue (i.e. the organ pipe), reed and mouthpiece subgroups. Membranophones and autophones are subdivided by Gevaert into instruments with definite and indefinite pitch. Gevaert's follower, Victor Charles Mahillon, also a Belgian, applied the acoustic viewpoint in his *Catalogue descriptif* (1888), although he was sometimes inconsistent in his systemization and basically used the ancient Indian classification system, dividing musical instruments into autophones, membranophones, chordophones and aerophones.

From Mahillon's system it was only a short step to a classification devised by Erich M. von Hornbostel and Curt Sachs in their *Systematik der Musikinstrumente* (1914), the only older classification still widely accepted. The authors replaced the term *autophone* with another of the same meaning, *idiophone.* The rest of their terminology as well as the classification system is more or less identical with the Gevaert system. However, theirs is basically governed by two viewpoints: idiophones and membranophones are subdivided according to the manner of playing while chordophones are classified according to external appearance and aerophones according to functional and construction features. Although the authors did come close to a system employing the features of the instruments in such a way that interrelations and family ties can be easily traced, the numerical classification forming the backbone of the system is not applicable to any instruments invented after 1914 nor to any combined instruments. However,

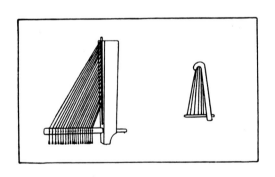 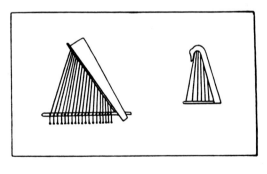

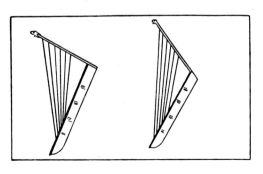 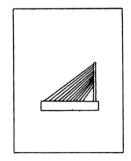 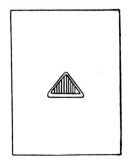

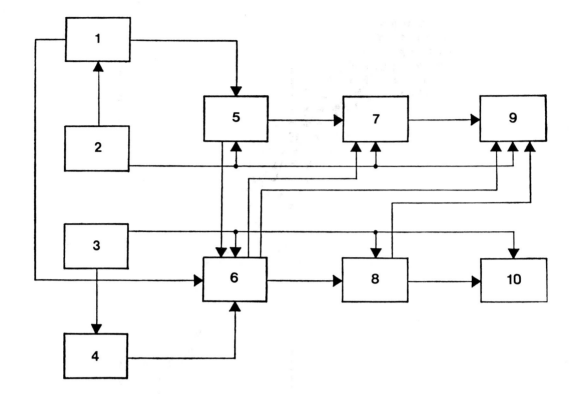

8 Schematic model of a musical instrument after P. Kurfürst
1 Main oscillator feeder 2 Main oscillator modulator 3 Secondary oscillator modulator 4 Secondary oscillator feeder 5 Main oscillator 6 Secondary oscillator 7 Main oscillator amplifier 8 Secondary oscillator amplifier 9 Main oscillator emitter 10 Secondary oscillator emitter

Sachs later supplemented and elaborated the system in *Handbuch der Musikinstrumentenkunde* (1930) and *The History of Musical Instruments* (1940).

André Schaeffner in his study *D'une nouvelle classification méthodique des instruments de musique* (1932) divided musical instruments into solid *(instruments à corps solide vibrant)* and wind *(instruments à air vibrant)*. Solid instruments are subdivided into solid bodies which cannot be tensioned *(corps solides flexibles)*, i.e. the reeds *(linguaphones)* and solid bodies which can be subjected to tension *(corps solides, susceptibles de tension)*, i.e. membranophones and chordophones. In contrast to the Hornbostel-Sachs system, the main criterion of the Schaeffner system is its consistent approach to classifying musical instruments which brings it close to the ancient Chinese classification.

Hans-Heinz Dräger in his *Prinzip einer Systematik der Musikinstrumente* (1948) defines a musical instrument as a sound-producing body or object consciously selected and shaped, and then he subjects each musical instrument to a thorough investigation beginning with its external description and with the principle of the vibration of matter and ending with information on the manner of playing and with individual player's styles. Dräger, a disciple of Hornbostel and Sachs, actually remains faithful to his teachers' classification although elaborating it more broadly and applying it to more areas.

Jeremy Montagu and John Burton of England made a remarkable proposal for musical instrument systemization in their study *A Proposed New Classification System for Musical Instruments* (1971). They hold that words are more easily remembered than long sequences of numbers (which is precisely why the Hornbostel-Sachs system has never become popular). Their new system uses very many definitions for the identification of musical instruments so that no term can be misunderstood, and the key can be therefore successfully used not only by organologists but also by any layman.

Some organologists have also attempted to systemize the classification of individual instrument groups. One such attempt was made by Johann Lehmann in the 1920's when he classified the stringed and flute instruments of non-European nations; Lehmann based his system on the development of the instrument shape, but he failed to discover a general unifying criterion. A system of chordophones based on organographic criteria was worked out by the Swedish ethnomusicologist Tobias Norlind and outlined in his work *Systematik der Saiteninstrumente* (1936—1939). Hans Hickmann, the Egyptologist, systemized ancient Egyptian harps according to their shape. A system which would consistently apply acoustic criteria and which could be classified by computer is the aim of Czech music theorist Pavel Kurfürst, who has elaborated a schematic musical instrument model incorporating all possible functional features and elements and all possible relevant connections, represented by feedbacks. The author has drawn on radioelectronic terminology, and by means of an acoustic analysis has attempted to determine which features of the model are inherent in individual instruments. Information and data obtained in this way will be processed by a computer which will perform a mutual comparison of instruments and facilitate a musical instrument classification according to all relevant features and feedbacks.

A new musical instrument classification is by the Section of Organology, ICOM (International Committee of Museums), which presented results of its work at the 1977 ICOM Congress in Moscow. These efforts are intended to improve the classical Hornbostel-Sachs systemization.

At present organologists, in cooperation with technologists, are concentrating on technological improvements, the further development of construction principles and a search for new possibilities in the traditional classical musical instruments utilizing air as the vibration medium. Another research field is concerned with electric musical instruments whose construction is determined by the properties of electricity as the sound-generating element. These instruments have recently shown heretofore unfathomed possibilities of further development. The classical reed organ probably represents the ultimate in traditional instrumentation; however, electric and electronic musical instruments are bound by no limitations imposed by matter. This opens new vistas waiting for full artistic exploitation.

If musical instruments represent a perfect creation in which art, technology and human ingenuity fuse in harmony, a really scientific classification can hardly be achieved by traditional methods. Yet our confidence that the world of sounds is after all measurable and analyzable gives hope that musicologists in cooperation with musical acoustics experts will at last discover the right key which will make a unified musical instrument classification possible.

I. THE DEVELOPMENT OF MUSICAL INSTRUMENTS FROM PREHISTORY TO THE PRESENT

PREHISTORY

Discoveries of prehistoric musical instruments are too rare to provide a clear idea of what prehistoric music and its instruments were like, yet the study of prehistoric music has been coming steadily into the foreground of archaeological interest. The foundation of this science, called archaeoorganology, was laid down by the research work of Curt Sachs, the famous German musicologist, Francis William Galpin and Arnold Dolmetsch. Recently, important advances have been made in the work of John Vincent Stanley Megaw. Archaeoorganology strictly observes the limitations of conclusive archaeological evidence and bases its

9 Clay drum. Late Neolithic

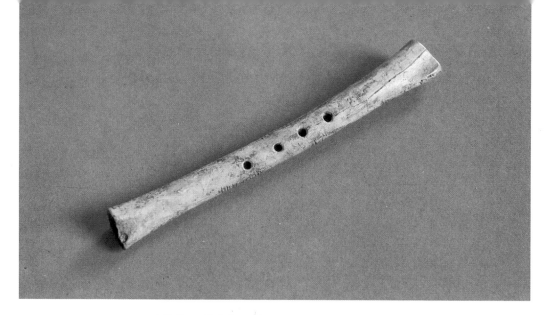

10 Bird bone whistle flute
Ryazan Region, Central Russia, 2nd millennium B.C.

Clay rattle and its sectional view, late Neolithic, Vykhva-tintse, Moldavian S.S.R., U.S.S.R.

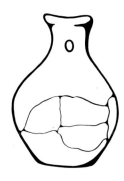

judgement only on preserved artefacts that can be subjected to research.

The first sound which inaugurated the long history of music was produced by prehistoric man with an instrument that may have been of any type: string, wind or other. Naturally, this primeval musical instrument has not survived, but we can make some guesses about it. Primitive musical or sound-producing instruments existed when neither tonality nor performance of a tune were yet known. What these instruments produced was merely a sound of a certain pitch with no aspiration as to pitch differentiation. However, even during the most primitive period, musical instruments must have undergone a considerable development.

Sound-producing instruments that have been preserved, i.e. *rattles, scrapers* and *clappers,* seem to testify that prehistoric man must have had some sense of rhythm, although the instruments were also used for functional purposes such as driving away evil spirits and to help cure the sick. It was only later when the dimensions of the instruments diminished that they came to be used also as children's toys; painted clay rattles discovered in child graves dating from the beginning of the second millennium B.C. were found in Vykhvatintse, Moldavia, U.S.S.R. Clay figurines of various shapes with rattling pebbles inside were used in dances, rituals and as toys. These instruments were excavated throughout the entire European continent in settlements of the Hallstatt period and especially numerous findings date from later settlements of the La Tène period. The Stone Age people knew also scraped instruments, the most important representative of which is the *scraper.* One such bone scraper dating from the Paleolithic period and discovered in the Pekárna Cave in Moravia has saw-like teeth or ser-

19

11 Musical bow
Cave painting. ca. 15.000 B.C., Trois Frères, France

Signalling whistles of reindeer bone, Paleolithic, Sveardhorg, Denmark and Csáklya, Hungary

rations across which a stick was drawn. A *gong* made of grey-green jade was discovered near Valencia, Venezuela, proving that prehistoric man could also differentiate between stones according to sound quality.

Simple *whistles, pipes* and *flutes* made from drilled animal bones and dating also from the Paleolithic age are undoubtedly older than any other known musical instrument. A rich variety of whistles and flutes have been found in archaeological excavations in Eastern Europe and have helped to verify that the flute must have been very important in the daily life of prehistoric man. A fragment of a bone flute dating from the third Aurignacian stratum (ca. 18 000 B.C.) and discovered in the Isturitz Cave in the Pyrenées has three fingerholes and is only slightly different in shape from flutes many thousand years younger. In the Paleolithic excavation station in Moldavia, Chernovtsy Region, U.S.S.R., the Soviet archaeologists have uncovered a flute made from a longitudinally-drilled piece of reindeer horn. There are four holes on the upper side of the very skilfully-executed instrument and two holes underneath, spaced quite far apart. The bore does not extend through the entire length of the piece of horn but goes only as far as the fourth fingerhole at the tapered end of the instrument. It is therefore an instrument with a stopped tube giving tones one octave lower than flutes with the tube opened at both ends (unstopped flutes). Ever greater workmanship can be seen on the so-called Bornholm flute which has five fingerholes and dates, according to some archaelogical authorities, from the European Neolithic period. Similar to the Bornholm flute is an instrument discovered in the territory of prehistoric Neolithic hunters and fishermen (second millennium B.C.) in the Ryazan Region of Central Russia. It is made of a hollow bird bone, with four fingerholes, and measures 10.5 cm in length.

In the prehistoric hunters' settlements *syrinxes* also called *panpipes,* were found. The instrument consists of a series of graduated bone pipes held together by wax or resin in such a way that the top is straight while the bottom end forms a slanting line. Tones are produced by blowing over the sharp edge of the free ends of the pipes in a similar fashion as in key whistling. The oldest specimens of discovered *syrinxes* come from a Neolithic burial ground in the southern Ukraine (2 000 B.C.) and from the Saratov Region in Russia. Both instruments consist of seven or eight hollow bird bone pipes in length from 4 to 11.5 cm and the pipes of the first syrinx are decorated with engraved ornamental lines. Syrinxes rank among the oldest wind instruments capable of producing many tones, and their importance for the further development of other musical instruments, especially the organ, was considerable.

Analysis of contemporary musical instruments from North Africa and Oceania suggests that prehistoric drums developed from wooden prototypes; the Bernburg clay goblet drums and spiral pottery binnacle (waisted) drums from the southern parts of the U.S.S.R. date from very approximately 4500 years ago. Recent reconstructions of these instruments proved to have outstanding sound qualities and bear comparison with today's similarly-shaped instruments from the Upper Nile region, made on a potter's wheel.

Hundreds of cave paintings about 15—10 thousand years old were discovered in the Trois Frères Cave in southern France near Ariège. Some paintings represent dancing shamans dressed in animal skins and wearing masks. One of the figures is masked as a bison and holds an instrument in his hand similar to a bow, which has been the subject of great discussions among experts. Some take it to be an endblown (longitudinal, vertical) flute, others hold that it is a *musical bow*. But so far only flutes have been discovered by archaeologists, although of course this does not disprove the existence of musical bows at that time, made probably of wood or bone and animal sinews. Naturally, such an instrument would have survived till today only under exceptional environmental conditions.

But there is no doubt that the regular hunting bow has been used throughout history and all over the world. When the prehistoric hunter noticed that the string launching an arrow produces a sound, he probably

12 Scraper
Ca. 15 000 B.C.

13 Reindeer bone whistle
Ca. 15 000 B.C.

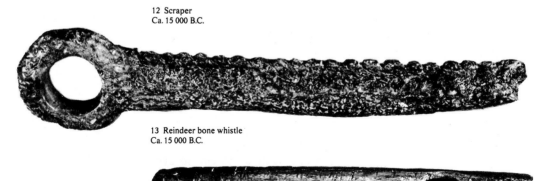

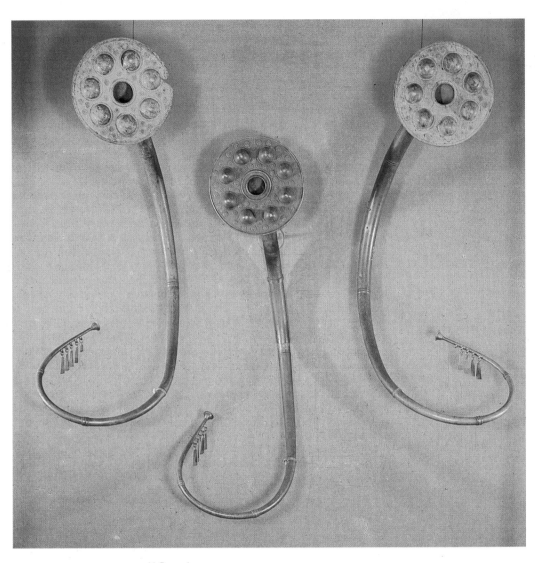

14 Bronze lurs
2nd millennium B.C.

started to pluck the string spontaneously to enjoy himself. Then in time
he discovered that bows of varying lengths and string tension produce
tones of different pitch. And if he placed one tip of the bow in his
mouth, holding it firmly, then tensioned the string and by plucking the
latter and listening to the tone pitch he tried to estimate the tension
with which the string would have launched the arrow, he would have
noticed that the mouth cavity amplified the sound of the string and in
this way he would have accidentally discovered not only the resonator
but also the musical instrument as such. The shaman depicted on the
cave painting in the Trois Frères Cave holds the top of the bow in his

Bone flute, Stone Age, Kent's Cavern, Devonshire, England

mouth, grasping the bottom end with his left hand while the right plucks the string. In contrast to a host of other French and Spanish cave paintings this particular scene lacks a distinctive hunting motif — a wounded or killed animal. Rather, the musician dressed in bison skins performs a ceremonial ritual with live animals, probably to charm a rich kill.

In time, the hunter discovered that if he sounded the string not by plucking but with another bow, the tone was longer, of a more flowing languid character and also stronger or weaker according to the pressure exerted on the string with the bow. This is precisely what can be seen on a cave painting in Cape Town, South Africa. A Bushman holds a bow in his right hand, touching the strings of seven other bows. The painting therefore documents a more advanced stage of development where the seven bows form one instrument and the bow held in the right hand of the Bushman serves already as a stick bow.

The Bulgarian musicologist Georgi Jantarski has described a cave painting in northwestern Bulgaria representing a bowed musical bow. The picture appears among a number of cave paintings in the Rabish Caves near Belogradchik and its composition is split into two planes. The upper plane shows a group of dancing women and naked men,

15 Golden horns
5th century A.D.

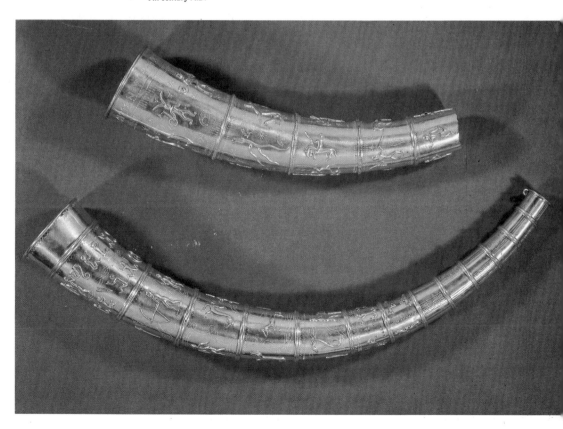

23

16 Carnyx trumpets of Celtic warriors
Relief on a silver vessel fragment, 2nd or 1st century B.C.

probably fingerpainted in dark ochre. Due to the humid conditions in the cave the rock surface was gradually etched off while the ochre acted as a protective layer of the painting which was therefore unaffected by erosion. In this way the original paintings were transformed into a plastic relief and nature itself quite unintentionally preserved the original painting, proving simultaneously its genuineness. In the centre of the lower part of the painting there are two musicians. One holds a bow in his left hand, positioned vertically and with the stick arch facing the musician's body, the right hand as if striking the bow string with some kind of a playing bow. The second figure had a *double-headed drum* on his chest and is beating it with both hands. In spite of

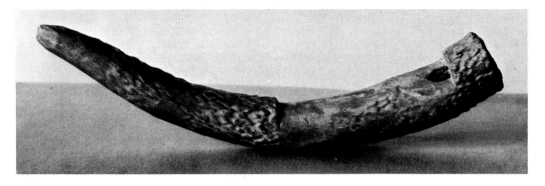

17 Stag horn flute
Southern Moravia, 9th century A.D.

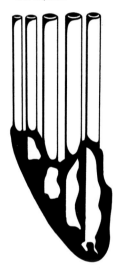

Panpipe, Stone Age, Klein-Küh-nau at Dessau, German Democratic Republic

the fact that the discovery has not been yet inspected in any greater detail nor dated, its importance for organology will undoubtedly prove immense. If Jantarski's theory proves to be true it will then be possible to shift the generally accepted date of origin of the bow from the eighth century A.D. back to the prehistoric era. And if what the second musician beats is really a double-headed drum, it would be an equally-valuable discovery since it would prove the existence of such a drum in a period from which only clay goblet and spiral ceramic waisted drums have survived.

It was also probably far back in prehistory when man discovered that taut twine, if divided into two unequal parts, gave two different tones. The string would have been divided either by means of another string tied to the first at a certain point, or a finger would be touched there causing the discovery of the flageolet technique. When the string was touched at various places musical intervals were discovered. Of course it took a long time before man learned how to tie two and then more strings of different length to one bow which finally resulted e.g. in the Sumerian lyre or a harp.

Prehistoric culture reached a high level of development in the

18 Bone fipple flute
Last quarter of the 9th century A.D.

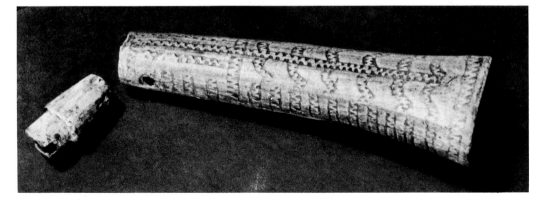

Bronze Age. As well as flute-type and reed instruments the first proto-types of mouthpiece instruments came into being. The considerable progress in metal processing achieved in the early Bronze Age made possible the manufacture of a bronze horn whose shape was derived from its ancestor and model, an animal horn. From the point of view of instrument workmanship as well as sound quality the most perfect instrument of this type is the bronze *lur* shaped like a mammoth tusk. These instruments are 150—240 cm long, the tube forming a gracious upward spiral ending in a forward-pointing bell. The tube is composed of two parts of unequal length and in the place where the two tube sections are joined eyelets are provided to a chain to carry the instrument. The mouthpiece is not separate but cast in one piece with the lower half of the tube and has a deep cup-shaped profile like today's tenor trombone mouthpiece. Both the mouthpiece and the bell are decorated with trapezoid pendants suspended on rings. When the lur was blown hard the pendants enriched the soft fine sound of the instrument with a brassy timbre.

Lurs are thought to have been used in rituals and the hypothesis is supported by the fact that their discovery has usually been in peatbogs in places where ceremonies used to be performed. Due to the preservative properties of the peat these beautiful instruments survived very well. With only a few exceptions lurs are always in pairs; lurs of each pair would be of the same size and tuning but always with opposite helices, and consequently they are thought to have symbolized the horns of a bull. Cave paintings also show lurs in pairs or fours with the tubes bent left and right. The majority of the lurs discovered so far come from Danish peatbogs and these specimens are nowadays among the most prized possessions of North European museums. The tuning is usually in C and E flat but tuning in D, E and G is not uncommon. When subjected to sound testing the lurs gave 17 partial tones but the number could be increased up to 24.

A slightly modified form of the animal horn is the so-called *Gaul horn* made of bronze and excavated near Nice. Only two-thirds of the resonator tube have survived. The length of the piece is 108 cm. The individual parts are joined by wide-profiled brass rings. This type of horn can be also seen on the marble statue of the *Dying Gaul* placed now in the Capital Museum in Rome, as well as on the Triumphal Arch in Narbonne, France. However, in both cases the original shape of the instrument was greatly distorted by poor restoration workmanship. The large number of small fragments unearthed in the Iberian Peninsula has made possible the reconstruction of the *small horn* of the Celt-iberians; the original of the flat (low profile) cup mouthpiece together with numerous other fragments from Numantia is now deposited in the Central Roman-German Museum of Rome. Although the Celts had taken over the *tuba* from the Romans, they greatly modified it as is proved by the unearthing of such an instrument in Neuvy-en-Sullies. The instrument consists of several parts joined by ornamented rings and the mouthpiece resembles those of today's trumpets.

A typical Celtic military instrument was the *carnyx* trumpet, called the *Galatean salpinx* by Homer. Typically, the bell of the instrument is decorated with the head of a horse, snake, wolf, etc. which was sometimes also hung with a rattling metal tongue. So far the only specimen of the carnyx to be found was discovered in the Witham River, Eng-

Musical bow, rock painting, Cape Town, South Africa

Musical drum and bow, rock, painting, Rabisha Cave near Belogradchik, Bulgaria

19 Bronze statuette of a Celtic trumpeter
Hill fort side, Stradonice, Czechoslovakia, 1st century A.D.

land, although many reports of the instrument can be found in the works of classical writers. The carnyx was also a frequent image on Celtic coins and can be seen on the Trajan Column. An image on a silver kettle discovered near Gundestrup, Denmark, shows three trumpeters with their instruments pointing straight up. The same type of instrument was discovered on an ancient Indian relief dating from the first century A.D., and Indian musicians still blow upright metal horns called *ranasringa* with the bell resembling the open mouth of a dragon. Interestingly, French instrument makers of the eighteenth and nineteenth centuries—still observing the ancient custom of their

Double drum, waisted, Eneolithic, southern U.S.S.R.

Celtic ancestors—shaped the bells of their trombones and bass horns as open mouths of various animals.

A ring of thick spikes on the bell of *Irish trumpets* from the Bronze Age, with the mouthhole located at the side of the tube, did not serve as an ornament but made the instrument a very dangerous weapon. The Celts modified not only the *tuba* but also the *syrinx* giving it a different shape so that one side is oblique and the top and bottom edges are parallel. A panpipe of such a shape with eight boxwood pipes was discovered in a well in the Gaul-Roman town of Alesie (now Alise-Sainte-Reine, France). An entire scale in D major can be played on the instrument. The Greek writer and historian Diodorus Siculus (first century A.D.) tells of Celtic bards accompanying their songs with a string instrument similar to the Greek *lyre*. An ancient Irish song celebrates a four-sided string instrument called the *crot* whose name seems to be echoed in the medieval rote (Latin chrotta, rotta) known already from the works of the Roman poet Venantius Honorius Clementianus Fortunatus (c. 540 — c. 600) — 'chrotta Britanna canat'.

20 Sumerian lyre
Relief, royal palace at Telloh, Iraq, ca. 2 400 B.C.

21 Large Sumerian frame drum with jingle discs
Stone relief. Telloh, Iraq, ca. 2 000 B.C.

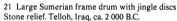

THE ANCIENT AGE

MESOPOTAMIA

One of the earliest civilizations was that of *SUMERIA,* which existed more than 5000 years ago in southern Mesopotamia in that tract of land between the rivers Euphrates and Tigris. Important relics of its culture are the epic poem of Gilgamesh, the legendary ruler of the city

22 Assyrian harp, lyre and double flutes
Relief, royal palace in Nineveh, ca. 700 B.C.

of Ur, and various hymns celebrating major deities and rulers. These hymns were recited to the accompaniment of musical instruments. Compared with ancient Egypt, the number of Sumerian instruments discovered is almost negligible and therefore an idea of the music and instrumentation of the nations of Mesopotamia can be formed only on the basis of preserved literary documents, reliefs, seal scrolls, votive stone tablets, shell-inlaid objects and so on.

A literary source tells of the existence of a flute whose Sumerian name *gi-gid* (*gi* = cane, reed) refers to the material the shepherds originally used for its construction. Later these flutes were also made of bronze, silver and gold. The Lagash king Gudea remembers how 'Enlulim, the goat shepherd used to fill the great courtyard of Eninn with the joyous mood of his pipe's sound' (F. Thureau-Dangin: *Die Summerischen und Akkadischen Königsinschriften,* 1907).

One of the most ancient pictures of musicians of the period is probably a fragment of a lazulite vase discovered during archaeological excavations of a Babylonian temple in Bismai. It dates from the third to

23 Semitic lyre
Tomb painting, Bení Hasan, Egypt, ca. 1900 B.C.

Silver Sumerian flute, ca. 2600
B.C.; University Museum, Phi-
ladelphia

24 Babylonian female lyrist and male dancer with tambourine
Relief, the reign of king Hammurabi, ca. 1700 B.C.

Sumerian lyre harp, after a mosaic standard, British Museum, London

fourth millennium B.C. and is now in the Istanbul Museum. The piece portrays three Sumerian musicians: One of them plays a *harp* resembling the modern bow (arched) harp common in Burma and Africa; the second player has a similar instrument but his is equipped with a triangular resonator box with long tassels and is similar to the later Assyrian harps. (What is most surprising about these harps is the sophistication of their construction which implies a long period of development. The number of the strings—five on the first instrument and seven on the second—allows a presumption that both a pentatonic (five-note) scale and a diatonic (seven-note) scale was already known at the time in question.) The third musician walking in the procession apparently keeps the rhythm with a *frame drum* held under his left arm.

In the Iraqi Museum in Baghdad there is a very precious specimen of a 4500 years-old harp discovered in the tomb of queen Pu-abi. The rectangular resonator box is embellished with lazulite and shell mosaic. Another decoration is formed by a bull's head made from embossed gold leaf on a wooden core with inlaid shell and lazulite eyes. The head is located on the front side of the harp in a manner of a ship's figurehead. If it could be proven that these figureheads, apart from being purely decorative, were also used to adjust the pitch of the instrument, then the Sumerians could be recognized as having reached a sophisticated level of harp and lyre construction.

The tombs of the kings of Ur unearthed in the 1920's disclosed not only harps but lyres, too, whose strings—in contrast to the length-graduated parallel strings of the harp—were of the same length, tied together at one end in a strand and arching out in a section. These harps were made of wood, silver and gold and were decorated with inlays and incrustations. Naturally, the wooden parts of the golden lyre frame have not survived but the golden pegs and broad bull's head mosaic decorations have. In the same tombs a mosaic was also found, a genuine picture book depicting Sumerian life prior to 3000 B.C. Among the figures formed by a mother-of-pearl and lazulite mosaic, a musician can be seen accompanying a lady singer with his eleven-string lyre decorated with a bull's head. (It was only until recently that the Georgians of the Caucasus used to play a harp embellished with an image of two horses and a bull forming a circular plastic relief, and the Hungarians have still retained their ancient custom of decorating their zither with an image of a horsehead.) The five to eleven strings of this lyre were mainly sounded with a plectrum and were stretched across the resonator box to the yoke (crosspiece) and fixed there either with pegs or leather thongs. A relief from the Sumerian summer palace at Telloh (2600 B.C., now in the Louvre) depicts a player with an unusually large eleven-string lyre, a sort of a *lyre harp*. The front part of the resonator box is decorated with an image of a standing bull, and the protruding front end of the yoke is in the form of an animal head. The construction details of this lyre harp resemble the psaltery harp of the European Middle Ages.

The invention of the *lute*, an instrument with a small pear-shaped body and a slim long neck, was ascribed by the Greek encyclopaedist Pollux to the Assyrians. The lute is often pictured in the hands of shepherds and is therefore presumed to have been a folk instrument.

In court ceremonies, *frame drums* were used, usually played by

25 Sumerian lyre harp, a reconstruction
Burial field, Uru, Iraq, ca. 2500 B.C.

Babylonian angle harp, after a relief in Ashurbanipal's Palace at Nineveh

women. Some pictures show drums up to 1.5 m in diameter, the skins nailed to the wooden drum frame. Similar drums can still be seen hanging in Chinese and Japanese temples, with skins tensioned similarly with nails.

Mankind is indebted to the *BABYLONIANS* for the immense progress in medicine, astronomy and also music which flourished especially during the reign of the famous Babylonian king Hammurabi (turn of the eighteenth and seventeenth centuries B.C.). The fact that the Babylonian culture was able to contribute to the further development of music stems from the ·great achievements of the older Sumerian and Akkadian civilizations.

No evidence has yet been unearthed of the music and instruments of the Middle Kingdom. Stone reliefs emerge only around the first century B.C., with images of musical instruments like a short *trumpet*, small *lyre*, a two-string long-necked *lute, double shawm* and *cymbals.* An earthenware *rattle* was discovered in Mari, a terracota figurine of a monkey with a *flute* has survived from the beginning of the second millennium B.C. Another preserved terracota figurine represents a woman playing a *syrinx (panpipe)*.

In the Museum of Archaeology in Ankara, Turkey, one can see a bas-relief of a musician playing a sort of *guitar.* The instrument bears a stri-

26 Hittite guitar. Stone relief, Alayn Häyük, Turkey, ca. 1350 B.C.

27 Assyrian musicians playing a frame drum, lyres and cymbals
Stone relief, Ashurbanipal's Palace, Nineveh, (ca. 626 B.C.)

king resemblance to a guitar painted some 2700 years later in the medieval Spanish codex *Cantigas de Santa Maria*. The relief, originally from the palace of the Assyrian king Ashurbanipal in Nineveh (now in the British Museum), shows a scene in which the king, accompanied by his bodyguards, performs a ritual of pouring sacred oils onto the bodies of some lions he had hunted down. The ritual is accompanied by a woman singing to the music of an *angle harp*. There are also very many neo-Assyrian reliefs showing *grand harps* with fifteen to twenty-two strings, which proves that nothing substantial was changed throughout the centuries as regards the looks and playing technique of these instruments.

The *HITTITES*, creators of one of the most unique cultures of the entire ancient period, became famous not only as being skilled metallurgists, brave soldiers and suave diplomats but also for their love of music, fully serving their religious cults. Their prayers to deities or songs celebrating individual gods, accompanied by *harps* and *lutes* are very poetic although some crudities and stylistic stereotypes show in places. A statuette of a man playing a *frame drum* reveals that these instruments were widely played and remained unchanged for millennia.

35

Egyptian trumpeter, after Champollion

EGYPT

We know considerably more about ancient Egypt that any other civilization of the epoch mainly because of two phenomena, the hot desert sand which preserved everything buried there and the impulse of the Egyptians to picture their daily life in sculpture and in tomb murals. The value of these illustrations is even greater due to the fact that the Egyptians accompanied the paintings with texts inscribed into any free space left around the picture proper and in this way all names of the ancient Egyptian musical instruments have survived. Furthermore, the texts not only mention their names but give complete descriptions of the duties of the individual musicians. Some were, for instance, required to clap their hands rhythmically while others are shown conducting whole instrumental and vocal ensembles. There are also pictures of priestess-musicians and singers who formed a separate caste and dedicated their life to service in innumerable temples. The inscriptions sometimes even give titles and texts of entire songs, topics of ritual dances and commentaries on their mythological meanings.

Prior to the ascent of pharaonic dynasties, a vertical (end-blown)

28 Egyptian female harp, lute and double shawm players,
Mural painting, Nakht Tomb, Theban necropolis, New Kingdom, ca. 1410 B.C.

Egyptian sistrum, after Champollion

Egyptian flute, after a painting in the tomb of Pharao Nencheftkal, 5th dynasty, Egyptian Museum, Cairo

Egyptian harp, after H. Hickmann

29 Harpist of Ramses III
Mural painting in the Theban necropolis, 1166 B.C.

flute known as the *m'at* with two to six fingerholes had been used in Egypt. The player would hold it slightly tipped to one side, blowing across the sharp edge of the top end of the tube. This type of flute has survived in the Islamic countries as the *nay*. In this period also the ancestors of the clarinet and oboe were born, i.e. instruments featuring either single or double reeds. Another specific feature of the ancient instrumentation which exists even today among folk musicians of the

37

Egyptian harps, after H. Hickmann

Near as well as Far East are doubled instruments consisting of two pipes held freely or tied together.

The mouthpiece instruments of ancient Egypt were basically of two types: cylindrical bore trumpets and conical bore horns. Naturally, trumpet instruments have never been in shape only cylindrical and organology has not stipulated the rate of conicity of the bore at which the instrument is no longer a trumpet but becomes a horn instead. In this book all instruments with a distinctive conicity will be considered as horns, the rest as trumpets.

Two *khnoue* trumpets were found in the tomb of Tutankhamen. They are half a metre long with a very narrow bore and ornamental ebossing on a funnel-shaped bell. Greek writers compared the sound of this instrument to the voice of a braying jackass.

Images preserved from the period of the Old Kingdom (2900—2473 B.C.) testify to the existence of wooden stick *clappers* bent at the end; the pair of sticks was held in one hand and struck together. There are also depictions of two-handed *clappers,* shaped as human hands and held by women worshipping the goddes Hathor. The *iba* rattle, sometimes also called the *sehem,* was also used in religious rituals. Later it acquired the name *sistrum,* a word of Greek origin. This instrument was used in the cult of Isis and was played throughout the Mediterranean, leaving traces even in Ethiopia and the Caucasus. However, in contrast to instruments found in territories other than Egypt, the genuine Egyptian *sistrum* had the shape of a temple front with rattling wires strung through holes in the sides.

However, Egyptian music is typically symbolized by the *harp.* The numerous variants of this instrument bear testimony to its popular character, proving also that the instrument was subject to adoration. (See the drawings on pages 14—15.) It is still unresolved as to whether the Egyptians adopted the harp from the Sumerians or vice versa. Nevertheless, the Egyptian and Sumerian harps did have many common features. The *arched harp,* which in the period of the Old Kingdom had a round resonator covered with skin, was played while the musician was sitting. Images dating from the New Kingdom (1580—1085 B.C.) show arched harps up to 2 m high with as many as 30 strings. These were truly royal harps, with the resonator box covered with leopard skin and played standing. Asia was probably the birthplace of the *angle harp* with a narrow upright body sewn into leather. The strings—there were 13 to 23 of them—were tightened by ropes tied to pegs, the ropes hanging down on the other side as decorative tasselling.

Tomb paintings in Bení Hassan show that at the beginning of the 2nd millennium B.C., Syrian nomads introduced into Egypt a *lyre* with a narrow four-sided resonator from which two arched arms extended, joined at the end with a yoke. The *lyre harp* was adopted by the Egyptians from the Sumerians as documented by a relief from the Philae temple dating from the lst century B.C. Together with the lyre, the *lute* also reached Egypt in the form of an instrument with a small elongated body and two to four strings plucked with a plectrum. The lyre and the lute have survived till today in Northeast Africa, Sudan, Ethiopia and some other Arabic countries.

Ancient Egyptian instrumentation was positively enriched around

30 Egyptian angle harps and double shawm
Stone relief, Abu Hasan, Egypt, beginning of 2nd millennium B.C.

31 Bell of an Egyptian trumpet
Tomb of Tutankhamen, 1320 B.C.

1500 B.C. when the kings of the 18th dynasty conquered Asia Minor and shipped female slaves to the Egyptian court together with their musical instruments. Female dancers used to beat rhythm on *frame drums* similar to the modern tambourines now common throughout North Africa and the Near East, although the ancient version did lack metal jingling discs. Reliefs from the 12th dynasty period (2000—1788 B.C.) also show double-headed *barrel-shaped drums* which were beaten with both hands.

A relief now in Cairo Museum represents three young Egyptian girls at dance while playing a lyre, a harp and a lute. In Sakkareh a very old relief has been preserved, dating from the Old Kingdom and proving the existence of simultaneous performance of several instruments: a lute, a shawm and a harp together with a group of singers. Actually it is nothing but a sort of mixed vocal-instrumental ensemble of a composition similar to modern Egyptian groups. The singers indicate the tone pitch with the fingers of the right hand, a practice also still used among modern Egyptian musicians just as an open palm held close to one's ear is a common gesture among Egyptian folk singers. The visitor to the Theban necropolis will be attracted to a fresco in the Kakhtu tomb depicting a blind musician and an all-girl 'chamber ensemble'. Similarly fascinating are paintings of royal trumpeters accompanying the Pharaoh's army, to be seen on the walls of Medinet Habu, and of two lonely harpists in the tomb known as *The Harpists' Tomb*. All these pictures show how immense was the Egyptians' love for music and what a great importance music was thought to have in daily life.

JUDAEA

We have only a very vague idea of what Judaean musical instruments looked like although the Old Testament and other literary sources do mention them. Since the Old Testament forbade the making of any images of men and objects and only two pairs of cymbals and one *sistrum* holder have been so far unearthed in Palestine proper, the evidence is rather scanty. However, Judaean music was in constant contact with the Egyptian and Mesopotamian cultures and it can be therefore safely presumed that there was no great difference in the construction of Egyptian, Assyrian, Babylonian and Hebrew musical instruments. Communication between these cultures is highlighted in

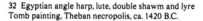

32 Egyptian angle harp, lute, double shawm and lyre
Tomb painting, Theban necropolis, ca. 1420 B.C.

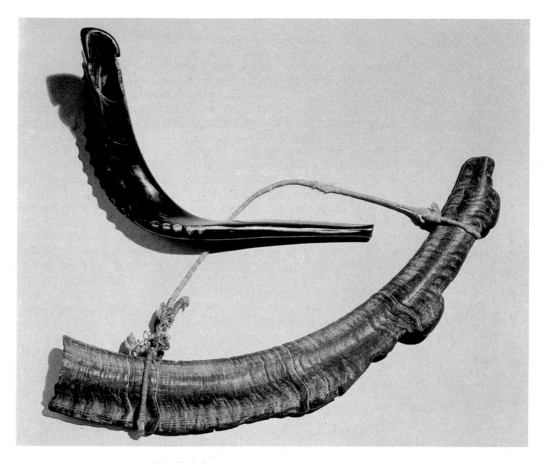

33 Jewish shofars
19th century

Egyptian harp, after H. Hickmann

the Talmud which says that Pharaoh's daughter whom king Solomon had married brought with her 'a thousand kinds of musical instruments' (Shabbat 56b).

Although there is much written evidence about the Israelis' love of music, sources on musical instruments proper are very scarce; and although the Psalms do mention some musical instruments, they never go into detail as to construction or design:

Sing praises to the Lord with the lyre (kinnor);
With the lyre and the sound of melody;
With trumpets and the sound of horn; (hazozra, shofar)
Make a joyful noise before the King, the Lord.

(Psalm 98,5)

Praise Him with trumpet sound;
Praise Him with lute and harp; (nevel)
Praise Him with timbrel and dance; (tof)
Praise Him with strings and pipe; (minim, halil)
Praise Him with sounding cymbals; (selslim)
Praise Him with loud clashing cymbals. (trud selslim)

(Psalm 150, 3—5)

41

Egyptian drums, after H. Hickmann

The *kinnor,* originally similar to the Egyptian or Syrian lyre, is today labelled *kithara* or *cithara.* According to the famous Jewish historian and general of the Roman army Josephus Flavius (1st century A.D.) the kinnor had ten strings plucked with a plectrum.

The only instrument which is still used in synagogues nowadays is the *shofar.* There were two kinds of shofar: one, made of a billy goat's horn was used on Rosh Hodesh (the first day of the month) while the other was made of a ram's horn and was used on Rosh Hashana (the Jewish New Year), a different tone of the shofar announcing each individual part of the festivities. To make a shofar, an animal horn was heated and shaped by flattening and bending. However, to sound a shofar is not an easy thing to do because the instrument can be blown only with difficulty and utters only a few uncultivated tones.

The Old Testament (Numbers, Chapter 10, Verses 1—8) states that the Lord ordered Moses to have silver *hazozra* trumpets made in case it would be necessary to go to battle. The Lord also instructed Moses in what manner, how many times, whether in pairs or singly and under what circumstances should the *hazozras* be blown. A scene on the Triumphal Arch of emperor Titus Flavius Vespasianus, erected in Rome after Jerusalem was conquered, depicts the emperor's triumphal return to Rome and among various kinds of war booty there are also short trumpets with funnel-shaped bells.

All we definitely know about the *nevel* is that it was a string instrument similar to the harp. Flavius mentions that the nevel had 12 strings and that it was played with bare fingers, i.e. without any plectrum.

The *tof* is an ancient Egyptian frame drum which—in contrast to the tambourine—had no jingling discs or pendants. This instrument, common to the entire Near East including Judaea, was usually played by women.

A Talmudic tract, *Ktubot,* relates that even the poorest people in Israel hired at least two *halil* players. The *halil* was most probably a kind of a *double aulos,* an instrument then common to the entire Near East. Earlier the halil used to have a cylindrical tube but later, just prior to the fall of the Jewish state, it acquired a conical tube similar to the Arabic *zamr.* The Arabic chronicle *Kitab al-Aghani* (Book of Songs) by Abu-al Faraj al-Isfahani (897—967) mentions the *mizmar* or *zamr* and the *deff* drum to be instruments used by Jewish tribal troops.

The *selslim* can probably be identified as cymbals. The *shama selslim* had a clear sound whereas the sound of the *trud selslim* was rougher. According to some organologists the *magrefah* was the Hebrew word for the *hydraulis,* or water organ, but there is no evidence for the existence of water organs in Judaea.

GREECE

Between the 5th and 3rd millennia B.C. when great cultures were flourishing in Egypt and Asia, Europe was still experiencing its Stone and Bronze Ages. The continent entered recorded history only as late as the 1st millennium B.C. in the lands around the Mediterranean which made possible not only the mutual contacts between the Greeks, the Etruscans and the Romans but also contacts with North Africa and the Near East.

Music historians often stress the incompatibility of ancient Greek music with the highly-sophisticated Greek poetry, sculpture and architecture. However, these arts have portrayed all aspects of Greek musical life and testify to the Greek interest in music. And it was the Greek theory of music which contributed most to the fertilization of European musical thought.

Athenaus, Pollux and other Greek writers mention a considerable

34 Jewish hazozras
Detail, Titus's triumphal arch, Rome, 1st century A.D.

number of Greek musical instruments of which the most important were the *kithara* and the *aulos.* Based on these two instruments, the Greek music was divided into two independent instrumental music styles: *kitharistics* (the art of playing string instruments) and *auletics* (the art of playing wind instruments). The first historical evidence on the playing of the *kithara* can be found in an ode by Terpander (7th century B.C.). The instrument was made entirely of wood and its sound was strong and clear. It was often decorated with carving and the late Roman kitharas rank among the most richly decorated instruments.

In the beginning the *kithara* differed only slightly from the other most common chordophone — the *lyre.* Greeks from Asia Minor as well as the Ionians inhabiting the Greek archipelago called the lyre therefore both the *forminx* as well as the *kitharis,* which is what Homer also called it. In the course of further development, both instruments retained some common features such as the shape, the number of strings and the manner in which the strings were sounded. Unlike the kithara, the lyre did not aspire to be an instrument of virtuosi and acquired instead the status of an entertainment and musical instruction instrument. The bottom part of the body was often formed by a tortoise shell stretched with skin and with two symmetrically-embedded antelope horns forming the arms of the instrument. The shape of the horn and the slightly upward curving outline gave the lyre its typical appearance which has been preserved till the present. The gut strings of both the lyre and the kitharis were stretched from the resonator box perpendicularly between the arms towards the yoke and to leather thongs wound

35 Greek kitharis (cithara)
Detail, Attica vase painting, 5th century B.C.

36 Aulos player. Detail, Attica vase painting, 5th century B.C.

around the yoke and tightened to obtain the desired tuning. The number of strings of both instruments was constantly increased from the original five up to eleven. A slimmer lyre type—the *barbiton* was used by Anacreon and other lyrical poets from the island of Lesbos to accompany songs performed at festival and feast time.

The *kithara* and the *lyre* were played either with fingers or with a wooden, metal or ebony piece called a *plectrum*. The strings were struck with the flat end of the latter which facilitated longer tone decay and increased the sharpness of the sound. As a common rule, singing was accompanied without a plectrum, but since the musician also had to perform solo intermezzos he had to switch between finger and plectrum plucking styles according to the immediate requirements of the piece performed.

Perhaps the most common Greek woodwind instrument was the *aulos*. A highly sophisticated type of aulos is described in great detail by the Greek writer Theophrastus (ca. 372—287 B.C.). The aulos was composed of three parts: the mouthpiece *(dzeugos)*, the middle joint *(holmos)* and foor joint forming the tube proper *(bombyx)*. The first and third parts were made of reed, the middle joint of bone or ivory. Other sources also list boxwood or metal as the material of the third joint and

37 Sambuke, cithara and lyre
Detail, Greek vase painting, late 5th century B.C.

38 Harp, aulos pipes, tambourine, lyre and lute
Greek plaque, 5th century B.C.

finally only the mouthpiece remained of reed. The Greek and Roman
aulos always had a cylindrical tube and older types of the instrument
lacked a bell. The long-discussed controversy over whether the aulos
had a single or double reed is still unsolved. The Greeks used four
types of aulos corresponding to the four basic pitches of the human
voice and also to the requirements of harmony with the *kithara*. The
fourth type was called the *kitharic aulos* and its pitch was between that
of the alto and tenor auloi. Other types were modified according to the
requirements of composition interpretation. This of course meant that
the solo player *(aulet)* as well as the accompaniment player *(aulod)*
each had to have an entire pitch—differentiated consort of instruments
to play in the prescribed mode. The number of fingerholes was gradually increased up to ten and even sixteen. The ancient writers hold that
each fingerhole enabled the player to play three tones of different
pitch; this implies that the ancient aulos players must have known not
only the principle of cross-fingering and partial covering of fingerholes
but also of overblowing into a higher octave. To facilitate overblowing
there was a device called the *syrinx*, actually a hole in the top (mouthpiece) joint of the aulos. It was called the syrinx because the higher
tones it emitted were similar to those obtained by the panpipe also
known as the *syrinx*.

The *salpinx* was a slightly conical trumpet with a narrow bore and
the earliest report of the instrument can be found in Homer's *Iliad.*

39 Roman trumpeter. Detail, mosaic, Piazza Armerina, Sicily, 4th century A.D.

Aeschylus mentions the instrument in his description of the battle of Salamis in his drama *Persae,* and Xenophon relates that the Athenian cavalry troops trained to the sound of salpinx signals, which implies that the salpinx was a military instrument. Thanks to its shrill sound, likened by Homer in the *Iliad* to the terrible cry of Achilles the salpinx was a favourite instrument for festivals and especially for solemn liturgical ceremonies.

Of the oldest wind instruments, the *kalamos* (reed) and *kalamé* (stalk) remained preserved in period folk music. The very names of these instruments reveal that they were made of reed and cereal stalks, and were later revived via the Latin word *calamus* in the French *chalumeau,* shawm. Another popular folk instrument pictured often by Greek art was the panpipe or *syrinx* whose design had remained unchanged since the prehistoric times, formed still by a series of graduated pipes held together with wax to form one instrument. This instrument is associated with mythological Pan who used to be a god of the

Salpinx, after a painting on a Greek cup, early 6th century, Rome, Museo Vaticano

Arcadian shepherds. During the day he roamed the mountains far and wide as a goat, but in the evening he blew his pipe so beautifully that nothing in the world could resist its charm.

No evidence has been discovered so far in literary or pictorial relics of any other Greek membranophone apart from the *frame drum.*

ITALY

Long before the ascendancy of Rome, the *ETRUSCANS* living in the heart of what is now Italy had developed a blossoming culture fertilized mainly by Oriental influences. Music played an important part both in their worship and in daily life and was also performed during sporting events and even when punishments were meted out. According to Diodorus Siculus, the Etruscans were the first to use a war trumpet called the *Tyrrhenian trumpet.* A mural painting in a tomb in Chiusi represents a burial rites scene (the mural is now kept in the Archaeological Museum, Florence) and shows a musician holding a trumpet with a slightly conical tube, bent like a smoking pipe at the end and reinforced with a crossband. The bend clearly shows a hole to allow saliva drainage. The shape makes the trumpet resemble the Roman *lituus* trumpet, a perfectly preserved specimen of which was found near Cerveteri and is deposited now in Museo Etrusco Gregoriano, Rome. It is 160 cm long and tuned in G.

The oldest representation of an Etruscan horn can be seen on a fres-

40 Cymbals and aulos
Marble relief, 1st century A.D.

41 Woman playing the aulos
Stone relief, southern Italy, ca. 460 B.C.

Lyre, after a painting on a Greek vase, ca. 480 B.C., Staatliche Antikensammlung, Munich

42 Etruscan flautist
Stone tomb relief, near Perugia, 2nd century B.C.

43 Etruscan aulos and barbiton players
Detail, Etruscan mural painting, Tomb of the Leopards, Tarquinia, 475 B.C.

44 Tibia, tympanon and cymbala
Mosaic, Cicero's villa, Pompeii, end of 2nd century B.C.

Greek cithara, after a painting
on a Greek vase, ca. 480 B.C.,
Museum of Fine Arts, Boston

co from Corveto-Tarquinia. A peculiarity of the instrument is a tube reinforcement crosspiece similar to that found on the Chiusi trumpet. An interesting point is that similar reinforcement crosspieces are found first on Etruscan brass instruments. This technological improvement was of great importance for the further development of mouthpiece instruments since it made possible instruments with much longer tubes, therefore also with lower tones and the possibility to sound a greater number of partial tones. The two horns found in a grave in Alba Longa attest to another technique unrecorded in Europe so far: the horns are not cast but hammered. According to Greek writers, the Greeks took over from the Etruscans a slightly conical straight trumpet used originally by Etruscan pirates for signalling at night or in fog. The Etruscans are also credited with the introduction of a detachable mouthpiece although no instrument with this improvement has survived.

Paintings on columns in the *Tomba dei rilievi* near Cerverti depict two *litui,* one of which has its mouthpiece differently coloured from the rest of the instrument body. From the Etruscans, the Romans took over technology of bronze trumpet and horn production and these instruments were later to become the dominant instruments of Roman mili-

51

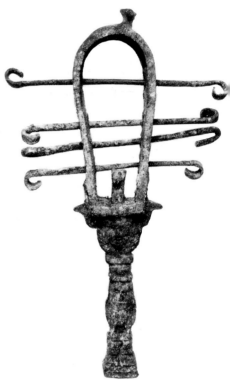

45 Aulos
Mural painting by a Hellenistic painter, Vigna Amendolo, Via Appia near
Rome

46 Bronze Roman sistrum
Pompeii, end of 2nd century B.C.

tary music; Etruscan mouthpiece instruments also found their way
northward to Gaul. An Etruscan stone urn dating from the 2nd century B.C. and unearthed near Perugia shows a relief of the head of
a musician playing a side-blown flute with a short tube of a wide bore
and fingerholes. The mouthhole is located about one quarter of the
total length of the tube along.

A favourite instrument of the Etruscans was the *double shawm,* an
instrument which originated in Asia Minor. An image of a musician
holding such an instrument has been preserved on a mural in the
Tombs of the Leopards of Tarquinia. The double shawm player is followed by another musician holding a seven-string *lyre.* As recorded by
Aristotle, the Etruscans used to hold boxing matches, knead dough or
punish their slaves to the sound of a *double aulos* and Etruscan musicians perfected the art of double shawm playing to unprecedented
virtuosity as did their Greek disciples with the single aulos. An Etruscan relief from the 2nd century B.C. (now in the Ashmolean Museum,
Oxford) pictures a ship followed by sirens playing kitharas with plectra, panpipes and double shawms.

The natural affinity of the Etruscans and Romans made the *ROM-*

Cornu and lituus, after an Etruscan mural painting, late 4th century B.C., Castel Rubello tomb, Orvietto

ANS discover in Etruscan art their own artistic leanings. Through the Etruscans the Romans came also into contact with the Greek culture, which then became a model for them.

Instrumental music soon acquired an important position in Roman culture and was considered superior to singing. Whenever a song or a dance was performed in Rome, the *tibia,* a short pipe of Etruscan origins, had to be there. Very often two tibia were paired together, the members of the pair being called *tibia dextra* and *tibia sinistra* (right and left tibia); the first had a narrower, the second a wider bore tube. Under the intensifying Greek influences, the tibia was being perfected in the same way as the aulos, but in the end it was totally driven out by the latter and its usage limited to ancient cult rites remembered fondly by Ovid and Horace as symbols of the good old days.

The Romans also took from the Etruscans the *transverse flute* (side-blown, cross-flute) which became a favourite motif for artists, but remained mainly a cult instrument in the hands of temple musicians.

47 Roman buccina
Detail, stone relief, Marcus Aurelius' triumphal arch, Rome, 2nd century A.D.

Roman aulos; after a sarcophagus relief, mid-3rd century, Praetext Catacomb, Rome

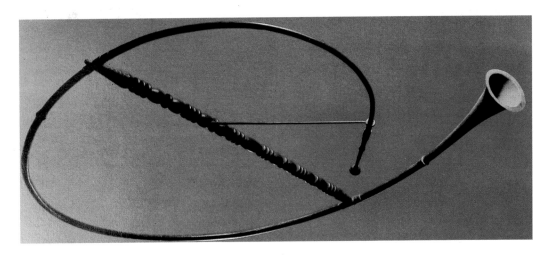

48 Roman tuba
1st century A.D.

The mouthpiece instruments were used primarily in the Roman armies. According to the so-called Servius' Constitution, there were to be 100 trumpeters and pipers to each legion, the task of the musicians being to give required signals and to entertain the troops with their music. When a victorious general returned triumphantly to Rome, the marching columns would be headed by a military band. To facilitate an easy recognition of the signal by sound only, the Roman armies employed many kinds of brass instruments. The majority of these were taken over from the Etruscans, but the Romans continued to develop them.

The main instrument of infantry troops was the *tuba* which had been quite common among ancient nations long before the Romans adopted it; its straight conical tube was about 125 cm long and ended in a flared bell. One of the scenes on the Trajan Column shows a tuba player whose instrument has a rope loop attached to the bell and in the middle of the body length. The rope was used to fix the instrument to the body when marching. The quality and strength of the sound of the tuba which could produce only six tones at the most was aptly described by the poet Quintus Ennius (239—168 B.C.): 'At tuba terribili sonitu taratamtara dixit' (With a frightening sound the tuba said 'taratamtara').

Cavalry troop for whom long straight trumpets would be unwieldy and cumbersome used a trumpet with a hooked bell called a *lituus.* The experts' opinion on the instrument—as well as the *cornu* and the buccina which are discussed below—varies greatly because of the unclear stylization of contemporary literary sources as well as imprecise period illustrations of the instrument. However, it is certain that the lituus, described already as having once been an Etruscan instrument, was shortened by the Romans and acquired its distinctive hook-belled shape. A perfectly preserved specimen of the *lituus* was discovered in the Rhine near Düsseldorf and is kept now in the Saalburg Museum.

Roman buccina; after a mosaic from a Roman villa at Nennig by Trier, West Germany, 230—240

The metal strip rings joining the individual parts of the instrument together are highly ornamented. Lituus and cornu player used to perform at weddings and funerals.

The *buccina* and the *cornu* will be treated jointly and their similarities stressed. The common feature of Roman mouthpiece instruments shown on Roman art relics is a narrow bore and slightly conical tube bent into a semicircle or an open circle, the bell being always funnel-shaped. Instruments forming a circle have the mouthpiece bent inside the circle while the bell is bent outside. Some circular instruments have a crosspiece which rested on the musician's shoulder while he was playing. It is debatable whether the instrument should be called a *cornu* or a *buccina*. The Roman writer Flavius Vegetius Renatus in his treatise *Epitoma rei militaris* defines the cornu as an instrument 'made of horns of a wild ox, skilfully joined by silverwork'. Another passage states that 'the *tubicines* blow the *tubae*, the *buccinatores* the *buccinae* and the *cornicines* the bent metal'. It is obvious then that the *cornu* must have also been a bent tube instrument made of metal. In the same chapter in which he deals with the *cornu*, Vegetius talks also of the *buccina* as an instrument which 'winds in a circle of metal'. This circular

49 King David playing a cithara
Late classical relief, 6th century A.D.

Hydraulis after Hero of Alexandria

instrument was carried by the musician in such a way that the middle part of the instrument's body ran under his arm and around his hip and the bell part rose above his shoulder.

The Romans are to be credited with an improvement in and popularization of the water organ which they called the *hydraulis,* an instrument which is indeed the most difficult to master and technically definitely the most intricate and complex of the entire classical period. Ctesibius of Alexandria, the famous ancient mechanic, is thought to have been the creator of the instrument. Although he lived in the latter half of the 3rd century B.C. the first description of the instrument is by Philo of Alexandria and dates from the 1st century B.C. Philo describes the water organ as something like a syrinx played by a water-powered mechanism. However, all this implies that to invent the *hydraulis* it was first necessary to replace the original syrinx pipes with flue pipes, to invent a mechanical device supplying air and to design a keyboard. In this author's opinion Ctesibius should be regarded as more of an improver than inventor of the instrument. He improved the system of air supply by means of water pressure which had the same function in the water organ as the weight of the bellows had for the mechanically-operated organ. The water organ *(organum aquaticum)* was never too popular in Greece, but it became very important in Rome and was

51 Roman cithara
Ivory relief, 5th century A.D.

50 Hydraulis
Pompeii, end of 2nd century B.C.

52 Roman cymbals
Pompeii, end of 2nd century B.C.

played by both men and women. It was used and played both in cult worship as well as household entertainment and was also used in circuses to accompany gladiator fights. Vitruvius in his treatise *De architectura* states—and his statement is corroborated in *Pneumatica* by Hero of Alexandria—that the *hydraulis* consisted of a water tank filled to more than half with water in which a spherical bell with water outlet holes was immersed. In the top part of the bell there were two pipes, one leading to a pump supplying the air into the tank, the other connected with the wind chest. When a key was pressed the air entered the selected pipe and sounded it.

So far two specimens of the *hydraulis* have been discovered, one in Pompeii, the other in Aquincum near Budapest. The Aquincum *hydra* — this name was found inscribed on the instrument — was made in 228 B.C. The ingenuity of the design and the small dimensions are very surprising: the height without base is only 62 cm and the instrument weights about 6—8 kg. Of the 52 flue pipes 39 are stopped and 13 unstopped, the pipe length is between 12 and and 36 cm, with diameters from 0.9 to 1.4 cm. The pipes are arranged in four registers facilitating play in various modes. Since the number of keys was identical with the number of the pipes in one register, the Aquincum *hydra* had 13 wooden keys covered with a brass sheet.

After the fall of the Roman Empire the hydraulis ceased to be used in the Occident while dying a slower death in Byzantium. The last image of the instrument can be found in the Utrecht Psalter from the 9th century, and although the picture is most probably a copy of an older model it means in any case that the instrument must still have been known at the time when the Psalter was made.

THE MIDDLE AGES

After the ovations for the Emperors and celebrations of the pagan gods ended, the musical instruments which had taken part in these triumphal pageants also fell silent and started to disappear into oblivion. From its beginnings, Christianity proclaimed its preference for vocal music and soon the majority of musical instruments of the classical age were forgotten. Those which had survived were stigmatized by the Church as belonging to 'Devil's musicians' who as 'Satan's sextons' were comparable to wild animals. Against them 'God's musicians' were those who played the instruments listed in the Old Testament. Nevertheless, early medieval painting and sculpture clearly prove that in spite of all the objections raised by the Church very many old instruments found their place and function in the daily life. Written records also inform us of the existence of these instruments, e.g. the spurious letter from Saint Hieronymus to Dardanus (9th century A.D.) lists twelve musical instruments as an aftermath of the Graeco-Roman instrumentation. Neither the instruments illustrated in the Utrecht Psalter or in the Bible of Charles The Bald were entirely free of classical influences. However, fiddles pictured in a manuscript in Madrid National Library

53—54 Drawing of musical instruments
M. Severinus Boethius: *De Musica*, copy, 10th century

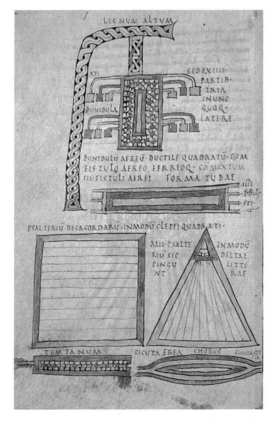
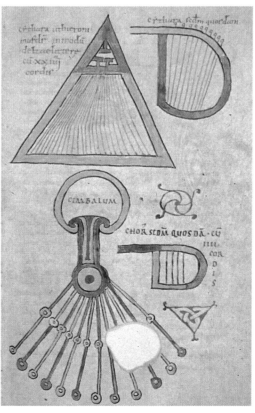

55 Cymbals, four-sided harp with resonators, harp, lute
Italian miniature, Abbazia, Monte Cassino, 11th century

(ca. 920—930; MS Hh 58) mark the first step of the dramatic development that was to culminate several centuries later with Antonio Stradivari. Nothing, even the cave paintings discovered recently in Bulgaria, can account for the origins of the bow. But the illustration in the
MS Hh 58 shows musicians holding bows in their hands. The bow is
simply suddenly here to cause a revolution among the whole string
family of later periods.

Medieval instrumental music was performed by jugglers and travel-
ling minstrels and 13th century Provençal jugglers were required to
master nine instruments: fiddle, bagpipe, fife, harp, hurdy-gurdy, gigue
(jig fiddle), decachord, psaltery and rote.

Among the oldest medieval idiophones were various wooden and
metal clappers derived probably from classical models. In the 13th
century, clappers can be seen in the hands of jugglers and still later
they became a device with which lepers were obliged to warn of their
presence. Among the instruments shown in the Bible of Charles The
Bald (A.D. 823—877) are metal *clappers* consisting of two small,
slightly convex cymbals on flexible arms and a common holder. The
player would hold one clapper in each hand, sometimes even playing
a wind instrument at the same time.

59

56 Horn, metal clappers, harp, cithara and lituus
Bible of Charles The Bald, 9th century

Double clarinet; after an illustration in MS Lat. 1118, 11th century, Bibliothèque Nationale, Paris

Cymbals were originally common only to the eastern and southern regions of the European continent and existed in two shapes. The first type had *convex plates* and can be seen on paintings and sculptural works up to the end of the 13th century. The other type, which existed parallel to the first, was of Oriental origins and featured *flat plates*. However, from the beginning of the 14th century onward only flat cymbals with central bosses can be found. From the surviving documents it has been ascertained that the cymbals were sounded always by concussion, i.e. striking them against each other and held either by handles or leather wriststraps. Until the 1250's the instrument was played only vertically but later on musicians can be seen holding cymbals horizontally and the cymbals were sounded either by concussion or by the top cymbal striking the bottom cymbal of the pair. Cymbals were played in this manner until the 16th century when they disappear from instrumentation entirely.

Handbells had been in continuous use ever since the ancient period while *tower* and *belfry bells* can be documented only as late as the 6th century A.D. In Latin texts, handbells are called *cymbalum* or *tintinnabulum*. Originally they were used solely for signalling and calling the adversary out in tournaments, but later they were introduced into liturgic music and were supposed to add—together with the organ—a mystic quality or halo to the earthly sound of medieval church music. In the Jaroměř Bible which dates from the end of the 13th century (now in the National Museum, Prague) we can see a three-bell *chime* although the majority of period illustrations show chimes consisting of a greater number of bells (usually 5—12). The *triangle,* made of a bent metal rod, was an instrument with a very refined sound that was not governed by any strict theoretical rules; its Latin name was *tripos colybaeus* and it existed in two shapes, as an isosceles triangle and as a regular trapezoid. A uniquely-shaped triangle can be seen in the Saint Emmeran MS from the 10th century (State Library, Munich): the shape is that of an openwork tripod. The triangle as such had apparently originated from the classical *sistrum* (rattle), and this assumption seems to be corroborated by its shape and by the jingle discs strung on the triangle base. When played, the triangle was held either by a handle or by a wrist strap and was sounded with a small metal baton.

Some very ancient wind instruments survived until the Middle Ages, e.g. the shawm, flute and fingerholed horns. The *shawm* acquired its

57 Oliphant
Property of Roland, nephew of Charlemagne, 8th century

medieval shape during the Crusades from the oriental conical tube *zamr* shawm. Reports of an instrument called the *chalamelle* or *chalemie* (from Latin *calamus* = reed) in French literature date as far back as the 12th century. Period illustrations show two types of medieval shawms. One, pictured in the Codex Manesse (ca. 1310, now in the University Library, Heidelberg) has a short, slightly conical tube, the second, as can be seen on a detail of the Gothic panel painting *Coronation of the Virgin Mary* by Paolo Venetiano (National Gallery, Prague), is longer and the bore is narrower.

Pictorial documentation also attests to a considerable spread of the use of the *bladder pipe* from the 13th to 15th centuries. The reed of this instrument was placed inside a bladder which had a similar function to the bagpipe airbag in that the reed could be sounded more easily than with the mouth, but the disadvantage of the instrument was that no overblowing into a higher octave was possible.

Very little is known about the *flute* prior to 1500. The oldest picture of it showing an end-blown (vertical) version with a cylindrical tube can be seen in an 11th century manuscript (Lat. 1118, National Library, Paris); its sound was said to be so gentle that in France the instrument became known as the sweet flute *(flûte douce).* It had reached Western Europe from Asia via North Africa, Hungary and Bohemia. The Slavic

58 Fiddle
Illuminated MS *Mater verborum,* 13th century

59 Harp, hurdy-gurdy, psaltery, fiddle
Miniature from a MS calendar of Irish origin, ca. A.D. 1300

60 Instruments permitted by
the Church *top, left-to-right:* monochord, glockenspiel, organ,
harp, panpipe, horn

Folk instruments
bottom, left-to-right: rebec, horn,
drum
Psalter of Abbot St. Remigius,
12th century

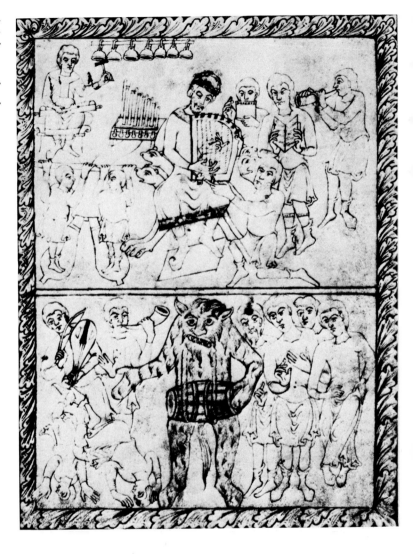

Straight cornett; after a bible
from ca. 1070, Gräfische
Schönbornsche Bibliothek,
Pommersfelden

background of the instrument is proved by Old French poetry and
prose celebrating it as the Bohemian flute — *flûte de Behaigne.* However, the flute is most commonly pictured in a flute and drum combination played by one musician. The poem *Frauendienst* by Ulrich von
Lichtenstein (1255) claims the homeland of this *pipe-and-tabor* combination to be France whence it spread throughout the entire European
continent. Guillaume de Machaut (1300—1370), the medieval French
poet and composer calls these two instruments *flaios* and *tabour* and
states there were more than twenty types of flutes, both 'thin and thick'
('tant de fortes comme de legieres'). Among the flaios group Machaut
ranks *fistules, pipes, soffles* and *fretiaux.* The *fretiau* was later known
as *galoubet.* Machaut was living at the court of the Bohemian king
John of Luxembourg and his description of musical instruments in his

61 Pipe-and-tabor combinations

62 Double-bladder pipes

63 Crumhorns

64 Fiddles

61–64 Miniatures from the codex of Alfonso el Sabio (Alphonso X The Wise) king of Leon and Castile
(Cantigas de Santa Maria)

65 Organ

66 Flute

67 Triangle

68 Tambourine

65—68 Marginal drawings from MS *Ponticale et benedictionale*, 14th century

Conquest of Alexandria documents the variety of instruments employed in musical performances at the Prague court.

The single hand flute had a short unstopped tube till the 14th century but later it was extended in length, became slimmer and acquired a beaked head. In spite of the fact that the instrument had only two fingerholes on the overside and one on the underside, by covering the resonator hole at the end of the tube and by using cross-fingering a chromatic scale of a two octave compass could be produced.

Once a different material than animal horn was used for the construction of a holed horn the *cornett* was born, although the instrument saw greater use only later during the Renaissance. A very important role in medieval daily life was played by the *trumpet:* it was used to call for bread and water at the courts of the aristocracy; also the trumpet opened and closed tournaments (as well as town gates). An equally important role was played by the trumpet in the military; cavalry troops used different trumpets than those used in fortified cities, castles and other strongholds and still other types were used in the navy. Basically, however, these instruments were always one of the two trumpet types known by the Latin names *buccina* and *tuba.* The tube of the *buccina* was more conical and the instrument had no bell so that the instrument had a more horn-like character, while the *tuba* was cylindrical and featured a flared bell.

The desire to produce lower and lower tones led to the tube length being progressively increased until the instrument was too cumbersome to handle and easily damaged. The tubes of the brass instrument therefore became curved and bent into all kinds of shapes until the curvature finally stabilized in the 15th century as the shape of the letter

Fiddle; after a miniature in a Catalonian bible, early 11th century, Biblioteca Vaticana, Rome

69 Bladder pipe
Mural painting, Karlštejn Castle, Czechoslovakia, 14th century

70 Fiddle, psaltery, lute, tambourine, portative, clappers, bagpipe, shawm, tympani, trumpets
M. Severinus Boethius: *De Arytmetica, de Musica,* 14th century copy

S. The era also marked the beginning of the great period of *clarinists,* trumpeters playing instruments called the *tromba clarina* or just shortly the *clarina,* who acquired a privileged position in the households of town and country nobility.

It is a well-established fact from the history of music that a great contribution to the development of the *pneumatic organ* in Europe is to be credited to the Byzantine emperor Constantine V (Copronymus) who in 757 sent to king Pepin the Short in Compiègne a present of a small portable organ with lead pipes. Called a *portative,* it was carried in processions on leather straps around the player's shoulders; the right hand played the 'keys' while the left operated the bellows in the back of the instrument. The portative had 8—32 pipes made of various alloys; each pipe had its individual key, or rather pallet or slide valve which was pulled out and pushed in during play so opening and closing the passage of wind to the pipes. From the 13th century, a system of levers came to be used instead of valves and when the lever key was pressed down, a flap opened in the back, allowing the wind to pass into the respective pipe. However, due to its small tonal compass the portative remained merely a supporting instrument in liturgic music and it was used mainly for Gregorian chants. After a period of bloom in the 14th and 15th centuries the popularity of the portative suddenly dropped and it was gradually replaced by a larger and non-portable organ called the *positive.*

No instrument in the hierarchy of musical instruments deserves more to be called 'royal' than the *harp,* indeed, medieval imagery associated the harp as closely with king David as the anvil with Juba or the monochord with Pythagoras. In the early Middle Ages, Irish musicians in-

71 Drum, flute, fiddles, psaltery and bagpipe
Detail, illustration of a song collection, Swiss, the so-called Codex Manesse, 14th century

72 Psaltery harp
Detail, fresco, Karlštejn Castle, Czechoslovakia, ca. 1365

Dulcimer; after a picture in *Les Échecs Amoureux,* late 15th century, Bibliothèque Nationale, Paris

troduced into Europe the broad *Irish harp* which later became the model for a similar but smaller instrument popular with the French *jongleurs* and the German *minnesingers.* The Provençal culture which reached the northern lands brought also poets and musicians who sang and played various instruments among which the most esteemed place was occupied by the small harp. This sized harp is commonly seen in medieval pictures, and only rarely does the instrument height exceed that of the sitting musician. However, an even smaller harp did exist, carried by the musician on a leather strap on his shoulder. The neck of this harp was extended in a serpentine manner and the musician rested the neck against his shoulder while standing to play it. This was another of the popular instruments used by minnesingers and troubadours for the accompaniment of their songs, and there was not a single *chanson de geste* through which the sound of a harp would not be constantly heard, or a presentation of chivalrous deeds and adventure nor introduced by a harpist.

Besides the harp another plucked instrument often depicted as being played by king David is the *psaltery* of the Middle Ages. Usually it was a delta-shaped instrument with several single and coarse strings made of metal. In the late medieval period the psaltery entered the domain of folk music and under the name of *salterio tedesco* became an ancestor of the *cimbalom* dulcimer. In fact, modern instrumentation is indebted to the psaltery which represents the earliest stage in the development of the later keyboard string instruments. Indeed, once a keyboard with

73 Ceteras psaltery and harps
Drawing from MS *Scriptum super Apocalypsis,* late 14th century

74 Trumpeter and drummer
Miniature from MS *Liber viaticus* by Jan of Středa, second half of the 14th century

a plucking mechanism was added to the psaltery the *clavicembalo* (harpsichord) was born: a version featuring tangents was called the *clavichord* or *manicordium.* Besides the psaltery proper, there were also semipsalteries or *micanons.* When the slanting side of the *micanon* became rounded, the instrument became wing-shaped, *ala* in Latin. One type of psaltery is found solely in documents of Czech origins and the instrument's provenance is proved by its attribute *bohemica—ala bohemica.*

When the harp and psaltery were combined a new instrument was born whose nature is buried under various Latinisms such as *tympanon, nabulum, cithara,* etc. What the instrument was actually like is known only from Czech and one South Slavic pictorial documents. It is the *psaltery harp* with two resonator boxes. In one body, with soundholes either in the soundboard or in the ribs, about 16 strings joined while the second body in the shape of a broad curved belt with a soundhole in

75 Bohemian wing (ala bohemica), cetera, fiddle and psaltery
Drawing from Velislav Bible, Bohemia, 1340

76 Psaltery harp, carillon and psaltery
Drawing from Velislav Bible, Bohemia, 1340

the centre took up the space between the first resonator box and the neck and substituted for the pillar. However, it did not occupy the entire space so that the shortest strings already ran outside the resonator box. A fresco in the Chapel of St. Cross in the Karlštejn Castle near Prague shows a psaltery harp in great detail.

From the typological point of view, the medieval chordophones equipped with a fingerboard can be arranged in two groups. The first is composed of three-part fiddle-type instruments whose resonator box consists of a soundboard or belly, a backboard or bottom and the ribs. The second group is made of two-part lute-type instruments with the resonator box consisting of a flat belly and highly arched bottom. The two-part instruments are usually plucked while the three-part instruments are bowed.

The main representative of the two-part chordophones is the *lute*. It is still not precisely known at what time and via what route the instrument had reached Europe after it originated in Arabia. The lute is easy to misidentify on pictorial material since the image can be also easily

77 Harp   78 Cetera

77—80 Details of Miniatures from Passional of Abbess Kunthuta, 1319—21

that of a similarly-shaped *rebec, cobsa, mandora* or *quinterne*. Genuine lutes with the distinctive neck, frets and back-bent pegboard can be found on pictures dating no earlier than the 14th century and neither the names *laudia, lautus* and *lutana* are much older. The lute body had first been pear-shaped, but its Italian makers later made it almond-shaped, the body was composed of many narrow maplewood staves. During the Renaissance, the period of the greatest bloom of the lute, the instrument was often made of santal and cypress woods. There are many exquisite works of art immortalizing the beauty of the instrument, be it the Giotto sculptures on the Florentine Campanille or the famous *Lutist* by van Dyck (the Louvre).

An instrument whose construction did not undergo any considerable structural change during its many centuries of existence was the *trumpet marine*. The instrument had a highly conspicuous body of a very narrow and long pyramidal shape whose length enabled the player to use the flageolet technique on the single string. The bridge of the instrument had two legs; the thicker and longer leg rested fully on the

79 Bohemian wing (ala bohemica)

80 Fiddle

81 Psaltery, trumpet marine lute, trumpet and shawm
Hans Memling: triptych *Angel Musicians,* late 15th century

sound board while the thinner and shorter one came only into very slight contact with it so that when the instrument was played the vibrations of the thinner leg gave the sound a curious timbre. Furthermore, the bow was not applied to the string above the bridge as on other bowed instruments but in the top part of the instrument between the head and the left thumb which stopped the string in critical points with very light touch. Also remarkable is the manner in which the instrument was held as attested by medieval pictures: it resembles the manner of trumpet holding. Can it be that this unorthodox and surely extremely uncomfortable manner of holding is somehow related to the other name by which the instrument was also known, i.e. *tromba marina?* Or is it that this seemingly contradictory name stems from the fact that the same natural scale could be played on this 'marine trumpet' as on the regular trumpet?

Although the *guitar*—a representative of the three-part chordophones—was to become extremely important only later in the 18th century, images of the instrument can be found on illuminations of Spanish books as early as the 10th century as the *guitarra latina, quinterne, guiterna,* etc.; it appears in a fully developed form as the *vihuela* in *Declaracion de instrumentos musicales* (Osuna 1549) by Juan Ber-

82 Straight trumpet, slide trumpet, portative organ. harp, fiddle
Hans Memling: altar piece (triptych) *Angel Musicians*, late 15th century

mudo. Michael Praetorius describes the guitar as an instrument of Italian comedians.

Johannes de Grocheo, a music theorist active around 1300 in Paris, wrote in his treatise *Theoria* (Darmstadt Library): 'The predominant position among musical instruments is occupied by the string family of whom the first is the *fiddle* because it has cantilena and also every other musical form in it.' The importance of the fiddle in the instrumentation of medieval music is also confirmed by its frequent pictures. Its Asia Minor origins are attested to by an 8th century ivory book cover showing the instrument held in the typical Oriental manner, as well as by the Utrecht Psalter where the instrument has a spade-shaped body. The first emergence of an oval-bodied fiddle dates from the 10th century and was developed among the Slavs. Its narrow elongated and waisted body later became common elsewhere.

Besides the fiddle, there was another bowed instrument which can be seen, for instance, on sculptural work decorating the Archibishop's Palace in the Spanish town of Santiago de Compostela. The instrument shown together with the fiddle had a wide oval body with low ribs and literary sources call it the *lira*.

83 Handbells, triangle, white cornett, jingle bells, trumpet, dulcimer, harp, shawm, fiddle, lute, mandora portative, vertical flute, harp, trumpet marine, psaltery, kettledrums, bell, glockenspiel, clavichord and hurdy-hurdy. Codex Casimirianum, 1448

Hurdy-gurdy; after a drawing in a psaltery from ca. 1170, Hunterian museum, Glasgow

A truly great popularity was enjoyed in the Middle Ages also by the *hurdy-gurdy* whose main design feature was the shortening of the strings by tangents. The mechanization of the bow action by means of a rotary wooden disc covered with resin and located in the lower part of the body was only a later improvement. Early illustrations show hurdy-gurdies of considerable dimensions which two men were required to play: one handling the tangents while the other turned the crank. However, the body gradually became smaller until only one man was needed to play the instrument. During the 14th century the popularity of the hurdy-gurdy steadily declined and today it is found only in European folk music.

Saint Isidore of Seville in his treatise from the year A.D. 600 called the drum *symphonia* and described it as a hollow log stretched on both ends with skins.

The illuminated manuscript *Liber viaticus* by Jan of Středa (National Museum, Prague) shows a drummer with the drum suspended around his neck. The instrument had the same dimensions as the modern side drum with the drummer using two drumsticks which beat the drumhead at the correct angle of about 75 degrees, the right elbow raised in the same way as is the practice nowadays. Medieval illustrations often show small drums in pairs, tied either above the drummer's knees or around his waist and beaten with two wooden drumsticks.

Kettledrums were introduced to Europe only after the Crusades, at the end of the 13th century. Guilaume de Machaut in his poem *The Conquest of Alexandria* calls these instruments *nacaires* (English *nakers*, from Arabic *naqqara*). Joinville, the chronicler of Louis IX of France, characterized the Saracen instruments in the following way when describing the Crusades: 'The quarrelling of their kettledrums and horns was a terrible thing to hear.' A picture of a double-headed elongated barrel-shaped drum can be found in an early 12th century manuscript kept at Cambridge while Italian manuscripts show hourglass or waisted drums. The so-called *margaretum* was a tambourine

84 Upright clavicytherium
Detail, wooden altar, parish church in Kefermarkt, Austria, late 15th century

85 Small kettledrums, fiddle, horn, triangle, lute and bagpipe
Miniature from Olomouc Bible, Bohemia, 1417

Drum; after a miniature in King Wenceslaus' IV Bible, 14th century, Staatliche Bibliothek, Vienna

with jingles sounded with a stick and was very common throughout the entire Mediterranean and especially in Italy and Spain. It is one of the most commonly depicted instruments in the works of 14th and 15th century Italian masters. However, during the 16th century the margaretum suddenly moved into the folk music sphere and was gradually forgotten by serious composers. As we can see, the Middle Ages knew all the types of drums used in modern orchestration. Since the greatest use of the drum was reserved for military purposes where the most important criterion was the volume of sound, there existed also a drum of considerable dimensions called the *bedon*.

Iconographic and literary sources prove the role of musical instruments in the Middle Ages to be much more important than has been realized so far. The Middle Ages did not have any genuine orchestra yet, and troupes of musicians as seen in various illustrations were formed only for each individual occasion, but despite this a definite attempt is discernible (especially in the age of polyphony) to aim at some instrumental grouping which would be based on the character of the sound combination. The lack of sources on the construction and design of musical instruments and on instrumental music performance in the medieval period still poses organology many unanswered questions.

THE NEW AGE

RENAISSANCE

The Renaissance marks the beginning of rapid progress in instrumental music which obtained the necessary stimulus from various court and aristocrats' orchestras. Various documents and preserved instruments allow us to form a clear idea of the instruments of the age. One is immediately struck by the fact that while string instruments had been predominant in the Middle Ages, the Renaissance was characterized by the splendid abundance of wind instruments of remarkable designs and high-precision construction. Moreover, the winds were now made more of wood rather than metal as in earlier periods.

The ever-growing demand for low tones provides the stimulus for the construction of large instruments, but these were handled only with difficulty as far as the playing techniques were concerned. During the Renaissance, entire instrument ranges called *consorts* were built from the descant to the subbass versions. The consorts were characterized by the same timbre; a typical example of a Renaissance consort would be that of 21 recorders described by Michael Praetorius.

This unprecedented development was greatly stimulated by attempts at timbre differentiation of instruments, but primarily by the invention of keys enabling the musician to reach the lowest fingerholes of the instruments. This revolutionary advance was of such an importance for the further development of musical instruments that entirely new mu-

86 Sordones
Late 16th century

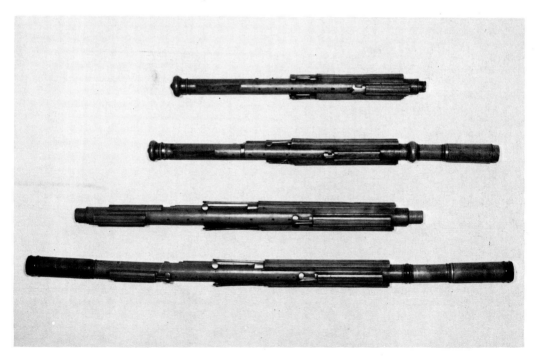

87 Slide trumpet and shawms
Maestro del Cassone Adimari, detail of the painting *Wedding of Adimari*, ca. 1450

88 Bombards, straight trumpets and curved trumpet
Drawing from the Richenthal Chronicle, the so-called Leningrad Manuscript, 1464

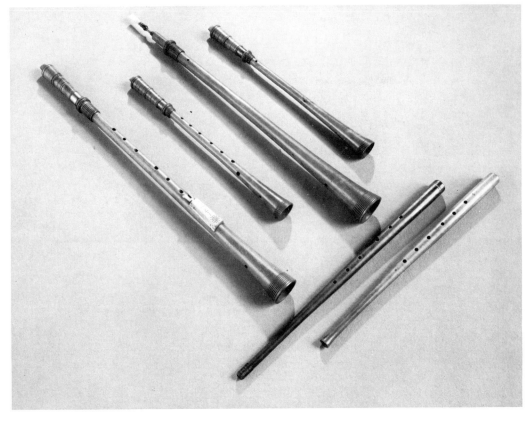

89 Two cornetts and four wind-cap shawms, 16th century

Great bass sordone
1 Mouthpiece hole 2 Fingerholes 3 Keys 4 Air hole
5 Resonator holes (bore ter-
minations) 6 Drainage hole

sical instrument types were born. Predominant among the latter was the *pommer* shawm whose consort, at the peak of its development in the 16th century, ranged from the small *bombardo sopranino* down to the great bass *bombardone.* The pommer had seven fingerholes and several other holes were manipulated with keys. In the lower, slightly conical part of the body there were two air holes and the bell edge was protected with a metal ring. Their popularity was transient, however; Abbé Martin Mersenne, French philosopher and scientist, in his book *Harmonie universelle* (1636) lists only three bombard sizes: *dessus, taille* and *basse* (the instrument was also known as the *bassanelli*). These clumsy double reed shawms produced a sound similar to the later bassoon which was to supersede them finally in the 17th century so that bombards were already unknown to 18th century musicologists. The great bass bombard was almost 3 m long.

The preference for low tones and a nasal timbre of the instrumental sound together with efforts to devise more sophisticated playing techniques provided the impetus for the creation of specially constructed woodwinds. One of these, called the *sordone,* is shown on the title page of Prae orius' work *Theatrum instrumentorum* (Wolffenbüttel, 1618). It is held by the musician standing on the right of the organ. Four pre-

Bass bombard
1 Double reed 2 Brass crook
3 Head joint with six fingerholes 4—5 Keys 6 Wooden
key covers called fontanellae
7 Brasswork 8 Brass fontanel-
la 9 Flare 10 Brass decorative
flare ring

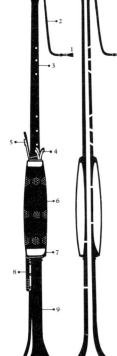

90 Cornett, racket, bass recorder, bombard, crumhorn, transverse flute, trombone, panpipe, bagpipe and recorder.
Shepherds making music with Pan, ivory carving detail from a mintbox of the Bavarian Elector Maxmili-an I, by Christoph Angermaier, ca. 1620

91 Touch table of cornett
Woodcut from J.F.B.C. Majer, Museum musicum theoreticopracticum, 1732

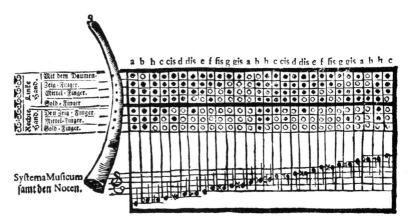

Tartold
1 Double reed 2 Crook 3 Fingerholes

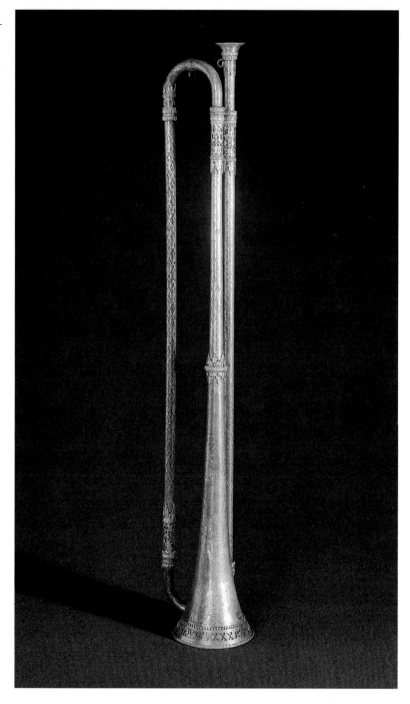

92 Trumpet in D
A. Schnitzer, Vienna, 1581

93 Tartolds in original case
From the Ambras Castle collections, late 16th century

served specimens of the sordone are kept in the Museum of Applied
Arts, Vienna. The bore of these unique instruments of Italian origin
doubles up three times in the body which is finely turned from a single
piece of boxwood. The instruments are sounded with a double reed.
Although the great bass sordone is a relatively small instrument the
lowest tone it produces is E_1; its sound is very weak and in volume does
not exceed the mezzopiano even when blown really hard. The same
principle of construction was applied to the *racket* whose body is
markedly short so that its descant consort measures only 12 cm in
length. Inside the short but broad body, there are nine interconnected
bores and the instrument has many holes although only 11 are used for

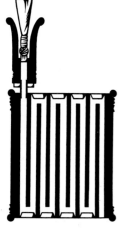

Racket
Bore system after J. Schlosser

94 Organ from 1575
Decanal church of The Holy Trinity, Smečno, Czechoslovakia

fingering. The racket suffered from the same malady as did the sordone, i.e. weak sound volume and indistinct tone pitch. However, the doubled bores of these instruments opened new possibilities for the woodwinds and thus marked a beginning which was to lead eventually to the bassoon.

An equally important family of woodwind instruments were the wind-cap woodwinds with the reeds protected by a wind chamber. This

95 Positive organ
Essaias Compenius, 1610

was a wooden receptacle in which the double reed was placed and the player blew wind into the wind chamber by means of a short crook without taking the double reed in his mouth. Once the bladder of the medieval bladder pipe was replaced by the wooden air chamber or wind cap, the *crumhorn* (French *cromorne,* German *krummhorn*) was born. However, although very popular it did not survive beyond the Baroque period and in Germany was soon ranked with the so-called 'rusty instruments.' In France it remained common up to the second half of the 19th century, although it had acquired a different design and was known as the *tournebout.*

The wind cap was characteristic also for that type of shawm which had retained the original features of the ancestral type, i.e. a short conical body with a wide bore. In the 16th century this instrument appeared in Germany with the name of *rauschpfeife* and can be seen on the famous woodcut: *Triumphal Procession of Maxmillian* by Hans Burgkmair. Specimens of *rauschpfeifen* can be today seen only in museums in Prague (where a unique great bass version is kept), Berlin and Leipzig. From these survivors, it was possible to reconstruct the entire *rauschpfeifen* consort from the sopranino down to the great bass instruments.

Since *rauschpfeifen* could not be overblown into a higher octave, the compass of the instrument was limited by six fingerholes and one key. Because of the wide bore the instrument had a weak and dull sound and was therefore unsuitable for performances of the ever more technically demanding pieces, so that its usage remained limited exclusively to the 16th century.

The recorder, not yet supplanted by the transverse flute, also had numerous pitch variants during the Renaissance, ranging from the 'little flute' as it was called by Praetorius down to the great bass version equipped with an S-shaped brass crook. Praetorius lists an entire recorder consort consisting of 21 instruments: 2 sopraninos, 2 descants

96 Black cornett
Late 16th century

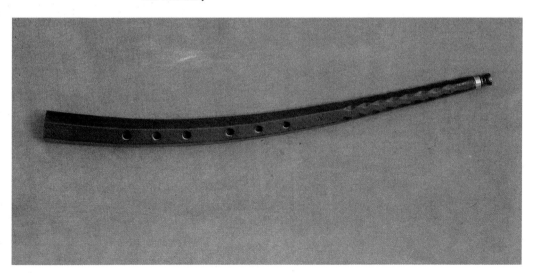

 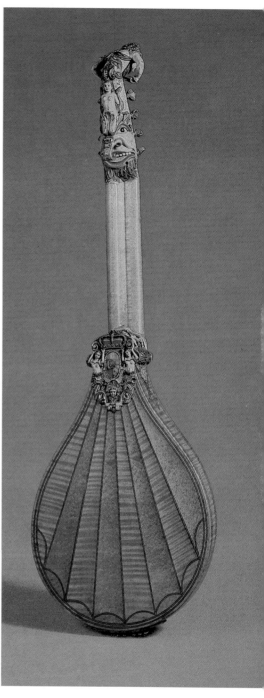

97—98 Cittern
Girolamo de Virchi, Brescia, 1574
Front and rear view

Great bass wind-cap shawm
1 Wind-cap   2 Mouthpiece
3 Double reed on staple 4 Fingerholes 5 Keys 6 Airholes

Wind-cup
1 Coat 2 Double reed
3 Pipe

99 Harp and lute
Detail of illumination of the Litoměřice Breviary, 1520

100 Tablature marks on a lute fingerboard
Sebastian Virdung: *Musica getutscht und ausgezogen*, 1511

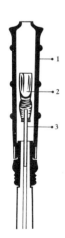

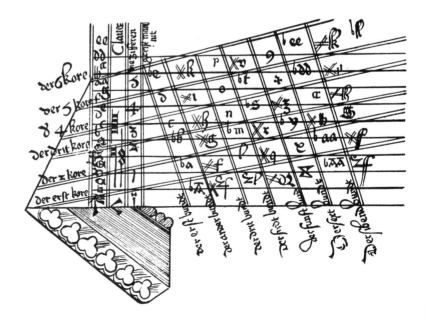

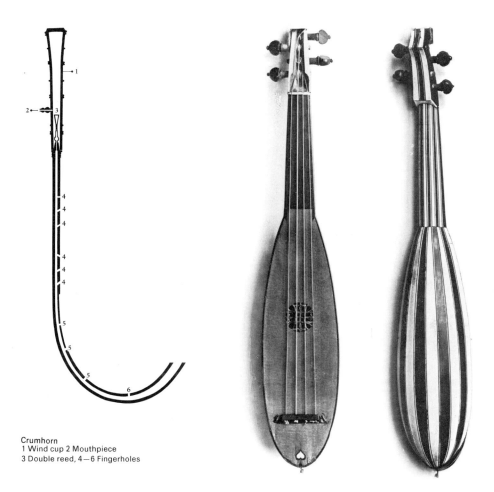

Crumhorn
1 Wind cup 2 Mouthpiece
3 Double reed, 4—6 Fingerholes

101—102 Pandorina. Italy, 16th century. Front and rear view

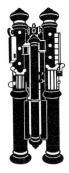

a fourth lower, 2 descants a fifth lower, 4 altos, 4 tenors, 4 bassets, 2 basses and 1 great bass. The 16th century practice did not call for precisely-fixed tuning of recorders and François Joseph Fétis, Belgian musicologist and musician (*Fabrication des Instruments de Musique,* 1855), discovered that Renaissance recorders of the same type had different pitch, giving as an example a descant recorder tuned as much as a third lower than other instruments of the same pitch type. Praetorius also complains that 'properly tuned' recorders are a rarity. Recorders survived in use until the mid-18th century when they were superseded by transverse (cross) flutes but continued in primitive folk instrument forms (e.g. Slovak *chakan* and *fuyara*) and as signalling whistles.

Since the bass recorder had a small sound volume and the great bass pommer could be played only with difficulty, a need arose for an instrument which could produce the required low tones but which could also be handled easily. These conditions were met by the *bassoon* whose invention is ascribed by a legend to Afranio degli Albonesi, an Italian. However, his instrument, which was also called the *phagotum,*

103 Chitarrone, organ, lute, violin, soprano and bass recorder
Laurent de la Hire (1606—1656): *The Allegory of Music. The Muse Euterpe,* The Metropolitan Museum of Art, New York

was a type of bagpipe. It was composed of two vertical pipes equipped with fingerholes and keywork and connected by a wooden block from which the wind supplied by a bag streamed onto metal reeds in the pipe heads. The third, centre pipe formed only an ornamental front of the block. Each pipe was split into two joints, the top part fitting into the bottom part which also served as a wind chamber and wind cap. The player would lay the phagotum on his knee and operate the bag in a way rather like playing the bagpipe.

The true inventor of the bassoon is unknown then, but he must have been familiar with the pommer, the bass recorder, the shawm, the crumhorn and also the trombone, since he combined some features of all these instruments to create a new instrument-type featuring the U-bore. From the historical point of view the Renaissance is that stage in the development of the instrument when it was still known as the *dulcian,* which typically had two connected bores worked in a single piece of wood, usually maple but sometimes also pear or cherry tree wood. The two bores were interconnected with a cross bore and the cross bore holes stopped with precision made and carefully-positioned wooden plugs. Apart from six fingerholes and one hole with an open (ring) key which were to be covered by the fingers of both hands,

104 Fretted clavichord
Germany, 17th century

105 Spinett regal
Anton Meidling, Augsburg, 1587

Dulcian

the upward bore had two additional fingerholes and one key for the thumbs. The dulcian had yet another interesting feature, a perforated bell cover serving as a mute. As with all Renaissance instruments, the bassoon was also made in entire consorts. Praetorius knew eight bassoon consort members: a descant, two piccolos, three choir bassoons, a quarto and a quinto. The name 'choir bassoon' stems from the bassoon usage in church choirs where it was used for a long time to support the bass. The modern bassoon is derived from this choir instrument whose basic key was C major.

The *cornett* occupied an intermediated position between the woodwinds, with which it shared material (wood) and design (fingerholes) and the brass instruments to which it actually belonged because its tone was produced with a cup-shaped mouthpiece.

Various cornetts were played as early as as the 11th century, for instance the *white cornett* which was straight and the *black cornett* which was curved and covered with black leather. From the 13th century the white cornett had only five fingerholes and an animal horn bell, and still later the instrument was turned from one or more pieces of boxwood and had usually seven fingerholes, six on the overside and one on the underside. The mouthpiece was also turned from horn or sometimes boxwood and came either separately or was an integral part of the pipe proper. This integral mouthpiece type had a less sharp

106 Virginal
England, 1575

107 Spinet. Murano da Pentorisi, 1590
Museo degli Strumenti musicali, Castello Sforzesco, Milan

108 Secretary desk virginal. German work, 17th century

109 Lute, harpsichord, sordine
Copper engraving by Václav Hollar, early 17th century

timbre than the first type and was therefore sometimes called the *mute cornett.* The curved black cornett was made of two pieces of wood in which the bore was pierced. Both joints were glued together to form a slightly curved pipe and the instrument was stretched with black leather.

The cornett-playing technique and embouchure is discussed in *Unterricht musikalischer Kunst* (Ulm, 1687) by Daniel Speer which gives a very interesting embouchure technique used with high-pitch cornetts and totally different from the brass instrument embouchure. Since the diameter of the mouthpiece rim on high-pitch cornetts was very small, musicians with thin lips could not apply the typical embouchure so that the mouthpiece had to be placed between the lips which were not to be pressed at all. The instrument was sounded by strong stressing of the

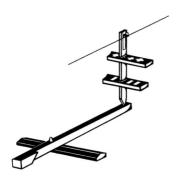

Harpsichord action

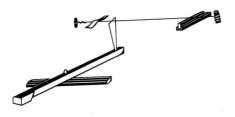

Clavichord action

110 Bass cittern
German work, beginning of 16th century

111 Lira da braccio and the master's signature
Giovanni d'Andrea, Verona, 1511

112 Violas da gamba and viola da braccio
Detail from the Isenheim altar by Matthias Grünewald, ca. 1500

 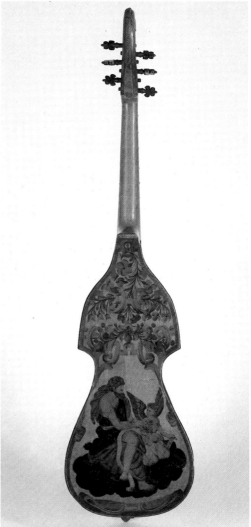

113—114 Bass viol
Gaspard Tieffenbrucker, Lyon, ca. 1560
Front and rear view

lips and the cheek muscles. This type of embouchure was customary in ancient times when instruments had no proper mouthpieces as we know them today, and when the pipe was simply inserted in the mouth. This particular blowing technique is still used on some folk instruments and high pitch trumpets (soprano cornett in E flat, Bach or piccolo trumpet).

The sound of the cornett was somewhat similar to that of the brass instruments: in highs it was more like the trumpet, in lows more like the trombone. However, the cornett sound had also something of the dulcian timbre, especially when played in the treble register. This indistinct, wailing and frankly boring sound, very unattractive when isolated but

In Padna Vendelinus Tieffenbruker.

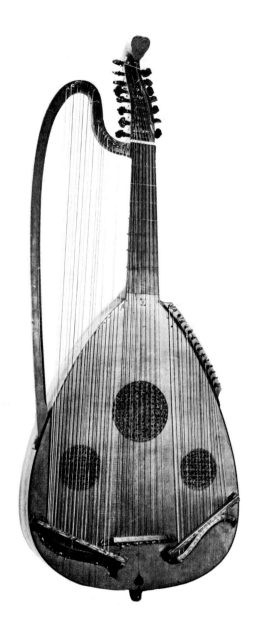

115 Harp cittern and its label
Vendelin Tieffenbrucker, Padua, ca. 1590

quite interesting if used for special sound effects and in concord with other instruments, was last used by Gluck in his *Orpheus*.

The bass cornett was called the *serpent* because of its serpent-like curved pipe which enabled the player to reach the lower holes. As the black cornett, the serpent was also stretched with black leather. As a bass instrument, it survived in church orchestras and military bands — especially in France — till the mid-19th century. The sound timbre of the serpent lacked glamour and the intonation was imprecise so that at the beginning of the 19th century instrument-makers attempted to improve it by introducing keywork. Rossini, Mendelssohn and Wagner com-

116 Harpsichord
Vitus de Trasuntinus, Venice, 1560

posed for this improved version of the serpent and in 1861 the Liverpool instrument-maker Jordan presented a contreserpent in London. However, all attempts to revitalize the instrument were in vain since it was finally driven out of the orchestra by instruments which were derived from this ancestral type, namely by the *bass horn* first and then by the *ophicleide* and the *bass tuba*.

The discovery of the technique of bending the resonator tube and the introduction of the slide mechanism created the conditions for the further development of the brass instruments. An important role in the development of the *trombone* was played by an older type of slide trumpet known as the *sackbut*, which was depicted often on medieval paintings, the most important being an altarpiece by Hans Memling (1433—1494) in Antwerp. The musician used to hold the sackbut right behind the mouthpiece while the other hand slid the entire trumpet in and out. A later type of this instrument already has the typical feature of the trombone: the player held the bell part of the tube in his left hand while his right moved the U-shaped tube. Once this slide was extended, the only thing that remained to be changed was the principle of the slide action and the trombone was born. In contrast to the sackbut, the trombone was held in the following way: the bell part was held by the left hand and the right hand operated the slide in the shape of an elongated U.

The best makers of trombones as well as of other brass instruments were those of Nuremberg. The first of these masters known to history was Hans Neuschel, who lived at the end of the 15th century. However, none of his masterpieces supplied to various noble and clerical households as well as court orchestras have survived. Long after Neuschel's death his outstanding reputation was emulated by other Nuremberg makers, especially those of the 17th century, such as Schnitzler, Hainlein, Ehe, Hass and others. Nuremberg was also famous for high-quality steel strings.

103

117 *From left:* trombone, harpsichord, violas da gamba and da braccio, violin, octave lute, sordine, black cornett, shawm, lira da braccio, violoncello, recorder, white cornett, black cornett and lute.
Right corner: handbells, jingle bells, hunting and postal horns
Jan (Velvet) Brueghel: *Das Gehör,* ca. 1620, Museo del Prado, Madrid

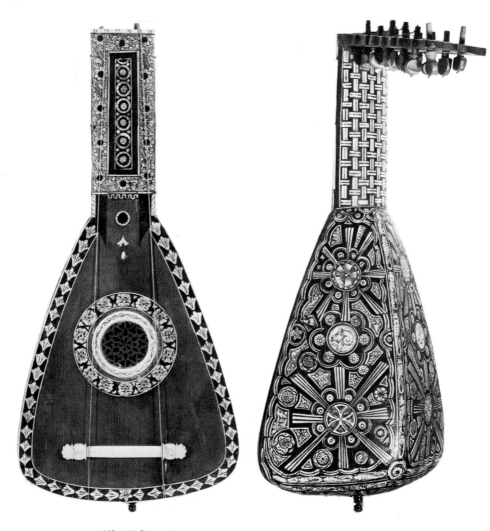

118–119 Soprano lute
Italy, 16th century
Front and rear view

The astounding variety and technical ingenuity seen in the wind instruments of the period is impossible to find in the stringed family. The variety of their medieval predecessors is perhaps reflected only in the shape variations of various plucked chordophones. The *lute* and its variants were extremely popular during the Renaissance and, indeed, this age represents the peak of their development and fame, unsurpassed since by any other instrument with the possible exception of the violin. The Renaissance raised the status of the lute to that of an *objet d'art.* The original pear-shaped body came to resemble an almond with edges inlaid with ebony and ivory. The flat soundboard of fine-grained spruce was retained but the ornamental carving of the soundhole, in the form of a rosette cut directly into the soundboard, was embellished with exquisite Gothic ornaments. The number of staves forming the back was also increased and the staves were often alternated with hair-thin

106

120 Chitarrone
Johannes Mantoya de Cardone, 1591

strips of ebony or other coloured woods. Ornamental carvings were also applied to the low bridge glued directly onto the soundboard and to the massive reflexed head or pegboard.

The number of strings of the lute was constantly increased. Originally the lute had four double courses, later a fifth pair and a single highest string were added so that the tuning was Aa, dd¹, gg¹, e¹e¹, a¹. The 16th and 17th century lutes had already eleven courses. The immense popularity of the lute gave rise to tablature notation which gives the fingering rather than notes. During the 17th century the cult of the lute and the social importance of the instrument somewhat decreased, but Bach still found a use for it in orchestral *(Trauerode, The Passions of Matthew)* as well as in solo parts *(Lute partitas)*, but by the middle of the 18th century the lute was finally quickly superseded by bowed and keyboard chordophones.

121 Tambourine, violin, lute, recorder
Bernardino Lanino (1510–1583): *Madonna Enthroned with Saints and Donor,* detail
North Carolina Museum of Art

As was the practice of the period, the lute was also built in various pitch consorts ranging from the small *octave lute* down to the *bass lute* whose bass strings were strung to a separate pegboard placed on the extended neck but misaligned with the main axis of the instrument. These instruments were called *theorbed lutes, theorbos, archlutes* and *chitarrones* with necks up to 2 m long. Thanks to the popularity the lute had acquired during the Renaissance, lute-making was to remain for long years to come one of the most profitable specializations in instrument-making. The centre of lute production was the small town of Füssen on the border between Bavaria and Tirol, and Nuremberg. In the 16th and 17th centuries, the centre of lute-making shifted to Italy, but Ernest Gottlieb Baron mentions also the Prague lute-maker Martin Schott, who was famous for his *Romance theorbos.* Another Prague lute-maker Ondřej Ott built exquisite instruments known under the name *chitarra battente.* It was basically a guitar with a vaulted back composed of staves. By this time, lutes were an attractive object for the art collector, and the greatest lute collection was in the famous Cabinet of Arts of the Fugger family.

The *fiddle* of the 16th century had a slim neck with a scroll head and a frontal peg system. The body of the *lira* became larger and a bass member of the consort was born under the Italian name *lirone perfetto* which had to be played while the musician was standing. These two bowed string instruments paved the way for the *viol,* an instrument which accepted and fused all the advantages of its predecessors: the vaulted soundboard with C-shaped soundholes, the flat bottom, slim neck and frontal pegs. The viol consort had also many members ranging from the descant *viola da braccio* to tenor *viola da gamba* to *great bass viol.* The 16th-century viols and gambas were not solo instruments, but were played in four to five member consorts. The Italians, however, soon opted for a viol type which permitted more expressive play, i.e. the *da braccio* instruments whose exclusive manufacture was in northern Italy. The viols easily dominated in the counterpoint texture of polyphonic music until the victorious onset of the violin family instruments. By the end of the 16th century, the highest-pitched member of the bowed instruments had developed from the viola da braccio, i.e. *the violin,* although the peak of its fame was to come still later. The rapid diffusion of and improvement in this most important musical instrument was due to 16th-century composers who immediately started to use the beautiful and gracious tone of the violin and its outstanding suitability for orchestral music so that some 50—70 years later the

122 Theorbed lute, tenor quinton
Bartholomeus van der Helst (1613—1670): *The Musician*
The Metropolitan Musem of Art, New York

first 16th-century master instruments were built in the Duiffopruggar workshops in Lyon and the Casparo da Salò shops in Brescia.

A quite common member of contemporary musical ensembles was the *dulcimer,* which used to be a popular instrument in musical ensembles performing at the courts of various Bohemian noblemen. Daniel Adam of Veleslavín lists it as a *sambuca.*

The Renaissance saw also a great improvement of keyboard chordophones. The application of a keyboard to a psaltery type of instrument had resulted earlier in the *clavichord,* which can be traced as far back as the mid-14th century. The 'tangents' of the clavichord ('tangent' being a name for a brass blade) were derived from the movable bridges of the monochord and sounded the string by striking while stopping it at the same time. This was the system of the so-called *fretted clavichord* in which each pair of strings served several tangents. In the later *unfretted* clavichord the double function was abolished and each pair of strings had its own tangent. The simple clavichord action with no registers or stops and no pedals encased in a narrow oblong box or case could produce only a very weak sound. On the other hand, since the tangent remained in contact with the strings until the key was released, a vibrato or 'bebung' could be produced by varying the finger pressure on the key. 400 years later, the German music theorist Jakob Adlung wrote in his book *Musica Mechanica Organoedi* (1768) that the clavichord, in spite of its weak sound, had a very fine tone and that no other instrument permitted ornamental play as well as this keyboard chordophone.

About a century later another keyboard chordophone came into being, mentioned for the first time by the Czech writer Pavel Zídek of Prague (Paulus Paulirinus de Praga) in the 1460's: the *virginal.* Its strings were plucked with raven quills or leather hooks called jacks and the instrument was made in several sizes and shapes. England and northern Europe preferred square virginals while Italy was the domain of virginals with the shape of an elongated pentagon. Small virginals were called the *ottavina* or *spinetta* in Italy and the *octave virginal* in England since this virginal was tuned an octave higher than other virginal types.

The keyboard had originally been parallel to the strings, but from the 15th century it was also built perpendicular to the strings and the plucking mechanism and thus became the harpsichord. The harpsichord had many advantages over the simple clavichord: a greater pitch compass and the fact that the majority of strings were in courses. Once the original harpsichord acquired another keyboard, possibilities of producing new sound timbres opened. The plucking action of raven quills or leather jacks generated tones that were sharper than those of the clavichord and the sound timbre could be modified by stops.

The leading position in the manufacture of keyboard chordophones was soon gained by the Flemish due to Hans Ruckers, Martin van der Biest, Hans Grauwels and other instrument-makers. Hans Ruckers' sons, Andreas and Johannes, are to be credited with the fact that in the 17th century Flemish master instruments were already being exported all over Europe. New instruments were also built which featured not only a built-in spinet but also a two-manual harpsichord with two registers, each operable by both manuals. The harpsichord then lived through three centuries of successive cycles of enthusiasm and neglect and disappeared finally by the end of the 18th century.

The envoys sent in 1457 by the Bohemian king Ladislav Pohrobek to ask the French king Charles VII for the hand of his daughter were also accompanied by players of large *kettledrums,* instruments heretofore unknown in western Europe. An explanation quite common in the literature on musical instruments holds that these instruments reached Europe via Hungary. However, the explanation is based on an erroneous interpretation of the first of Ladislav's formal titles as 'king of Hungary'. In fact, Ladislav's royal seat was never in Hungary and the envoys in question were dispatched from Prague. By the early 16th century the original rope-tensioning system of the kettledrums had been replaced by another using an iron band tightened with screws. Tympanists—tympani being the most important membranophones of the European orchestration—used to enjoy the same privileges as trumpeters and buglers.

124—125 Lira da braccio
Giovanni Maria da Brescia, 1540
Front and rear views, Ashmolean Museum, Oxford

123 Lira da gamba
Vendelin Tieffenbrucker, ca. 1590

111

126 Violin, tambourine, trombone, bombard, viola da gamba and lute. Peter Lastman (ca. 1583—ca. 1633): *Concert*, oil.

THE BAROQUE AND CLASSICAL ERAS

The musical art of the Baroque period is marked by the *continuo,* or thorough bass practice. The victory of Italian monody over the polyphony of the Low Countries represents an important change in direction for European music. The old church modes were replaced by the major and minor scales known already for some time in folk music. Besides melody and harmony, instrumentation (or orchestration) becomes the most expressive factor in music, and following the example of the *concertante* instrumental style, instrument differentiation and individualization takes place within its framework.

The extraordinary importance of the *continuo* and its practical application increased the role of the *continuo* instruments: the organ, the harpsichord and the lutes. *Maestro al cembalo,* the harpsichordist, becomes the leader and in fact conductor of the entire instrumental ensemble. The numbered bass part made such a deep impression on the entire Baroque musical literature that music between 1600—1750 is rightly called the period of the thorough bass.

Instruments were acquiring a progressively solo character as *obbligato* voices, and therefore the first to disappear from the orchestra

127—128 Trumpet and its detail
Jan Bauer, Prague, late 18th century

129 Recorder
Jan Kupecký (ca. 1667—1740): *Recorder player,* oil

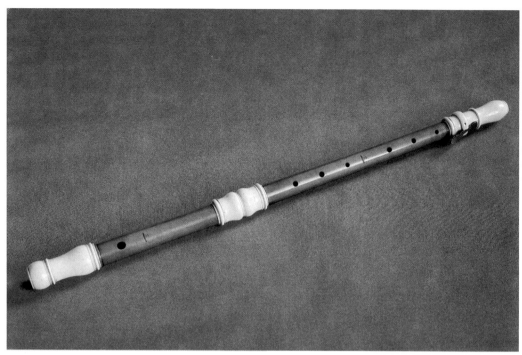

130 Flute
Louis Hotteterre, late 17th century

131 Ivory and boxwood clarinets
J. Schlegel (1733–1792), Basel

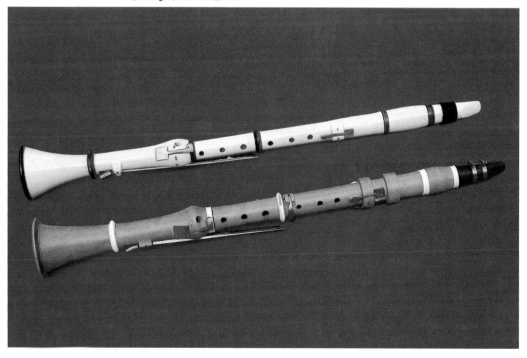

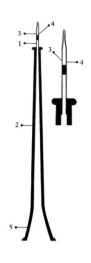

Sectional view of oboe
1 Mouthpiece 2 Barrel (bore)
3—4 Double reed 5 Flare
(bell)

were all technically and musically obsolete woodwinds of the wind-cap type (wind-cap shawms, crumhorns, etc.) Next to go were the bombards, sordones, rackets and finally also the cornetts. Only three instruments of the entire group survived, namely the *shawm* from which the *oboe* developed following a long and complicated developmental process, the *bassoon* and the *transverse* (cross, side-blown) *flute.* The transverse flute was one of those few instruments which had 'only' three sizes during the Renaissance. During the Baroque period, this instrument became one of the most important solo instruments. Among the brass family, the greatest stress was laid on high-pitched *trumpets (clarinas)* and variously-pitched *trombones.* The only newcomer to the group was the *French horn* which developed from the earlier *cor* (or *trompe*) *de chasse* (hunting horn) through an extension of the tube and acquisition of a smaller diameter body. The French horn (also called the orchestral horn) reached Bohemia as early as 1661 thanks to Count František Špork who dispatched two of his servants to Paris to master this 'splendidly pompous instrument' as the horn was described by Mattheson.

Another important instrument of modern music was also created at this time: the *clarinet.* Although Johann Christoph Denner cannot unambiguously be cited as its inventor any more, to him remains the credit for the great improvement of the shawm. Any attempts to trace the origins of the existence of the instrument, its name and usage in orchestral practice are hindered by the fact that *shawm* had been first a name used also for the clarinet. The word clarinet itself is derived from the Italian *clarinetto* and it used to designate a high-pitch trumpet called the *clarina* whose place the clarinet was to usurp. The Denner clarinet retained the funnel-shaped flare and the original seven finger-holes of the shawm and Denner himself introduced only a single reed and two keys which extended the compass of the instrument down-

132—133 Cors de chasse
B. Fürst, Ellwang, 1770 and Goutrot, Paris, late 18th century

135 Positive, violone, tenor viols
Rear: trumpets and trombones
Hanging on the wall: French horn, triangle with metal rings, oboe
d'amore, pandora
Liturgical music concert in the Weimar church in 1732, engraving, 1732

134 Bassoon and French horn
Viennese porcelain, 18th century

Sectional view of clarinet
1 Single reed 2 Barrel (bore)
3 Mouthpiece 4 Flare

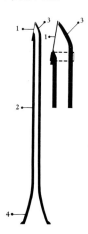

ward. The Bohemian composer Jan Stamic (Johannes Stamitz) used clarinets in his symphony 'avec clarinettes et cors de chasse' in 1775.

At the beginning of the 18th century an instrumental ensemble played in the gallery of the Weimar church. A period engraving of this event by Johann Gottfried Walther in his *Musikalisches Lexikon* (1732) shows that the ensemble is conducted by a conductor following the organist's score.

The picture manages very well to capture the atmosphere of a musical production and the play of the instrumentalists supported by the *continuo* provided by the organ. After the Thirty Years' War the Catholic Church utilized all the means at the disposal of both secular as well as ecclesiastical power to restore the old glory of the Church. Magnificent churches were constructed everywhere in which liturgical singing was accompanied by the organ. The *positive*, which had had two pumping bellows and a few stops during the Renaissance, continued to live for some time yet, but it could not keep up with the

136 French horn, porcelain
Germany, 18th century
The Metropolitan Museum of Art, New York

ever-growing musical requirements of festive liturgical occasions, and huge organs began to be built with numerous stops and several manuals. While Renaissance organ practice stressed the perfectly built-up principal diapason, Baroque organ builders aimed to have a rich representation of the flute choruses. By various combinations of these stops and their perfect sound fusion, new timbres were obtained. The organ action was constantly improved by introduction of new technical and acoustic inventions such as the air pressure gauge or tempered tuning. The keyboard compass became stabilized at the range $C—c^2$ for many years to come. The undying fame of organ building art was greatly contributed to by many an outstanding master, among them, for instance, the organ builder-cum-organist of the Duke of Wolffenbüttel's court, Essaias Compenius, or Eugen Casparini, the ancestor of the fa-

137 Trumpet, G. F. Glier, Markneukirchen, 1801. French horn, C. F. Eschenbach, Markneukirchen, 1792

mous Silbermann family of organ builders: Andreas and Gottfried, Zacharias Hildebrand, Anton Gärtner and others.

Secular music raised the harpsichord, which had acquired another set of strings, to the status of the main *continuo* instrument. As a result, the body of the instrument was considerably extended in length, and consequently the sound gained more depth and fullness. To create a more powerful sound, two and even more harpsichords were sometimes used, supported also by other *continuo* instruments such as lutes, a harp, and sometimes even with bowed bass instruments.

Thanks to the Romance nations, a great and unprecedented development of the guitar took place from the second half of the 18th century. The instrument's shape became stabilized, with a maple back and spruce belly, high ribs and a circular soundhole. The fingerboard was divided by frets into semitone intervals and topped with a flat pegboard. The six strings were tuned in E, A, d, g, h and e, although the notation was written an octave higher. The great popularization of the guitar at the close of the 18th century is to be credited to the Weimar violin maker Jacob Augustus Otto who also added the sixth, lowest string. However, long before Otto's time Europe had already had something of a vogue for the instrument. The guitar was an instrument played by and composed for by outstanding performers and composers such as Schubert, Boccherini, Weber and Paganini.

A weaker competitor to the guitar was the *cittern,* existing since medieval times under the name of *citola* with a pear-shaped body; in

139 Portative
Late 18th century

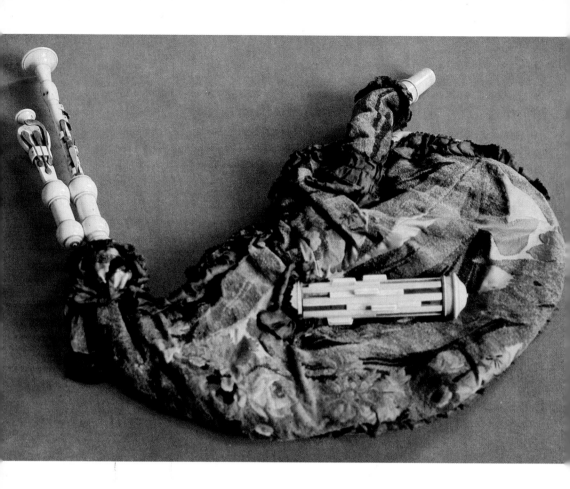

140 French concert *musette* bagpipe
Late 18th century

16th- and 17th-century England it was also known as *cithern* while the Germans called it *Zitter*. By 1800 the cittern with its five metal double courses, *capotasto* and plectrum plucking style was a popular lady's instrument. Especially beautiful citterns equipped with an ingenious tuning mechanism were created by the Prague violin-maker Jan Michael Willer. A version of the cittern called the *pandora*, a *continuo* instrument with seven metal double courses and a deeply scalloped body outline is thought to have originated in England. An even more complex body shape is to be found on the *penorcons, bass citterns* and *orpharions* with 7—9 double courses and in rare cases even up to 13 double courses and single strings. However, these polychordic instru-

141 Organ. H. Sieber, St. Michael's, Olomouc, Czechoslovakia, 1706

Pandora

ments were never very popular, and because of their extremely difficult tuning did not survive beyond the Baroque era.

Late 18th-century France witnessed the creation of the *lyre-guitar,* an instrument in the shape of the classical lyre with six strings, played almost exclusively by ladies. In contrast to the guitar proper, the lyre-guitar was played on the left knee, the left foot resting on a footstool. Although the instrument was never a practical one, it saw some use for several decades of the 19th century. A sort of substitution for the guitar was to be the *harp-lute,* an upright board zither, called also the *diplo-kithara* and invented around 1800 by Edward Light of England, but coming more in vogue after a patent had been granted on the instrument in 1816.

142—143 Theorbo and detail of the rosette
Tomáš Edlinger, Prague, 17th century

Orpheoreon

144—145 Chitarra batente. Italy, early 18th century. Front and rear views

Not much is known of the origins of the instrument known originally as the *gravicembalo col piano e forte*. The principle of the hammer action had been known as early as 1400 and the *échequier* mentioned by Guillaume de Machaut must have had some sort of hammer or striking action (Fr. *écheck* = strike).

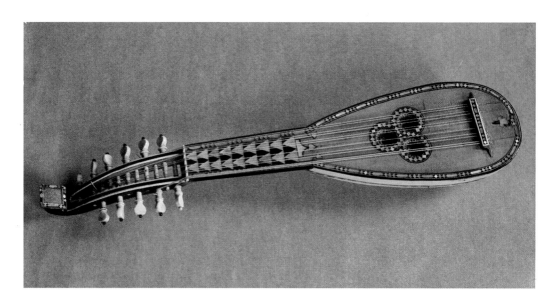

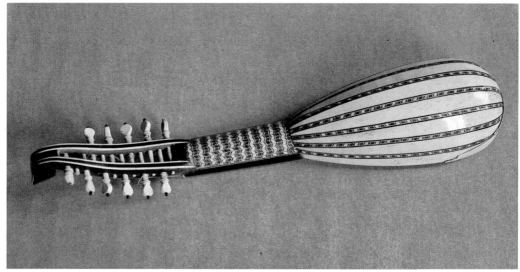

146—147 Pandorina
Ignazio Ongaro, Venice, early 18th century. Front and rear views

In his work *Interpretations of the Music of the XVIIth and XVIIIth Centuries,* Arnold Dolmetsch wrote in 1915 that he had seen a piano which had been made in 1610. Such an instrument would have proceeded the first instruments built by Bartolommeo Cristofori by more than a century. The instrument was said to have looked like a large dulcimer with tiny hammers fitted to keys in a similar fashion as in a simple form of the later Viennese or German action. Once music started to feel the small dynamic range of the existing keyboard chordophones such as clavichords, harpsichords, virginals and spinets to be too limiting, the birth of the *piano* became inevitable. This is the reason

148 Guitar. Jean Voboam, Paris, 1687

149 Bottom (backboard) of the previous guitar

Main parts of guitar
1 Head with pegs (pegbox)
2 Machine head 3 Finger-
board with frets 4 Neck
5 Bridge (or nut, see picture)
6 Soundboard with soundhole
7 Ribs 8 Bottom

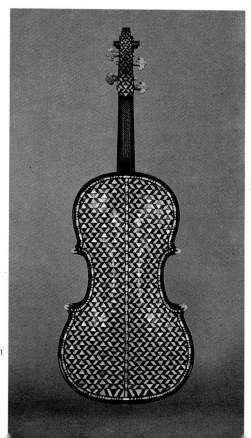

150 Violin
Nicóla Amati, Cremona, 1681

151 Double guitar
Alexandre Voboam Jr, Paris, 1696

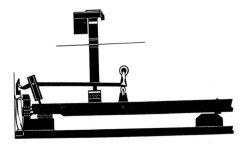

German piano hammer action,
A. Stein, 1772

English piano hammer action,
(double), R. Stodart, 1777

why Pantaleon Hebenstreit, a dulcimer virtuoso, received such an unexpected success in 1705 in Paris with a dulcimer of his own construction, named the *pantaleon* in his honour by Louis XIV.

The German organist and writer Gottfried Schröter wrote that he had been the inventor of the hammer action in 1717, and one year before him Jean Marius of France had demonstrated to the Royal Academy in Paris a model of his *clavecin à maillets* employing the hammer action. Nevertheless, the historical fact remains that the first hammer action piano was made by the Florentine instrument-maker Bartolommeo Cristofori in 1709.

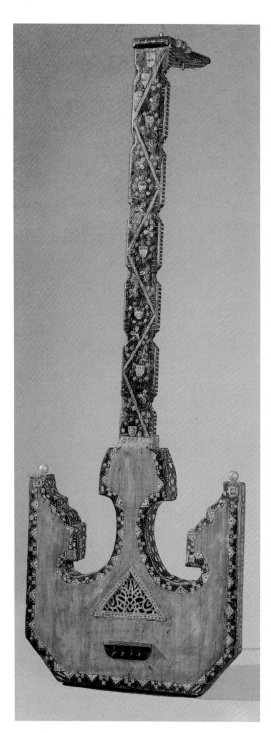
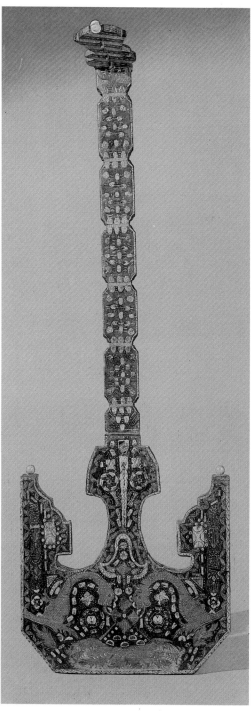

152—153 Guitar
Fedele Barnia, 18th century
Front and rear views

129

From the technical description of the Cristofori piano action published in *Giornalle dei letterati d'Italia* in 1711, it is apparent that this action was actually quite similar to the English action since the hammer covered with chamois escaped after having struck the string, and was engaged by a check to prevent it from reverberating and striking again.Apart from this form of escapement, the instrument featured individual dampers for each key. The credit for a greater popularization of the hammer action is to go to the famous organ-builder Gottfried Silbermann, who opened the way that was to lead to John Broadwood, the inventor of the modern English action. The Viennese action was designed in 1778 in Augsburg by Silbermann's pupil Johann Andreas Stein, although the system was made really famous by his son-in-law,

154—155 Guitar. Georgius Sellas, Italy, 17th century. Front and rear views

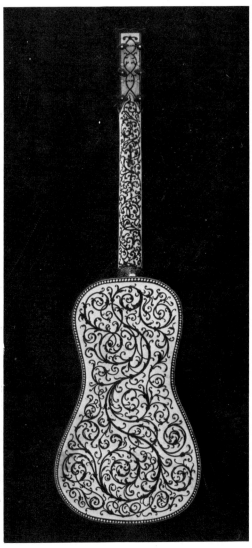

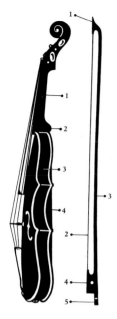

Violin
1 Neck 2 End block 3 Ribs
4 Bottom (back)

Bow
I Point 2 Bowhair 3 Stick
4 Frog 5 Screw

Violin
1 Scroll   head   2 Pegbox
3 Pegs 4 Nut 5 Soundboard
(topboard, belly) 6 Soundholes   7 Bridge ' 8 Tailpiece
9 Button 10 Chin rest

156 Archcittern
17th century

131

157 Lyre guitar
G. M. Pace, Catania, early 19th century

158 Lyre guitar
Mlle Rivière: *Lady with a lyre* oil, ca. 1820

Violino piccolo (piccolo violin)

Tenor violin

159 Viola bastarda, recorder
Domenichino (Domenico Zampieri, 1581—1641): *St. Cecilia,*
ca. 1620. Musée du Louvre, photo Musées Nationaux

the outstanding Viennese piano-builder Johannes Streicher. The Viennese action features chamois padded hammers fitted directly to the end of the key, whereas in the English action hammers are tipped with felt and pivoted on a separate bar quite independently of the key.

Whereas the best harpsichords of the 17th century were of Flemish designs, the most perfect bowed strings headed by the *violin* hailed from Italy. The violin family of instruments produced in the workshops of the Cremona masters Nicóla Amati and his pupils Antonio Stradivari and Guiseppe Guarneri, known as del Gesù, reached the pinnacle of perfection. No other instrument can match the refined beauty, the sin-

133

Pardessus de viola

Viola pomposa

160 Milanese mandolina
Francesco Plesbler, Milan, 1773

161 Neapolitan mandolina
Johann Jobst Frank, Dresden, 1789

Quinton

ging tone quality and the technical versatility of the violin. Naturally, not every violin has these attributes since a lot depends on the maker. Violins made by the famous 17th and 18th century Italian masters are actually works of art comparable to Raphael's paintings or Michelangelo's sculptures. As a blind man will never be able to perceive the beauty of the harmony of colours, so nobody who has not had a chance to hear a virtuoso playing a truly great instrument can imagine the delightful, unique effect of that instrument's sound.

The violin also had very many variants with different pitch variations ranging from the *violino piccolo,* which was slightly smaller than the regular violin and tuned a fourth higher (hence the name *quart violin*), down to the *contrabass violin.* However, a *double bass viol* or *violone* was used more often instead, and later the *double bass* came to reign in the bass parts. Of the original six-member violin consort the first to be forgotten—and unjustly, too—were the *piccolo* and then the *tenor violins.* The nonexistence of these two instruments is a drawback

162 Pointed harp
German work, late 18th century

163 Harp-lute (dital harp)
Edward Light, late 18th century

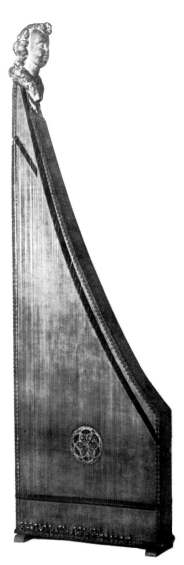

135

164 Pedal (single action) harp
French work, late 18th century

165 Pedal harps
Jean-Baptiste Mauzaisse (1784—1844): *Harp Lesson*
Photo Musées Nationaux

that is felt not only in the interpretation of Bach's opuses, since Bach liked to orchestrate for them, especially for the piccolo violins, but they are also missed in the orchestra in general, where the tenor scores have to be divided between the *violas* and *violoncellos.* It is also very interesting to note that the violoncello made only very slow headway against the commonly used *viola da gamba* since the gamba, which had played a great role in the history of improvisation was fading only very slowly and kept obstinately surviving in home music and as a solo instrument. The gamba with its high ribs and the flat bottom had great drawbacks in design as compared with the cello. On the other hand, its greater number of strings (5—6) and the special way in which the bow was held (similar to that used on the double bass) permitted three and even four strings to be played simultaneously on the gamba because of its flat profile bridge. Only as late as the end of the 17th century when Stradivari stipulated the classical violoncello shape was the latter able to succeed over the viola da gamba.

The importance of lacquer was also discovered first with the violin instruments. Lacquer protects the instrument from harmful external influence such as unstable ambient temperature and humidity but it also affects — though to no substantial degree — the quality of the tone. The lacquer gives the instrument its beauty: the deep colour, its lucid transparence, that hard-to-define quality called the 'play of light' in gems. This is also why the secret of the lacquer composition — presumed to have been buried with the old Cremona masters — has always ignited the imagination not only of violin makers but also chemists and dilettantes.

The important status that the violin instruments enjoyed was further manifested by the fact that new variations were being created. How-

166 Spinet. 17th century

167 Harpsichord-spinet. Johannes Ruckers, Antwerp, 1619

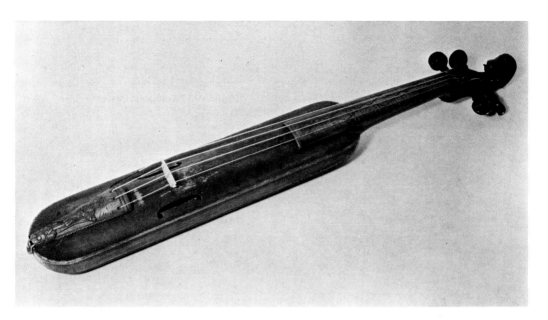

168—169 Sordine and detail of its bottom board
Italy, 17th century

ever, these instruments never had the vitality of the violin family, and
after a short time were usually forgotten. In this way the viola da
gamba and the lira da gamba gave birth to a lyra viol called the *viola
bastarda,* which acquired sympathetic strings at the beginning of the
17th century only to abandon them some decades later. A small-sized
kit remained in use until the 19th century in dancing instruction (hence
the name *dancing master's violin*). Originally the pochette violin had
a narrow boat-shaped body and was known in this miniature form as
the *sordine* in Italy. Due to Bach's instigation, the five-string *viola pomposa* was built in Germany while five-string gambas called *quintons*
were made in France. The *basso di camera* had also five and sometimes six strings; a treble viol developed in the mid- 18th century was
called the *pardessus de viola.*

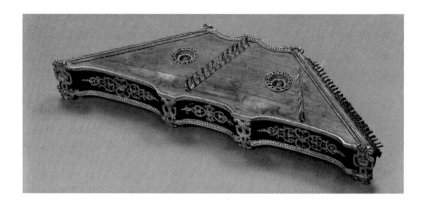

170 Dulcimer
French work, 17th century

171 Harpsichord
Late 17th century

As we can see, it is not only musical compositions that are suscep-
tible to changes of taste but also musical instruments which are born
and reach the culmination of their development only to fade away and
make way for new and more vital instruments. That is one of the reasons why instruments featuring—besides the fingered (stopped)
strings—also metal sympathetic strings could not survive for long.
A delicate and handsome representative of these bowed strings was
the *viola d'amore* although a more proper name would be *viola da
more,* i.e. the Moorish viol. There are indeed certain ties between the
viola d'amore and the Indian *sarangi* and *esrar* featuring also a number
of sympathetic strings. It is slightly larger than the violin, the flat bottom recedes somewhat towards the neck, and the soundholes are
shaped like tongues of flame. The six or seven fretted strings and the
same number of sympathetic strings are stretched across the bridge

140

and along the slightly vaulted neck to the pegs. The elegance of the instrument is enhanced by a long pegbox with a number of pegs and topped with a carved head of a woman or a *putto* to symbolize its gentle and warm sound. The fingered and the sympathetic strings were tuned in D flat major. Johann Sebastian Bach who liked to use the key of E flat minor for the viola d'amore usually followed the common period practice of tuning the instrument in the key of the performed piece. By the end of the 18th century when the general interest turned to instruments of greater sound volume, the viola d'amore was declining in popularity because it had too weak a sound. An *alto viola d'amore* with a larger body and a double set of sympathetic strings is called the English *violet.*

The English makers also built a bass viol called the *barytone* (or *viola di bordone*) with up to 40 sympathetic strings, some of which

172 Harpsichord
Hercule Pepoli, Bologna, 1677

could be plucked from behind the neck by the left thumb. The size and tuning of this instrument corresponds to those of the tenor gamba; apart from the stopped strings, it had 9—27 sympathetic strings running over a massive bridge glued directly onto the soundboard and leading further in a massive pegboard topped with the carved head of a man. The baryton fingerboard was fretted as were all gamba instruments. The high point of the instrument coincides with Joseph Haydn's presence at the court of Duke Nicholas Esterházy in Eisenstadt in 1765—1775; the instrument was much favoured by the Duke and Haydn wrote 175 opuses for it.

INSTRUMENTS OF THE MODERN ORCHESTRA

If Baroque music had a more or less universal character, the 19th century is the period when national musical cultures were born. The widespread use of brass instruments led to the creation of folk and popular orchestras whose composition and sophistication of playing techniques usually reflected the standards of military or marching bands. The period efforts to seek new tonal timbres and colours somewhat resembles the Renaissance and its aims, but the real objective was not the polyphonic contrast and subtlety but an interest in creating a new sensitivity, a new emotionality. These requirements of expressivity and emotionality demanded new instruments and their consorts. Clarinets are made in eight sizes, saxophones in six. In order to fulfil any

173 English violet
Jan Oldřich (Johannes Udalricus)
Eberle, Prague, 1727

174 Quinton
Thomas Hulinzký, Prague, 1754

175 Viola da gamba
J. O. Eberle, Prague, 1740

176–177 'Le Messie' violin
Antonio Stradivari, Cremona, 1716
Shirley Slocombe: *Le Messie,* 1890

178 Kits (dancing master's violins)
Late 18th century

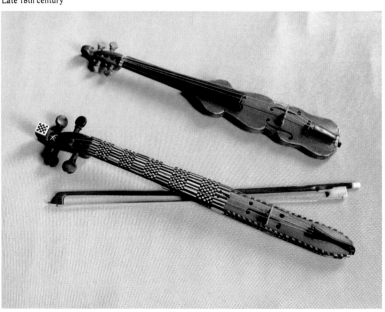

musical requirement the musical instruments, especially the winds, have had to undergo considerable changes and modification. Thanks to F. Blühmel and H. Stölzel of Germany, the *valved trumpet* was developed at the beginning of the 19th century and soon became the dominant descant brass instrument. Even the *harp*, accepted by Berlioz as an almost constant member of the symphonic orchestra, suddenly shed its ancient design and became an instrument playable in all desired keys. On the

180 Bass viola da gamba, later modified to four strings
Joachim Tielke, Hamburg, 1687

179 Baryton (viola di bordone)
Viennese work, late 18th century

other hand, the classical-romantic period almost totally eliminated the plucked chordophones from orchestral instrumentation and the idiophones met with a similar fate to be rediscovered only by Neoromanticism and Impressionism.

Superficially viewed, it may seem that our century has simply taken over the sound source heritage of the Romantic period without any change whatsoever. However, this is not really the case, although the innovations of Richard Strauss actually do stem from the Berlioz theory of instrumentation. But the mid-20th century has again rediscovered the plucked string sound, this time in the form of a *pizzicato* of the bowed strings, and idiophones and membranophones now form an integral and important component of the sound of contemporary music: in *L'Histoire du soldat* we find six melody instruments plus an equal number of percussion instruments. But this development is hardly surprising since for centuries rhythm was subordinated to harmony.

About one fifth of the total number of musical instruments kept in world museum collections are the so-called friction instruments featuring wooden, glass or metal bars, rods, strings, tubes, bowls or bells

181—182 Violoncello
Domenico Galli, Parma, 1691
Front and rear views

183—184 Viola d'amour
Thomas Hulinzký, Prague, 1769
Front and rear views

185 Baryton (viola di bordone)
18th century

which are not struck but rubbed. The rubbing is provided by a resined bow, a rotating cylinder, an air stream or moistened fingers of the player. Business-minded instrument-makers, acousticians and mechanics flooded the 19th-century market with scores of novelty instruments which they had 'invented' or at least 'improved', giving them romantic names vaguely reminiscent of Greece, for instance the *euphone* featuring glass tubes, or *terpodion* in which a resined cylinder rubbed wooden bars, or *akukryptophone, bellarmonic, clavicylinder, coelestine, uranion,* etc. The sound of these novelties was usually very weak and the instrument lacked any sufficient expression modulation, consequently most had become obsolete by the 1850's because of these drawbacks and their difficulty of production.

Among the innumerable scores of friction idiophones, the *nail violin* (also known as the *nail harmonica*) enjoyed a short-lived popularity after the 1850's. The instrument was invented by Johann Wild of St Petersburg, Russia, and had a wooden resonator box with nails of

186 Angelica Kauffmann, glass harmonica virtuoso
Engraving, first half of the 19th century

187 Nail violin
First half of the 19th century

different length sounded with a bow. Later the instrument was also fitted with sympathetic strings and long after it had been forgotten it was revived in Vienna at the beginning of the 20th century only to fade quickly away for good. The most typical representative of this class of instruments is the *glass harmonica,* or *armonica* as it was called by its inventor, the famous American physicist and statesman Benjamin Franklin. Franklin fitted chromatically tuned glass bowls of different size on a common shaft over a trough of water and rotated them by a wheel driven with a treadle and belt. The wetted glass bowls could be sounded only if the player's fingers pressed against the glass were absolutely grease-free. It was not enough just to wash one's hands, for they had also to be rubbed clean with chalk, which caused very unpleasant dryness of the skin. Some bowls would sound if pressed with a finger tip, others required the entire first link, etc. The problem of how to play the instrument without any direct contact between the player's fingers and the vibrating glass bowl while preserving a reasonable sound quality was not solved even by the invention of the *piano harmonica.* The rumours of the harmful effect the glass harmonica was

149

188 Violoncello, violin, serpent, piano, French horns, oboe and theorbo
John Zoffany: *Family with Musical Instruments*, oil, 1781

reputed to have on the human organism caused banning of public performances on the instrument in several cities. However, both musicians
and the public were enthusiastic about it, because the glass harmonica
was thought to reflect precisely the general mood of this oversensitive
period, and the instrument proved to be an influence on poetry and
prose (Jean Paul, Wieland, Schubert, and others). After 1830, however,
its ethereal sound died away, being displaced by the so-called *physharmonica*, which was invented in 1818.

The physharmonica invented by Anton Haeckl in Vienna (1810) was
one of the forerunners of the harmonium group. In it free metal reeds
were fixed at one end to a sound plate and vibrated by a stream of air
supplied by foot bellows to the wind chest from where it went through

key-operated valves or flaps to the individual reeds vibrating up and down through a slot in the plate. Recent research has proven that the sound wave in the free reed glass instruments is generated by a periodic pressure drop around the narrow slot in which the reed is fixed. The tone pitch depends on the thickness and length of the reed while the timbre is determined by its shape and location.

Although the *harmonium,* another representative of the free reed instruments, is sometimes called the ·*reed organ,* it has only a little in common with the regular pipe organ. The harmonium was improved by Gabriel Joseph Grenié of France who built his *orgue expressif* in 1810 and by another Frenchman, Alexandre François Debain, who had the instrument and its name *harmonium* patented in 1840. To permit the player to control the sound volume, the Paris company of Alex-

189 Glass harmonica
Late 19th century

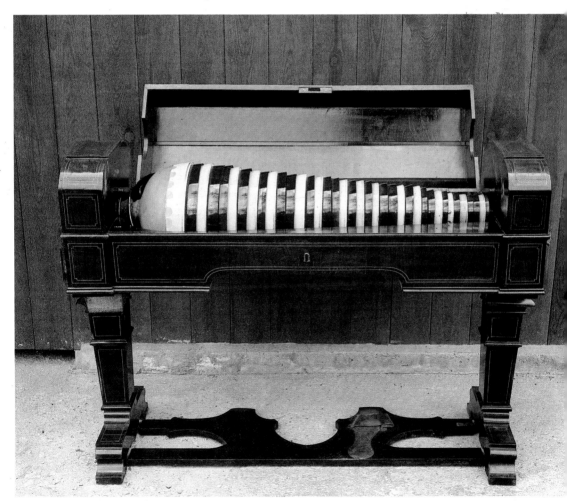

190—191 Terpodion and an internal view of the instrument
First half of the 19th century

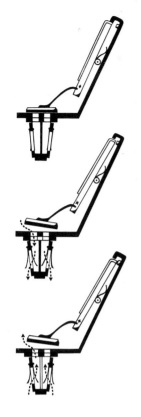

Generation of tone in the accordion

192 Physharmonica
Early 19th century

Sectional view of harmonium
1 Pedal 2 Bellows 3 Wind trunk 4 Reservoir 5 Wind chest 6 Stop pallet 7 Knee (swell) lever 8 Compartment (channel) 9 Pallet 10 Manual 11 Stop crank 12 Forte stop knob 13 Reed chamber

153

193 Serpent. Early 19th century

Triangle

Cymbals

Gong

andre père et fils introduced a stop called the *expression* which closed the bellows so that the reeds did not start vibrating immediately but after a short delay. The majority of modern harmoniums have the same feature, but this action does not permit playing of rapid passages. This was the reason why a Parisian instrument-maker Martin equipped his *orgue à percussion* with a hammer action called a *percussion* and with a *prolongement* stop which permitted longer tone decay. A perfect instrument called the *harmonium d'art* was built by another Frenchman, Victor Mustel. His type featured all the improvements described above, but it was also equipped with a double expression and knee-operated shutters permitting the typical *swell*. The precisely-stipulated specifications of the Mustel harmonium formed the basis of independent musical literature written specifically for the harmonium. World-famous instruments were manufactured by the Viennese harmonium-builder Kotykiewicz.

Harmoniums can have one or more sets of reeds of the same timbre called ranks. Each rank consists of 61 reeds covering the compass of five octaves. The pitch is given in feet as in the case of organ pipes, but the footage does not designate the length of the pipe but the pitch of the reed corresponding to the pitch of the organ pipe of the same footage. To gain a greater fullness of the tone colour, or to double the tones, several tones of various octaves can be coupled as in the regular pipe organ. A fundamental feature of the harmonium which has a bearing on the playing technique is the fact that the keyboard is divided into two independent but mutually complementing halves, bass and treble. The ranks are controlled by numbered stops located above the manual.

The volume of the reeds is determined by the speed of the pedal action. Just as a good pianist will be recognized by his touch, the qualities of a harmonium player are revealed by his pedal work. Concert

194 Clay ocarina
Late 19th century

195 Double English flageolet
Late 19th century

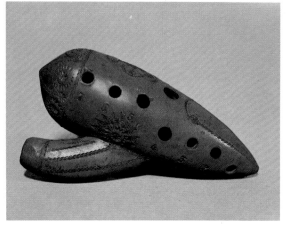

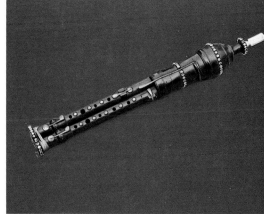

Xylophone

harmoniums feature also some other improvements such as percussion and prolongement which keeps the tone sounding even after the key is released. The Mason and Hamlin Company of Boston developed a harmonium known as the *American organ* which differs in the direction of the air flow, the bellows exhausting the reservoir instead of filling it. Since the instrument was intended to replace the pipe organ, it was also named the *cottage organ* and equipped with a pedal and several manuals.

The free reeds are the main feature of the *accordion* and its earlier versions known as the *concertina, lap organ,* and *mellodeon.* The archetype of the instrument was built by David Buschmann in Berlin and called the *Handeöline.* In 1829 Charles Wheatstone changed its rectangular shape into a hexagonal one and called it the *concertina.* In contrast to the Handeöline the concertina intonation did not change with the direction of the bellow action, i.e. the same tone was sounded both on the press and draw alike. Button keys were arranged in horizontal rows on both sides and a chromatic scale could be produced depressing the button keys alternately with each hand. At the end of the 1840's the new shape was changed back to square in Germany and the keys ar-

196—197 Piccolo flute and flute
Amati, Kraslice, Czechoslovakia

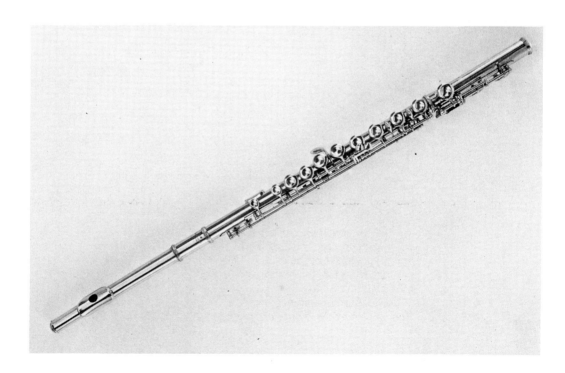

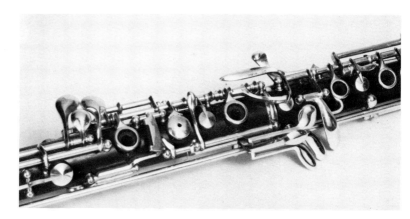

198—199 Oboe and detail of the keywork
Amati, Kraslice, Czechoslovakia

ranged in vertical rows. This type of the instrument was the basis for
Heinrich Band's *Bandonion.*

By the gradual extension of identical tones to the press and to the
draw and by the chromatic arrangement of tones, the way was paved
for chromatic concertinas called *accordions.* Since the time of its invention, the *piano accordion* with the righthand piano style keyboard has
remained in the foreground of makers' interest. The instrument is cur-
rently being perfected by extension of the bass registers, their chromatic arrangement (baryton basses), by extension of the tonal compass
through octave registers, of different footage and by introduction of
various combination registers, shaft resonators and shutters. Through
an introduction of an ingeniously designed master-coupler changing
the regular bass keyboard into baryton basses, the Scandalli Conserva-
torio model gained heretofore unprecedented technical versatility and
musical expressivity.

David Buschmann was also the inventor of the *mouth harmonica,*
known also as the *mouth organ* and the *Mundäoline,* although at first it
was more a novelty than a genuine musical instrument. However, it
was constantly improved and finally it gained a stable position among
other regular instruments. Mouth organs are classified as diatonic,

200 Cor anglais (English horn)

201 Home organ. Georg Hammer, Schierz, Switzerland, 1838

Flexatone

202 Hook harp
Severin Pfalz (1796—?): *Prague harpist Josef Häusler*

Castanets

chromatic, accompaniment and special. Good examples of diatonic mouth organs are the Richter, the Knittlinger and the Viennese models. The Richter mouth organ has 10—12 simple tone channels, each with two different tones, one played by blowing, the other by sucking the air in. The Knittlinger model has the compass of one or two octaves and features double channels, each tone sounded both by blowing and sucking is doubled with an upper octave tone. The Viennese model is of a vibrato design and has a compass of one octave. For each tone of this vibrato type mouth organ there are two tones tuned in unison, but differing slightly in frequency which results in tone vibrato. Chromatic mouth organs are actually two diatonic models in one and are tuned a semitone apart. The desired tone is selected by a push button slide which opens and closes the appropriate channels. A recent innovation is the application of a keyboard to the mouth organ principle, the resulting instrument being called the *melodica.* The chord harmonica is a kind of accompaniment harmonica consisting of two harmonicas

159

204 Bassoon
Amati, Kraslice, Czechoslovakia

203 Contrabassoon
Amati, Kraslice, Czechoslovakia

about 60 cm long which are placed parallel in a metal fixture allowing the harmonicas to be opened or closed together.

A popular instrument of this family in West Germany is the *harmonetta* with 32 keys producing a three octave chromatic scale. A Czechoslovak invention is the *polyphonic* consisting of two chromatic

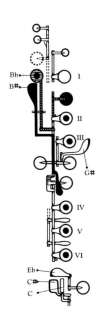

Flute with the Böhm keywork
(Böhm keywork flute)

Clarinet with the Böhm keywork (Böhm keywork clarinet)

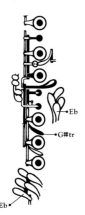

harmonicas joined together by a fixture and permitting four-part harmony in all keys. The instrument is so small that it almost disappears in the player's hands. Special mouth harmonica models feature non-European tonal systems or combine melody and accompaniment harmonicas in one instrument.

A metal idiophone lending the orchestral sound a clear ringing quality is the *triangle* made of a round-profile steel bar shaped into an isosceles triangle with one apex open. The triangle is freely suspended by this apex and is sounded with a steel baton. Since the fundamental tone decays due to the disproportion of the steel bar thickness and length and since no partial tone is predominant over other partials, the triangle has indefinite pitch. *Cymbals* also have indeterminate pitch and were used for the first time by Gluck in his opera *Iphigenia on*

205 Zithers
Lying: early 19th century
Standing: Georg Tiefenbrunner, Munich, 1850

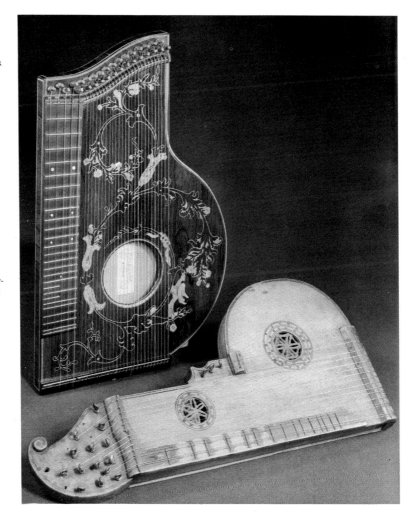

Tauros (1799). The use of the instrument in military bands dates from the beginning of the 19th century. Cymbals are made of bronze or bell metal alloy. They are held in the following way: the four fingers but not the thumb are inserted through the leather wrist strap which is then tightly held by the thumb and the index finger, or the stretched thumb is rested on a felt pad. The cymbals are rotated during play not for a mere visual effect but primarily for acoustic reasons since rotation increases the tone prolongement. The plates are dampened by pressing them against the abdomen. Basically there are three cymbal types: Turkish, Chinese (which are thinner and have therefore a deeper sound than the former) and Italian used in pairs or singly in jazz *(high-hat cymbal)*.

Oboe keywork articulation　　　Heckel's bassoon keywork articulation　　　Saxophone keywork articulation

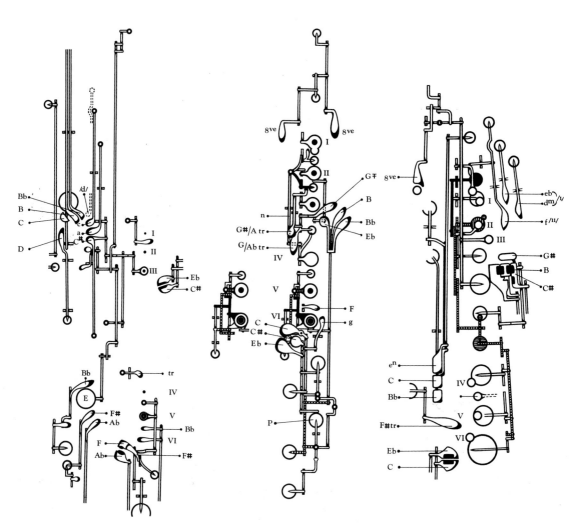

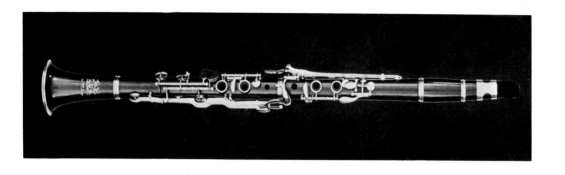

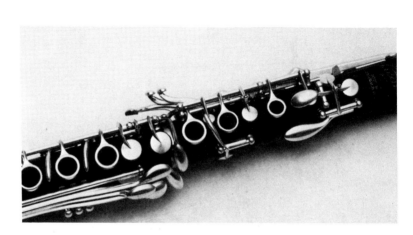

206—207 Clarinet and a detail of the Böhm keywork system
Amati, Kraslice. Czechoslovakia

The *gong* used for the first time in orchestral practice by the French composer François-Joseph Gossec in 1791 reached Europe from China via Indonesia. It is shaped as a shallow bowl or plate and made in different sizes from bronze, with upturned rims two to five centimetres wide. The gong is tuned within the compass c—c¹. The instrument is suspended on a silk cord and sounded with either a soft or a hard (leather covered) beater. Larger gongs are sounded with a wooden mallet which is struck at the centre of the instrument. The gong has a clear bell-like tone, and large gongs can easily match regular bells in sound volume. A variation of the gong is the *tam-tam* in the form of a shallow bowl with a slightly upturned rim. Its main difference from the gong is that it has no definite pitch.

Bells are commonly replaced in the orchestra by a set of 4—13 brass or steel tubes graduated in length, stopped at the top and tuned chro-

208 Bass clarinet
Amati, Kraslice, Czechoslovakia

Piccolo heckelphone

matically in one octave. These *tubular bells* are struck with a wooden mallet covered with thick leather. The bells are struck near the point of suspension. Luigi Cherubini (1760—1842) was the first to use them to stress the festive mood of a piece.

Ever since Handel used the keyboard chime or carillon in his *Saul* (1738), the *glockenspiel* has been a standard member of the modern orchestra. The instrument consists of two rows of chromatically tuned metal bars arranged rather like piano keys. The bars are supported with wooden blocks or strings running through metal pegs, and the instrument is struck with two moderately hard beaters with round or hammer heads of various sizes and materials. There is also a keyboard-operated model.

Another version of the glockenspiel is the *tubaphone* featuring metal tubes instead of bars and sounded by a hammer action. The sound of the tubaphone has a gentle chime-like character, and a unique sound effect called circular glissando can be produced on the instrument with the hammers tracing various closed loops along the surface of the tubes. The sound and the technical potentiality of the instrument have not been fully utilized in the symphonic orchestra so far and it remains more or less restricted to the use of musical artistes and clowns.

The *celesta,* invented by Auguste Mustel in 1886 in Paris, somewhat resembles a small harmonium, but inside the case there are small metal plates supported by individual tuned resonators and sounded by a hammer action. The instrument features a single pedal controlling the dampers. Recently, the instrument has been equipped with an electro-mechanical vibrator. The sound of the celesta is of a more gentle and less ringing character than that of the glockenspiel.

209 Bowed zither
Late 19th century

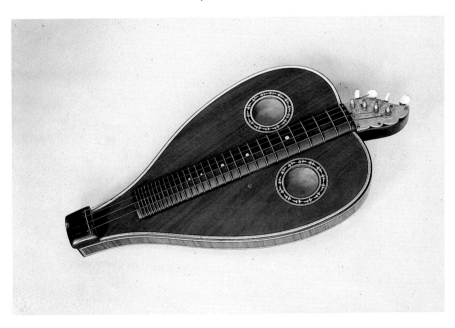

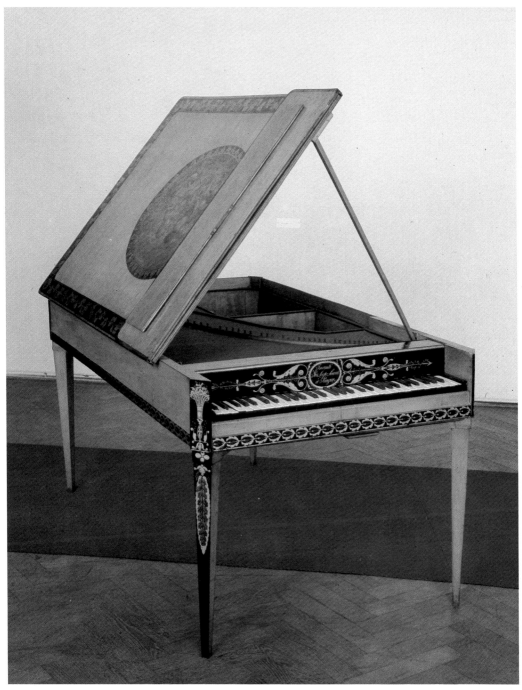

210 Table piano
Leopold Sauer, first half of the 19th century

165

Another idiophone of this group of instruments is the *vibraphone* built by H. E. Winterhoff, an American, in 1927. Graduated aluminium bars are arranged in two rows and supported by an independent metal frame. Under each bar there is an individual resonator tube. In the top of each resonator is a small fan, and all these fans are mounted on a common shaft and rotated by an electromotor. The fans control the passage of sound waves into the resonator tubes and a dynamic vibrato can be produced in this way. The vibrato frequency as well as the tone decay can also be controlled.

Sarrusophone

The year 1840 marked the arrival of the *xylophone* in the modern orchestra. The modern xylophone consists of 36 maple or palisander wood blocks tied together with a string. The blocks are freely supported by wooden bars, forming four rows and supported by rubber blocks in nodal points of vibration. Some woodblocks are doubled for easier play. The blocks are sounded with spoon-shaped beaters and produce a hollow sharp sound. Tones can be sustained by tremolo beating, a technique utilizing rapid successive strikes by both hands.

The *castanets* used in symphonic orchestra practice are formed by a wooden spoon-shaped plate inserted between the two nutshell-shaped castanet halves. This handle facilitates better control of the instrument. Sometimes two castanets are fitted to a common handle, and then the connecting string has to be replaced with a rubber band keeping the halves slightly apart. Rhythmically complex passages are played with castanets without the inserted part, the fingers beating the rhythm on the castanets worn on the middle finger and supported in the palm.

Modern composers sometimes call also for other less common idiophones such as the *flexatone* featuring a metal plate fixed at one end in a frame with a handle. There are two wooden balls containing springs, and when the instrument is shaken the balls beat against the plate. The pitch varies with the deflection of the plate, and the instrument produces a wailing glissando sound. A speciality of French com-

214 Keyed trumpet fingering chart

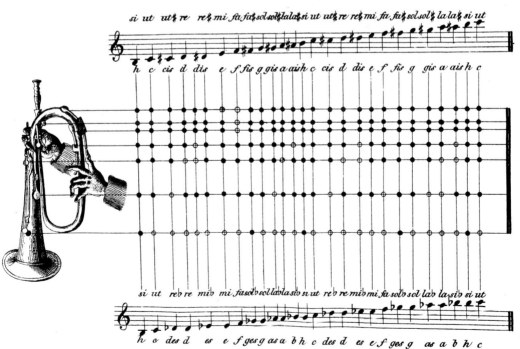

posers such as Debussy and Ravel is the inclusion of the *crotals*, a pair of small bronze plates tuned a fifth apart to produce a ringing tone. Special sound effects can be also produced with the *anvil, jingle bells, cog wheel (ratchet) rattle* etc.

In England in the first quarter of the 19th century, the *English flageolet* became extremely popular among amateur musicians. It was a vertical whistle flute somewhat resembling the recorder, but the latter's beaked mouthpiece was replaced by a bone or ivory nozzle with a cap

215 Giraffe piano
Josef Seufert, Vienna, ca. 1820

168

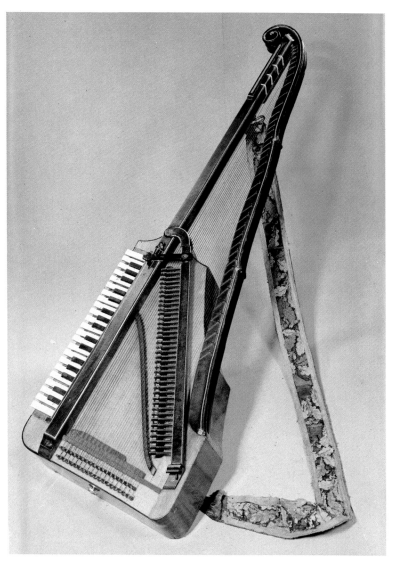

216 Orphica
Joseph Dohnal, Vienna, ca. 1800

in which a tiny sponge was placed to trap the saliva. There was also a *double flageolet* with a doubled bore and a mechanism which could render a half of the double bore ineffective. At the turn of the century, amateurs in Italy and other western European countries enjoyed playing the *ocarina* as it was called by its inventor Donati. It was an oval globular or vessel flute made of earthenware or porcelain and having 8—10 fingerholes, and sometimes even one or two keys.

The most respected instrument in the wind section of the modern

Keyed bugle

Aida trumpet

orchestra is the modern *transverse flute* perfected around the first half of the 19th century by Theobald Boehm, flautist of the court orchestra in Munich. He gave the flute back its original cylindrical shape, improved the keywork and set forth new principles of articulation which were later applied to the majority of the woodwinds. The flute sound has a gentle and, in lower register, even moody character. Silver and cheaper substitute alloys of copper and nickel are now used more often for flute manufacture than the original granadilla wood. The highest-pitched member of the orchestra is the little flute called the *piccolo* of which more and more is required nowadays as far as technique and performance are concerned, and the instrument is also often used as a solo instrument.

Ever since 1867 when the *clarinet* acquired the Boehm articulation keywork system, the instrument has been widely utilized because of its possibilities as far as the tone formation and compass are concerned. Clarinets come in several sizes and types, the smallest E flat clarinet is used mainly in brass marching bands, while concert clarinets are usually in A or B flat. Apart from the Boehm clarinet the Heckel clarinet is also sometimes used, with different articulation and therefore different fingering. The *bass clarinet* made in 1890 by Fontaine Besson of France was used by Vincent d'Indy in his opera *Fervaal* (1895) and by Antonín Dvořák in his opera *The Devil and Kata* (1896—99).

Adolphe Sax of Belgium was granted a French patent for his *saxophone* in 1846. The popularity of the instrument quickly grew and the saxophone was constantly improved until it acquired the Boehm keywork which lent it universal appeal. The original saxophone family had two lines, one intended for the symphonic use with instruments tuned alternatively in F and C, the other being restricted almost totally to military and citizen marching bands and tuned either in E flat or in B flat. The first line soon became obsolete, while the second survived and was used later especially in jazz music. Saxophones have a single reed like the clarinet, but they differ from the latter in tone character and construction. They can be overblown an octave higher rather than a duodecim (twelfth) like the clarinet, are entirely of a metal construction and feature a wide conical bore.

The instrument to which all other instruments of the orchestra are adjusted as far as the fundamental frequency pitch is the *oboe,* developed in 17th-century France from the shawm by narrowing the bore. The instrument was first used in 1659 by Cambert in his opera *Pomone.* Between 1844—50 the oboe acquired the Boehm articulation as did other woodwinds and was tuned in C as was the flute. The quality and firmness of the oboe tone is determined by the quality and the proper scraping of the double reed made of cane and mounted on a metal staple which in turn is inserted in the head joint of the instrument. Most oboists scrape their reeds themselves. Prior to play the double reed must be properly moistened in the mouth otherwise the oboe could not be played. The player controls the reed vibration only by slight lip pressure and gentle tightening of the mouth muscles. The oboe is the instrument of romantic and love cantilenas and of natural motifs, for example it is used to simulate the sound of shepherd pipes. Slightly larger than the oboe is the *oboe d'amour* which is equipped with a bulbous bell. Johann Sebastian Bach used to compose for the instrument

Bass horn

which later slid into oblivion to be rediscovered by Debussy *(Gigues)* and Richard Strauss *(Sinfonia domestica)*.

The *cor anglais* developed in the first half of the 18th century from the earlier *oboe da caccia*. As the name implies, it was curved but the modern version of the instrument is straight while only the crook is curved slightly to permit vertical holding. A 17th-century arrival to this family is the *baritone oboe,* and the *bass oboe* has been used in orchestration ever since it acquired keywork articulation at the close of the last century. A serious rival to the baritone oboe was the *heckelphone* designed by W. Heckel in 1904 and used in Richard Strauss' operas *Salome* and *Electra.* Johann Heckel made also a *terzheckelphone* and a *piccoloheckelphone* and was the founder of the world-famous wind instrument manufacturing company in Biebrich on the Rhine.

Heckel also won undying fame for his improvement of the intonation qualities of the *bassoon* which—in spite of numerous efforts—never worked well with the Boehm keywork system. The only genuinely deep bass fundament among the woodwinds in modern orchestration practice is provided by the *double bassoon,* or *contrabassoon,* an instrument in existence as early as the 18th century, but impractical until Heckel improved it. Musicians nicknamed it 'central heating' because of its

217 Tenor trombone in B flat
Ramis, Madrid, early 19th century
The Metropolitan Museum of Art, New York

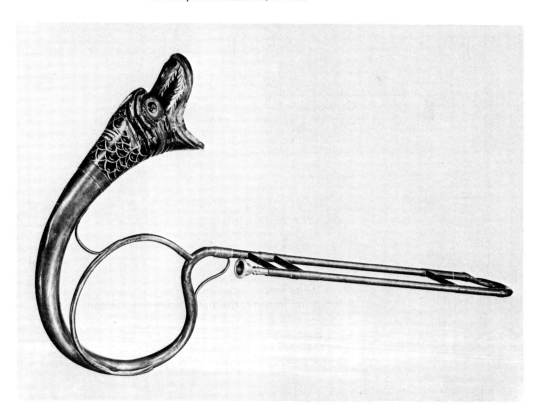

Sudrophone

Euphonium

218 Walking stick violin
Ca. 1810

construction of wooden tubes joined by metal U-shaped pieces. The metal resonator tube extension of the butt joint points downward while the bell at the end is slightly turned to the side. A *subcontrabassoon* was built in 1872 by the Czech instrument-maker František Václav Červený: the theoretical bore length of the instrument was quadruple that of the regular bassoon. However, due to the enormous requirements on the playing technique the instrument never became practical.

With the exception of the slide trombone, the modern brass wind instruments are equipped with valved mechanisms consisting of valves, pistons, ports and crooks or loops. The valve mechanism is either of a piston or rotary valve type. The first system employs pistons with ports deflecting the air through the extra length of tubing when the piston is depressed, whereas the second system features rotary valves which open the passage of the air to the extra tubing when the valve is rotated around its axis after the key is depressed. The rotary valve system is predominant in the symphonic orchestra instruments and in Central European marching bands while the piston system, basically E.F. Périnet's improvement of older designs, is used in French *cornets (cornets-à-piston)* and *tubas.* The tone character of the brass instrument

219 Glockenspiel
Amati, Kraslice, Czechoslovakia

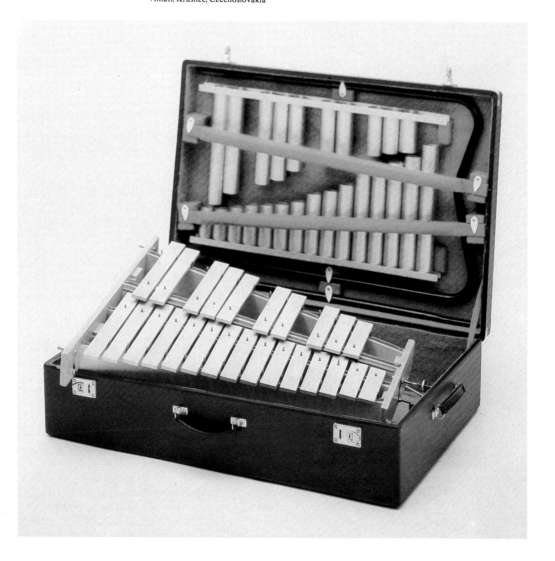

220 Valved trumpet. Lídl, Brno, Czechoslovakia

Ophicleide (bass)

depends mainly on the material, size and profile of the mouthpiece which can be either funnel or cup-shaped, and last but not least it is determined by the conicity of the bore.

The fine sound of the French horn, capable of expressing a whole range of moods, whether used as a solo instrument or in full orchestration concord, makes the instrument probably the most attractive of the brass winds. Its mechanism is usually of the rotary valve system. Recently the *compestating horn* has been rapidly gaining grounds, and this is also capable of producing pedal bass tones.

Prior to the definite victory of the valved brass instruments, A. Weidinger in 1801 in Vienna had applied the woodwind keywork to the trumpet, but after a short vogue the keyed trumpet died a quiet death. The lack of success of this instrument was caused by its dull sound which lacked expressivity, a result of a mechanistic application of a basically pipe-articulation system to an instrument whose character was fundamentally horn-like. A somewhat greater success was the *keyed bugle*, patented by Halliday in Dublin in 1810, although even this instrument was soon to be ousted by the *flugelhorn*.

The modern *trumpet* used in symphonic and marching orchestra alike, is most commonly played in B flat and employes a rotary valve mechanism. The clear stirring festive sound of the trumpet fuses well with the rest of the brass family instruments. Furthermore, various sound effects can be produced by a large number of mutes. Marching

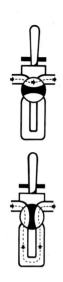

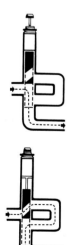

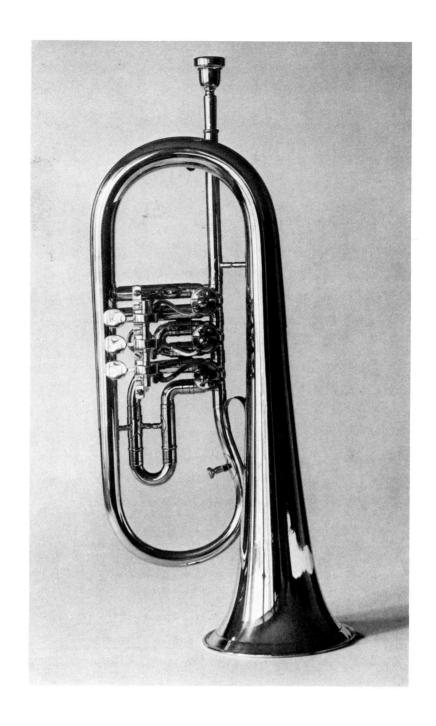

221 Flugelhorn, Lídl, Brno, Czechoslovakia

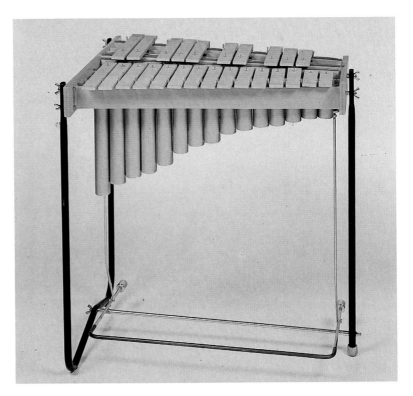

222 Vibraphone

Organ
1 Front positive 2 Great organ with metal pipes 3 Swell organ
with wooden pipes 4 Pedal organ 5 Console 6 Manual I Manual II 8 Pedal board 9 Pedal board tracker action 10 Stop
cranks (knobs) 11 Bellows 12 Wind trunk

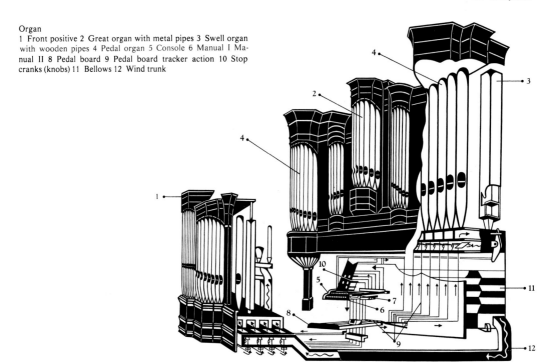

176

Schematic diagram of slider chest tracker action organ
1 Keys 2—3 Stickers 4 Pallet 5 Pallet chest 6 Stop crank
7—8 Stickers 9 Slider

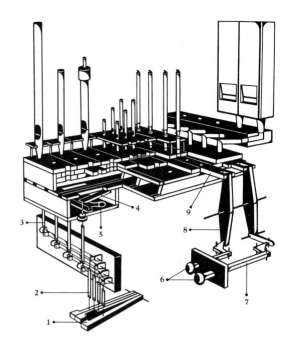

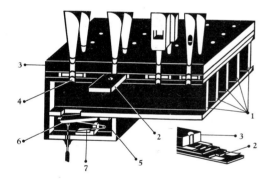

Organ slider chest
1 Tone compartments 2 Sliders 3 Soundboard 4 Pallet hole
5 Pallet chest 6 Pallet 7 Steel spring

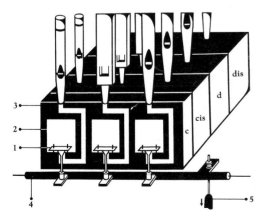

Sliderless chest (Pitman chest)
1 Pitman 2 Stop compartment 3 Soundboard 4 Double-arm
lever 5 Sticker

177

223—224 Organ and organ console
Rieger and Kloss, Krnov, Czechoslovakia

bands sometimes use a lower pitched member of the *trumpet in E flat* which usually provides accompaniment. The lowest pitched member of the trumpet group is the *bass trumpet*, now almost exclusively a marching band instrument. For the interpretation of the high *obbligati* parts of scores by Bach and Haendel, the so-called *Bach trumpets* or *piccolo trumpets* used to be made in D, while a replacement crook allowed the player to adjust the tuning to C. However, most commonly these parts are played by small trumpets in B flat with the tube length equalling one half of that of the ordinary B flat trumpet. Fanfares in Verdi's *Aida* are played by so-called *Aida trumpets*, each of which has one piston valve.

The modern trombone has remained unchanged since its creation as the slide is a perfect mechanism that could hardly be improved. Of the entire consort of trombones used in the past only the *tenor* and *bass trombones* have survived, although there were some efforts on the part of Schönberg, Mahler and other contemporary composers to revive the *alto trombone*, which had been in use till the latter half of the 19th century. The lack of its unique clear sound represents something of a loss to orchestral sound. Trombones for symphonic use are made with a wider bore and bell, while marching and dancing bands have

instruments characterised by narrower bores and bells. The Leipzig instrument-maker Sattler built in 1839 a combination of tenor and bass trombones by introducing a crook to the bell part of the instrument. This *tenorbass trombone* soon became so popular that it finally drove the bass trombone almost entirely from orchestral practice. The *contrabass trombone,* required for instance by Wagner, was handled only with great difficulties and this historic instrument is now rarely seen. Military bands, especially those of the cavalry, replaced the classical slide trombone with the *valved trombone* featuring either piston or a rotary valve mechanism.

France is the land of the *cornet,* but in other countries the instrument is almost entirely confined to brass, military and jazz bands. Since the bore of the *cornet-à-piston* is similar to that of the French horn, the first instruments of this type were usually performed on by horn-players. Its construction and sound character place the cornet somewhere between the trumpet and the horn. Interpretation of parts requiring perfect embouchure is entrusted to small *piccolo cornets* pitched in sopranino, but the most common member of the group is the *soprano cornet.* Some western European military bands still use *alto cornets* in E flat or F, in England rather in C, to fill in the harmony part.

Cornophone

A special place among the brass instruments is reserved for the *flugelhorn* group whose major member is the *flugelhorn,* the queen of Central European brass bands. The instrument originated in Austria-Hungary when the rotary valve mechanism was applied to the simple signal bugle to create a tone that is darker and less shrill than that of the trumpet, but has a more singing quality. It sounds well in brass band music, but is only rarely found in the symphonic orchestra (Mahler). The bass *flugelhorn* remains exclusively a marching band instrument where it provides the tenor part. In lower pitch the *bass flugelhorn* part is sometimes reinforced by the *euphonium,* said to have been invented by the instrument-maker Sommer of Weimar, although occasionally a *baritone horn* (which is similarly shaped) is used. In 1835 instrument-maker Moritz, using a design provided by the Inspector-General of the Prussian military bands Wilhelm Friedrich Wieprecht, built an instrument called the *bass tuba* which also soon found its way into the symphonic orchestra, and soon replaced the earlier serpents, bass horns and ophicleides. In quick succession other variants of the tuba appeared in the form of huge subbass and even contrabass pitch brass instruments, but their handling required superhuman strength and

225 Compestating horn
Lídl, Brno, Czechoslovakia

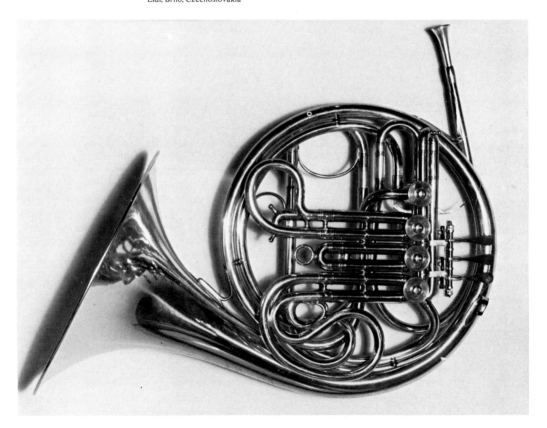

180

226 Helicon
Amati, Kraslice, Czechoslovakia

stamina and thus the instruments did not last long. The lowest-pitched brass instrument was therefore the *contrabass tuba,* built successfully for the first time by the Czech instrument-maker Václav František Červený. Circular tubas called *helicons* (Greek helix - winding) in bass F_1 and even contrabass B_2 were made for military bands. The name *bombardon,* originally describing a tuba of Viennese origins in E flat bass tuning with a wide conical body, was later applied to all kinds of tubas and helicons. Another peculiarly shaped version of the bass tuba is the *sousaphone* named after its inventor, the famous 19th-century American bandmaster and composer John Philip Sousa. Sousaphones found a place in marching and jazz bands.

The mid-19th century, rich in various improvements to musical instruments, also brought into existence a plethora of brass instruments the majority of which are long since forgotten. Such is the fate of the *sudrophone,* devised by the Parisian instrument-maker Sudré, and of the *fonikon* and *baroxyton* of F. V. Červený, whose *cornon* built in 1844 is said to have been the model for Wagner's proposition for the construction of the *Wagnerian tubas* to be used in Wagner's tetralogy. Wagnerian tubas have an oval body and a very open bell and are used in pairs in tenor and bass in the orchestra. The French instrument-maker Fontaine Besson built a whole range of Wagnerian tube type instruments at the end of the 19th century, calling them *cornophones.* And Adolphe Sax designed a whole consort of the so-called *Sax horns* for the French military bands ranging from the piccolo in A flat down to the contrabass in B flat.

Ever since the Baroque era, the *organ* has been rightly thought of as a regal instrument. Indeed, no other instrument produces such a rich spectrum of sound colours, none surpasses the organ in design complexity and none is so closely connected with so many arts and crafts.

227 Organ
Rieger and Kloss, Krnov, 1973
in Nevolné, Czechoslovakia

228 Piano key accordion
Hořovice, Czechoslovakia

Although the Romantic period did bring a whole number of improvements, these innovations affected mainly the playing technique and the mechanical function of the instrument. Attempts at simulating the sound of the instruments of the symphonic orchestra and the period fashion for peculiar and bizarre sound effects led to a dramatic fall in the organ's reputation as a serious musical instrument, and it is only due to Albert Schweitzer and to the collaboration between the musicologist Willibald Gurlitt and the organ builder Walcker as well as to other organ experts that the modern organ has regained its enormous technical and sound qualities. Despite this, however, modern music still has not shown any great interest in the instrument.

The main parts of the pipe organ, the pipe assembly, the bellows and the console, form the organ case whose front is called the prospect. The console is the control panel of the instrument and it contains several keyboards. Hand-operated keyboards—there may be up to five of them—are known as manuals and are arranged in a terrace-like fashion one above the other; there is also a bass keyboard operated by the organist's feet and called the pedalboard. The console is also fitted with controls of both the individual pipe ranks and the various sets of

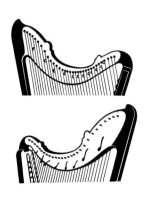

Mechanism of hook harp

229 Banjo
Cremona, Luby, Czechoslovakia

Function of tuning discs on a double action pedal harp and a detail of the pedal action 1 String in full length 2 Pedal in first notch (half-depressed), pitch raised by a semitone 3 Pedal in second notch (fully depressed), pitch raised by a further semi-tome

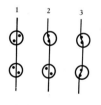

pipes and their combinations. These controls are called stops, which may be sliders, pushbuttons or rocker switches. Other instruments enclosed in the organ case may also be operated from the console, e.g. kettledrums (tympani), drums, glockenspiel, etc. Indeed, a common practice during the Romantic period was to include a thunder-making sound machine, featured, for instance, in Verdi's opera *Othello*.

The connection between the keys and the individual pipes is provided by the action. Old organs have a mechanical action powered by the organist himself, and consisting of a complex system of cranks, levers, shafts and stickers which in total are known as the tracker action (Latin *trahere* = pull). The disadvantages of the tracker action is its heavy operation which deteriorates: as the number of coupled stops

184

increases, with humidity and with fluctuations in temperature. However, the advantage of the traditional action is that it is more sensitive to touch. Modern instruments operate on the principle of a pneumatic or electric action. The first is controlled by compressed air supplied by lead air tubes, and this action is sometimes called tubular pneumatic. In the electric (or rather electro-pneumatic) action, a depressed key will close an electric circuit which will energize an electromagnet. The electric current thus carries the control impulses immediately to the wind chest, but the valve opening the passage of air into the pipe is actuated pneumatically. Modern actions of this type are more reliable and are easier to operate, but these gains have been made at the cost of responsiveness to touch since the varying pressure on the key will no longer permit different tone attack.

230 Chromatic harp
H. Greenway, Brooklyn, USA, second half of the 19th century

231 Harp
A. Červenka, Prague

The wind needed to sound the pipes is supplied by delivery bellows (in modern organs electrically-driven rotary blowers) to reservoir bellows fitted with a blow-off valve and appropriately weighted to keep the wind supply under constant pressure. From there the wind goes into an airtight box called the wind chest. The passage of the wind is controlled by valves called pallets, and to prevent all the pipes from sounding simultaneously only those pallets will be opened which are coupled to the correct stops.

There are two types of wind chest. The older type has a frame construction and is divided internally into numerous compartments called slider chests which support the individual pipe boxes, and there are foot holes through which the air passes into the individual pipes. When a key is depressed the pallet will admit the air into the appropriate slider chests, but the desired pipes will sound only because there is a slider controlling the entry of the wind to the selected pipes. The slider is a thin strip of wood with bored holes registering with the foot holes of the pipes and when the organist pulls a stop knob, the slider will allow the passage of the wind to the pipes of the stop.

The other type of wind chest has a separate valve for each individual pipe. These 'pitman' valves are of a floating type so that when a key is pressed the pitman valves in the appropriate compartments will open.

Organ pipes are made of wood (fir, spruce, pine) or metal (tin, zinc, lead, copper). According to the formation of the tone, the pipes can be divided into flues (stopped and unstopped)·and reeds.

The pipe pitch is derived from the length of the longest pipe, the unstopped C pipe measuring 8 ft. This dimension is called the speaking

232 Button accordion
Hlaváček, Prague

233 Jazz trumpet
Amati, Kraslice, Czechoslovakia

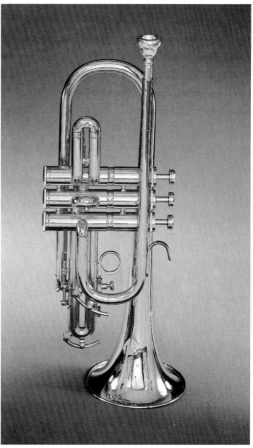

234 Cornet (cornet-à-piston)
Amati, Kraslice, Czechoslovakia

length. If a pipe twice this length is connected, i.e. a 16 ft. pipe, its tone will be one octave lower. And in contrast, a 4 ft. half-length pipe will sound one octave higher. The tone character of the pipe is determined by many factors such as the diameter (scale), foothole size, flue width, mouth height and so on, relative to the speaking length. Flue pipes can be also stopped or unstopped (open), a stopped pipe sounding an octave higher than an open pipe of the same speaking length.

The number of pipes in a large organ is enormous, around 10,000, but 40,000 pipes can be found in the greatest instruments. Naturally, the pipes have to be ingeniously arranged and grouped so that the individual keyboards produce self-contained choruses of a distinct sound character and permit a perfect fusion of all in the grand *tutti* of the organ. All this is the responsibility of a tonal designer who must work closely with the voicer and the pipe maker.

Simultaneously with the new trends in organ building has been a considerable development of other synthesizing or composite keyboard instruments, especially of the electronic organ. However, the

235 Piano
Weinbach, Hradec Králové, Czechoslovakia

similarity of this to the classical pipe organ is in name alone. These instruments, although producing organ-like tones, work on other functional principles and their construction is totally different. Such instruments will be dealt with in the chapter on electric instruments.

An established member of the symphonic orchestra and now its sole plucked chordophone is the *harp,* which after an existence of several thousand years had its design radically changed at the beginning of the 19th century. The old diatonic harp could not produce semitones and various mechanisms were introduced to shorten the strings as required. At the end of the 18th century, the Parisian harp builder Jacques-Georges Cousineau came up with the ingenious idea of the double-action pedal. Although the *double-action pedal harp* appeared very soon after that, a really practical instrument of this type was built by Sebastian Erard only in 1820, and this instrument's design has largely been retained till the present time. The modern orchestral double-action harp consists of a supporting pillar topped with an ornamental head, the neck shaped like an elongated letter *S* and the conical resonator with a soundboard with three soundholes. In the centre of the resonator runs the stringboard in which the strings are fixed. The resonator and the pillar join in the pedal box which serves also as the base. The action mechanism controlled by the pedals is mounted inside the pillar and the hollow neck and rotates discs with two studs. Each string has an individual disc and when the disc is rotated by the pedal, the string pitch will be raised by either a semitone or a full tone. The brass neck bears the tuning pins and the nuts, limiting the pitch of each string. The pedal box contains seven pedals, each adjusting the pitch of all the same lettered strings. The harp has usually 47 strings tuned diatonically. All C flat gut strings are red, while F flat strings are blue for easier identification.

However, even the modern double-action harp has some drawbacks. The complicated mechanism to shorten the strings contains a relatively large number of moving parts which can be under great stress, the playing technique does not always permit complicated pedal work, there are certain problems in playing chromatic passages, etc.

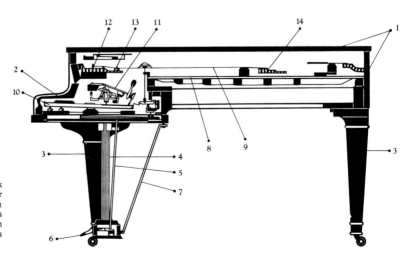

Piano
1 Case with lid 2 Note rack
3 Legs 4 Pedalier 5 Pedalier bar 6 Pedals 7 Pedalier strut
8 Soundboard   9 Strings
10 Keys 11 Hammer action
12 Wrest pins 13 Agraffes
14 Hitch pins

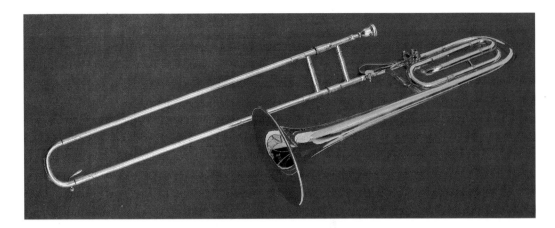

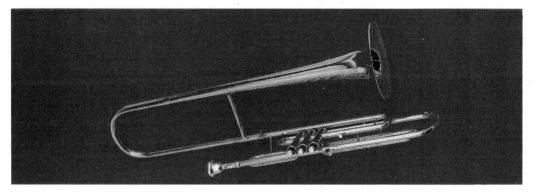

236 Tenor trombone
Amati, Kraslice, Czechoslovakia

237 Trombone
Amati, Kraslice, Czechoslovakia

Consequently, there have been attempts to resurrect the *chromatic harp,* especially since composers now use key transpositions and harmonic and melodic chromatization to a larger degree than before. The Frenchman Jean Henri Pape attempted to build a chromatic harp in 1845, but with little success. Independently of him, Gustave Lyon patented a design in Paris in 1894. The Lyon harp could play all major and minor scales, arpeggios with comfortable fingering, etc. and soon there were composers (Charles Lefebvre, George Enescu and others) who wrote specifically for it. However, certain difficulties with the tuning, the enharmonic glissando and the fact that the strings crossed did not allow the chromatic harp to survive long.

The *orphica,* an invention of the Viennese instrument-maker Karl Leopold Röllig, was a type of keyboard harp, and could be played on a table or suspended on a strap around the player's neck. The instrument was very popular in the early 19th century, but today is seen only in museums.

Like the flageolet in England or the ocarina in Italy, the most popular instrument among 19th-century German and Austrian amateur musicians was the *board zither.* Its flat low body is usually laid on a table, or it can also be played on the player's lap. The straight side of the instrument facing the player bears a fingerboard with metal frets and five metal melody strings stopped with the left hand, and plucked with a ring plectrum worn on the right thumb while the accompaniment gut strings (24 or more) are plucked with the right fingers. Johann Petzmeyer, the zither virtuoso performing at the court of duke Maximilian of Bavaria, invented the *bowed zither*. This instrument has no accompaniment strings and has usually a heart-shaped body with a raised fretted fingerboard with two sound holes running through the centre of the body. The four metal strings were tuned like those of the violin and were bowed with a violin bow. The instrument was also made in tenor and alto versions.

238 Sousaphone
Amati, Kraslice, Czechoslovakia

Sax horn (baritone)

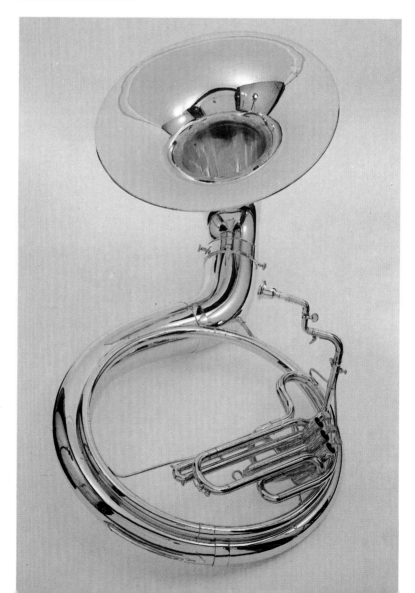

Long before the invention of the piano, instrument-makers had tried to overcome the short austere sound of the keyboard chordophones by systems producing sustained tones. (A classical example of these attempts was the manufacture of the *Geigenwerk* by Hans Haiden from 1575.) The trend culminated in the 19th century in the construction of bowed pianos called *wheel cymbals* in England. One of these was the *piano sostenente* of Isaac Mott patented in 1817. The *piano éolien* of Henry Herz was sounded by comporessed air while Philippe de Girard solved the problem of tone prolongement by repetitive hammer strikes in his *piano trémolophon.* The Turin company of Caldera and Bossi marketed in 1873 their *melopiano,* a mechanism which could be used with any piano and which prolonged the piano tone by a rapid succession of strikes by tiny hammers driven by a fine spring clockwork. For an exhibition in Vienna in 1892, Kühmeyer built a bowed piano in which a bow pressed against the selected string by means of an electromagnet.

However, no make of sostenente piano was able to displace the orthodox *piano,* which retained its popularity while being constantly improved. In 1823 Erard in Paris presented his double escapement piano while concurrently Streicher in Austria devised a hammer action, striking the strings from the top. The modern piano action is located below the strings strung in steel frame capable of withstanding extreme tension. In the higher octaves the strings are trebled, the lower strings are doubled while the lowest bass strings are single but copper-wound. The strings are tuned with wrest pins and run through holes in metal plates called agraffes, across the fir soundboard and end on steel

239 Harmonium
Petrof, Hradec Králové, Czechoslovakia

hitch pins. There are three pedals: the right pedal is used for sustaining tone, it lifts the dampers away from the strings; the left pedal is the soft pedal since it moves the hammer closer to the strings which then produce a softer sound when struck; the centre pedal sustains only those notes whose keys were depressed when the pedal was applied. The return of the piano to the orchestra (chamber orchestration stressing the strings and winds) may seem a new trend in 20th-century music, but is in fact a continuation of 19th-century trends.

In the string section, there have been attempts to replace the missing middle part handled as late as the 17th century by smaller *alto* and larger *tenor viols*. In the 18th century the tenor string part was taken

240 Bass tuba in B flat
Amati, Kraslice, Czechoslovakia

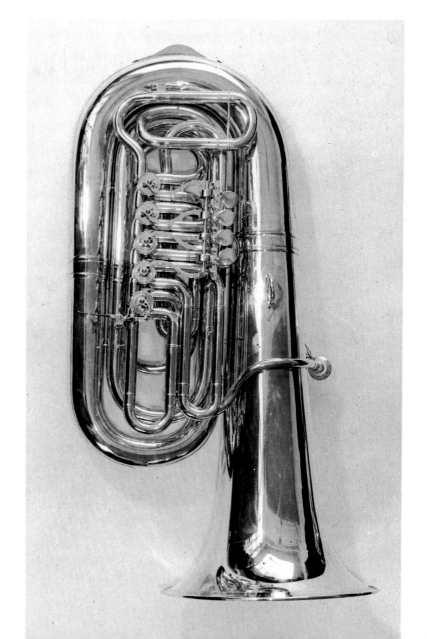

Contr'alto
of J. B. Vuillaume

Violotta of A. Stelzner

over by the violoncello and the treble viol disappeared into oblivion surprisingly quickly to be replaced by instruments of varying design and size, often produced by violin makers at the direct proposals of active performing musicians. Such were the origins of the *violon ténor* of the Paris Opera double bass player Dubois, the *contr'alto* of Vuillaume, the violin-maker, Henry's *baritone*, Stelzner's *violotta*, etc. None of these instruments were successful as they were too big for viola players to handle while violoncellists refused them for the discrepancy between the instrument size and the natural arm movement. On the suggestion of the violist Hermann Ritter, Karl Adam Hörlein, the Würzburg violin-maker built at the end of the 19th century a *viola alta* with an additional e^2 string. Ritter came with a revolutionary proposal to form the string quartet exclusively with violin instruments. He used his viola alta instead of the second violin, the third member was to be a *tenor (treble) viola* and the fourth a *viola bassa* also of a violin shape, larger than violoncello and tuned an octave lower than the *viola alta*. Ritter's requirement of instrument proportionality was later verified by acoustic research studies which proved that the body size of the bowed instruments is insufficient for generation of resonant low tones. Ritter is also credited with creating a counterbalance to Wagner's orchestral reforms based mainly on changes in the wind section. So far the greatest practical success has been the viol of the English violin virtuoso Lionel Tertis who stipulated the dimensions of the instrument in collaboration with the instrument-maker Arthur Richardson in 1937. The Heidelberg Bach-Quartett has been trying to introduce into practice the *tenor violin* made by the Frankfurt violin-maker Eugen Sprenger in the 1930's. The American violin-maker Carleen Hutchinson built her eight-member violin consort ranging from sopranino to contrabass pitches in 1969.

The basic classification criterion of the membranophone-type instruments is the number of membranes. Single-headed membranophones can be pitch-tuned since the sound waves produced by the single vibrator cannot be disturbed by waves produced by another vibrator. On the other hand, in the double-headed membranophones there occur constant collisions of waves propagating from two membranes so that the sound has indefinite pitch.

In the orchestra, the leading position among the membranophones has always been retained by the *kettledrum* despite its cumbersome nature. In the past, whenever the tympanist wanted to adjust the pitch of his instrument he had to use a key or wrench by means of which he turned six to eight tuning screws. The composer had to bear this in mind and to leave sufficient pauses to allow the tympanist to retune. This was so awkward a process that there were numerous attempts after 1800 to find a technical solution permitting a quick and reliable retuning of the instrument; the final solution, the modern pedal-operated machine ketledrum is the invention of the Parisian instrument-maker Gautrot from 1855. The system was improved in 1881 by a Dresden musician named Pittrich and a mechanic named Queisser whose pedal kettledrums could be retuned so quickly that even a simple one octave melody could be produced on the instrument.

Kettledrums are commonly used in pairs in the modern orchestra and each consists of an open-topped capper shell known as a 'kettle'

Snare drum

across which is stretched the 'head' (either calf or kidskin vellum or plastic) held in place by a metal hoop at the top bearing the tuning screws which tension it. The whole instrument is supported with massive struts and a base. The tone is produced when the stretched head is struck with a stick so causing it to vibrate, with the copper shell acting as the resonator. Modern kettledrum sticks have metal or wooden heads covered with flannel or felt. Various changes of tone can be achieved by placing a piece of cloth opposite the spot which is struck, however the practice of beating the kettledrum directly through the cloth has ended. The roll is achieved by a quick succession of strikes with both hands.

The *bass drum* has a low shell, two skins wrapped on thin wooden or metal hoops, two clamping hoops and 8—12 single or double-shanked tensioning screws. Its sound is deep and has no definite pitch. During performance the instrument is supported on a stand and the player strikes it with his right hand, starting at the bottom and continuing upward clockwise, using a drum stick with a round chamois-covered head. Orchestral bass drum players use sticks with heads of several sizes. A short tone is produced by immediate dampening of the vibrating skin. In jazz bands the bass drum is sounded by a foot-

241 Military side drum
Amati, Kraslice, Czechoslovakia

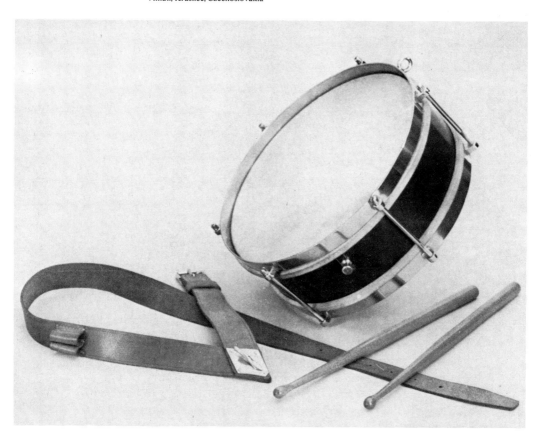

Congas

Timbales

operated pedal with a pivoted and springed felt-padded beater striking a vertical flannel cloth strip stretched permanently over the skin. The other head is fitted with special disc mutes but recent drums incorporate mutes installed within the shell.

The *side drum* has a low metal shell of copper sheet with two calf or donkeyskin heads. One or both heads are stretched with a set of 2—12 snares (gut strings wound with tinsel thread). Modern side drums are fitted with a mechanism which will lift the snares off the skin, giving the sound a deeper timbre. The side drum is usually beaten with two slim hardwood sticks in about one third of the diameter where the sound is sharpest. Both sticks must strike the skin immediately next to each other at an angle of about 75°. Instead of sticks wire brushes may sometimes be used, especially in jazz music.

Jazz has had a great influence on those drums which form the basic drumkit. The bass drum is today only half its previous size, the side drum has a separate stand, and there are several single and double cymbals operated by foot or struck with stick or wire brushes. The modern jazz band drum kit has also acquired some other drums, usually of Latin-American origins, including single-headed tunable *timbales* of various sizes, untunable double-headed *tomtoms,* and various *conga* and *bongo* drums.

For special effects in the orchestra the *tabor* will sometimes be used. It has a wooden cylindrical shell twice as high as that of the side drum, and is beaten with sticks similar to tympani sticks. A version of the tabor drum is the *tambourine de Provence* fitted with a snare and beaten with a single stick with a large bone head. In theory, the instruments

242 Pedal tympani
Musikinstrumente VEB, Dresden, GDR

243 Jazz drum kit
Amati, Kraslice, Czechoslovakia

discussed below can be tuned to a definite pitch but in practice are not, and their pitch varies from one instrument to another.

The *tambourine,* a type of frame drum which is used in the symphonic orchestra, has a metal frame and is sounded by being struck against the first of the other hand, an elbow or a knee. The same goes for the *tambour de Basque.* A rough rolling effect is produced by rapid shaking with the instrument while a fine roll is achieved by running a moistened thumb over the tambourine skin. Rhythmically intricate passages are performed while the instrument is laid on the player's knees with the skin down, the sides being gripped by the elbows. Then the instrument is slightly raised in this way and the rhythm pattern is beaten with the fingers on the frame rim. The roll can also be produced in this fashion. Modern composers sometimes write for other kinds of membranophones, especially non-European drums such as the Cuban *bongoes,* congas and other Latin American drums, and Chinese *goblet drums.*

Bongoes

The formation of the modern orchestra has been the result of thousands of years of tireless effort and ingenuity. The resulting full orchestral sound gives a unique auditory experience based on a harmonious combination of a multitude of instruments. However, attempts to improve the existing musical instruments go on even today, being constantly spurred on by the ever-increasing improvements in instrument construction, tone quality and in sophistication of playing techniques.

197

II. NATIONAL AND FOLK MUSIC INSTRUMENTS

ASIA

INDIA AND PAKISTAN

Instrumental music has always held an important place among the three parts of the Indian *Sangita,* comprising singing, music and dancing. Indeed, Indian instrumental music has a very ancient lineage the origins of which can be traced as far back as the 3rd millennium B.C. The Dravidian people who settled in India in those times had very lively trade connections established with Egypt and Mesopotamia. Records on Indian music exist already in the ancient treatise *Natya Shastra* by Bharata (6th century B.C.); music is thoroughly discussed in another of the major Indian writings on the topic, the *Sangita Ratna-*

244 *Surnay* shawm
Bombay

245 Indian instruments: *dhola* drum, *jhanja* cymbals and *nagasuaram* shawm

kara treatise by Sarngadeva from the 13th century A.D. Another ancient treatise entitled the *Raga Vibhoda* discusses not only certain melodic forms called ragas but also provides instruction on playing string instruments plus an appendix listing some 50 tunes as well. The stages in the development of Indian musical instruments have been preserved for posterity by works of ancient Indian artists who — influenced by Greek sculpture — cut reliefs into the stone walls of the Bharat Temple in the 2nd century B.C. Scenes depicting the musical life of the ancient Indians have been also preserved in the numerous stone reliefs

Indian tubri clarinet

in the vast Buddhist Borobudur Temple, built in the 8th century A.D. by Indian colonists on the island of Java. Later, during the times of the Muslim conquest, India fell under the influence of Perso-Arab music. Actually, musical instruments of the Islamic culture arrived almost simultaneously both in Europe and in India.

Compared to other Asian nations, the Indians have relatively few idiophones. For rhythmic accompaniment, bronze cymbals called *jhanja* are used, similar in shape and sound to Turkish cymbals. They are flat, with a central boss, and are joined with a silken cord running through the centres. Thick-walled cymbals called *tála* or *mandira* are bowl-shaped. The *kurtar* or *chitike* is a bunch of jingles or metal

246 Indian drums and lute. Miniature, late 18th century

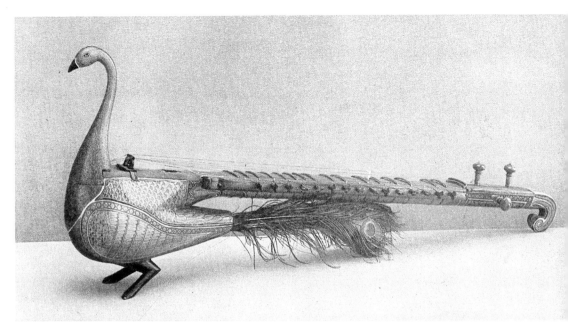

247 Indian bowed instrument, the *tayuc*

jingling discs suspended in a wooden frame, flat on one side and arched on the other. They are held in one hand, the flat end clashing as the fingers are opened and closed.

The wind instruments have remained practically unchanged throughout the millennia of development of Indian music and are similar to those of other musical cultures. In India, however, these instruments have acquired an unmistakeable national character. Archaeological findings prove that the flute had been played in India long before the arrival of the Aryans (1500—1200 B.C.) Its charming tone is echoed in the poetry of Rabindranath Tagore and in the legends of the god Indra. At marriage ceremonies and in religious processions the shrill sound of the *surnai* double shawm (sometimes also called the *shahnai*) can be heard. The South Indian version of the *surnay* is the *nagasuaram,* with a conical bore and a metal bell. Its double cane reed is fitted with a piruette against which the lips are rested. The instrument has 12 fingerholes of which only seven are actually fingered, the rest being plugged with wax and used for precise pitch adjustment. The *tubri* (or *tiktiri* or *jingivi*), known as the typical instrument of snake charmers, is common throughout India. It is basically nothing but a double clarinet consisting of two cane pipes with a common reed fitted in a wind chamber, usually a gourd. India is also the home of the bagpipe. The *shruti upangi* or *bhezana shruti* is the South Indian bagpipe with a single chanter and a goatskin bag incorporating a short mouthpipe. In North India and Kashmir a bass drone is added and the instrument is called the *moshuk.* The large brass horn called the *ranasringa* consists of two curved sections fitted together, forming either one large or a double S-shaped bend. The *ranasringa* is played during temple rites and various festivities.

The foremost position among the stringed instruments is reserved for the *vína,* one of the most ancient Indian instruments, a sophisticated stick zither. The name is derived from the *bin,* the ancient Egyptian harp. All *vínas* have a long and wide neck forming also the axis of the instrument, numerous frets and two resonators. The instrument is very attractive, usually richly carved and inlaid with gold, silver and ivory. Four of the seven strings are fingered and the remaining three run along the left side of the neck. The *vína* is played either on the lap or supported by the left shoulder; the player always sits crosslegged. The strings are never plucked with a plectrum but with fingernails grown extremely long. There are several variants of the instrument, but their designs differ in minor detail only. A *vína* variant called the *taus* or *esrar* with a peacock-shaped body is also equipped with sympathetic strings and movable frets.

Many of the Indian chordophones are played with a simple stick bow without any nut. One such chordophone is the *sarangi* whose body is shaped like the figure 8, hollowed from a single piece of wood and stretched with parchment. The neck is short and wide to accommodate three stopped and 15 chromatically-tuned sympathetic strings. The *sarangi* of North India is more elaborately sculptured, the head carved in the shape of a swan neck. The *sarinda* is common in Bengal, Pakistan and Afghanistan. It is somewhat narrower than the *sarangi* fiddle and

248 *Vicitra-vína*
Bombay

249 *Surbahar*
Calcutta

the belly is not covered with parchment but remains open.

Perhaps no other ancient culture developed such an intricate system of rhythms as is seen in Indian music. The fine drumming techniques provide a matching rhythmical answer to the moralizing drone of the Indian tunes. The drumming techniques have always been extremely elaborate and complex, and even today Indian musicians astonish their Western audiences with the complexity and perfection of the rhythm section work. Medieval India was the birthplace of the drum set composed of drums of various pitch, although the drum set was later perfected in Burma. The Borobudur Temple reliefs show several types of cylindrical drums dating from the pre-Islamic period. Kettledrums are an Islamic import into India so that today both types can be found.

A representative of the double-headed wooden barrel drums tuned by lacing and chocks is the *mridanga* or *mathala,* invented according to legend by Brahma himself. In North India, the *tabla* is preferred, actually a pair of drums differing in shape, size and pitch. The larger, cylindrical *daina* is played with the right hand, the left beats a smaller barrel or kettle-shaped *bayan.* The body of the drum is made from one piece of wood and the head is formed by three layers of skin. The bottom skin stretches over the entire head, then comes a second layer glued to the first but with a circular cut-out, the third top skin having a cut-out of an even larger diameter than the middle skin, so that there is a thick treble layer of skins around the periphery only. The centre of

203

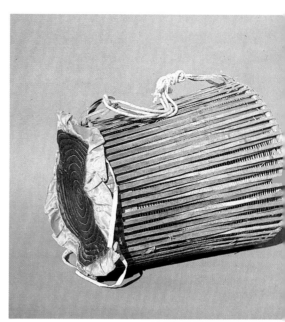

250—253 Indian drums

Indian *bansari* flute

the head is covered with a thin film of smooth black paste mixed from mango powder, boiled rice and tamarind juice which lends the *tabla* the fine muted sound so suitable for the accompaniment of the *sitar.* Folk instrument groups use the *dhola* and *dholak* drums with heads reinforced with hemp rope hoops and tensioned with leather thong lacing. The dhola is beaten with a drum stick or with the hand. The *naqara* kettledrum with copper or iron-riveted shell can be heard during state ceremonies, in processions and temples. The membrane is attached to the head by means of a metal hoop and is tensioned with a wet rope which shrinks as it dries, making the membrane taut. Palace ensembles play huge kettledrums the diameter of which can reach up to 180 cm and whose weight may be well over 200 kg. The instruments are transported on elephants' backs and are draped with free-hanging drapes.

For several thousand years the musical culture of Pakistan has been developing side by side with the music of India. No wonder then that the Pakistani instruments are quite similar to and sometimes even identical with their Indian relatives. The *sitar,* a lute instrument popular in both nations is a combination of the Indian vína and the Persian *tambura* and it is said to have been invented by the famous musician Amír Chusrau who lived at the court of a 13th-century Delhi sultan 'Ala-ud Din. The resonator of the sitar is made of wood or from a gourd cut in the direction of the kernels, the belly made of thin wood. Originally, the sitar used to have three strings (*si* = three, *tár* = string), but the modern sitar has seven strings plucked with a plectrum worn on the index finger. A combination of the *sitar* and *sarangi* is the gentle and fine sounding *esraj (esrar).* This light fiddle-type instrument with a fingerboard and 18 adjustable frets originated during the period of Muslim rule as a ladies' instrument.

254 Pakistani *bansora* flutes

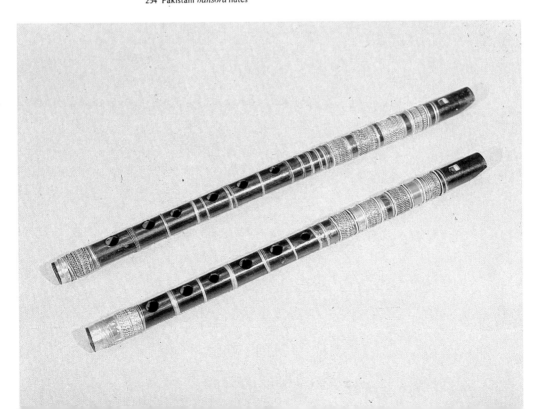

255 Indian singer with *sarangi*

Indian *sringa* horn

256 Indian drum and single hand *pena*
Assam, India

257 Indian *baya* and *tabla* drums

Indian *sarinda*

MONGOLIA AND SOVIET CENTRAL ASIA

Musical instruments depicted on murals in the Erdonidzú Temple in *MONGOLIA*, the small drum seen in the hands of the Indian magus Mahasiddha as well as modern instruments all reveal the strong Chinese and Indian influences on Mongolian music. When in the 13th century the great Mongolian ruler Genghis Khan laid the basis of the huge Mongolian empire, the Mongolians were exposed to different cultures in their wars of conquest. The cornerstone of Mongolian literature, a chronicle called *The Secret History of the Mongols* written in 1204, as well as reports from European envoys at the Mongolian court, mention the existence of a distinctly Mongolian folk music and of the *morin-chur* fiddle which even today is considered the national Mongolian instrument.

The body of this low-ribbed, trapezoid fiddle with its parchment belly and back is reminiscent of the Arabic *rebab* fiddle. The two horse-hair strings are tuned a fifth apart. Other typical Mongolian instruments are the three-string *shanza* lute and the *iochin* dulcimer beaten with sticks in a similar fashion to the European, or rather Hungarian, *cimbalom*. The 14-string *yatag* is somewhat similar to the Chinese *ku-ch'in* zither, and is plucked with fingers. The *limba* flute as well as the

207

dudaram gong chimes are used both as solo and accompaniment instruments. Lamaistic rites are known for use of the *temur chur* jew's harp and the *damar,* a rattle drum of Tibetan origins.

The typical instrument of the shepherds in *KAZAKHSTAN,* a vast region of the U.S.S.R. stretching between the lower Volga River and China, is the end-blown *sybyzgi* flute with four to six fingerholes. Folk singers in Kazakhstan accompany their epic songs with the *dombra,* a two-string lute with a long neck. Like the dombra, the bowed *kobyz* in the shape of a ladle is also made from a single piece of wood. The *daulpaz* kettledrum, suspended from a horse saddle, used to be a military and hunting instrument.

In *KIRGIZIA* the men play two types of flutes: a wooden one called the *choor* and a brass flute called the *sarbasnay.*

The *temir-komuz* jew's harp is exclusively played by women. In the Tien Shan mountain range the three-string komuz sounds today as it did long ago. The middle string of the instrument is tuned to sound higher than the two side strings. The *kiyak* with a flat elongated body resembles the Kazakh *kobyz.*

Images of musicians and musical instruments on silver bowls dating from the 3rd century B.C., terracota figurines of musicians with instruments found in the little town of Ajrtam as well as treatises on music by the famous Central Asian scholars al Farabi (Alfarabius), Ibn Sina (Avicenna), Djami and others testify to the richness of the musical

258 Priestesses playing flute, lute, drums and handbells
Deatail, painted base of a ceremonial chest, 18th century
Choidzhin-lamyu-suru. Monastery, Ulan Bator, Mongolia

Afghanistani *rebob* fiddle

259 Musical instruments of Turkestan

Central Asian jew's harp

heritage of the *UZBEK* and *TADZHIK* nations. Among the great variety of instruments, a prominent position is held by the two-string *dutar* with a pear-shaped body glued together from bent mulberry wood staves. Extensive vocal-instrumental works called *makoma* are usually accompanied by a three-string plucked chordophone called the *tanbura*. The two *rebab* types, i.e. the Afghan and Kashgar versions, are identical both for Uzbekistan and Tadzhikistan. The same is also true for the less common *dumbrak*. The *chang* is a type of dulcimer with a flat trapezoidal box and three-string courses tuned diatonically. The chordophone family is supplemented by the *gidzhak* and the *kobuz*. The gidzhak is a fiddle with a metal spike and belly stretched with a membrane; the instrument has three strings. It is quite similar in construction on the Tadzhik and Turkmen versions. The kobuz is identical to the Kazakh *kobyz*, but can be found only in certain areas of Uzbekistan.

Apart from the *nai*, a cross (side-blown) flute whose name testifies to its Arabic origin, the most common wind instrument is the *surnai* shawm, played exclusively as a solo instrument unlike its relative the *zurry* which is always used in pairs in the neighbouring countries.

The tones of the large brass *carnai* trumpet used to announce the commencement of grand ceremonial occasions. Today, the *katnai* is played in parades, ceremonies, processions and folk festivals.

Quite common to the entire Uzbekistan and Tadzhikistan as well as other Central Asian regions is the *doira* tambourine with jingling discs in a wooden frame. The jingling effect is increased by metal caps worn on the fingers. The *nagora*, a pair of small kettledrums of Persian orig-

209

Uzbek *carnai* trumpet

260 Mongolian fiddle *morinchur*

Kirgiz *komuz*

261 Kazakh *kobyz*

262 Uzbek *kashgar*

Dagestani *agach-komuz*

ins have the same role as the *doira.* The *nagora* used to announce ceremonial entrances of emirs and khans to the city.

DAGESTAN, the southernmost autonomous republic of the U.S.S.R. has a cosmopolitan population. The Kalmyks and Djargins often use a three-string plucked chordophone called the *agach komus* (or *temur* by the Avar peoples), with a body shaped like a spade and fitted with a trident-like spike at the lower end of the body. The *tar,* a lute instrument, is played in southern Dagestan. (The same instrument is called the *tara* by the Lezgian peoples, and the *chongur* by the Kumyks and Aktins.) The *chagana* is common among the Avar and Lak peoples, and is related to the Georgian *chianuri.* It is a type of spiked fiddle with a flat body stretched with ram skin.

A very popular reed instrument in Dagestan is the *iasti-balaban* which is similar to the Azerbaidzhani *balaban.* Basically a solo instrument, the *iasti-balaban* nevertheless finds great use also in folk ensembles for the accompaniement of song and dances. Equally widely used is the *zurna* whose Dagestan form differs from the zurnas of all other Central Asian regions only in dimensions and the location of the finger holes. The *concertina* as a folk instrument found its use in Central Asia at first in 19th century-Dagestan. The *komuz* is a type of the so-called Asian or 'Oriental' accordion or concertina, similar in design to the Vyatka concertina with the only difference that the pitch does not change with the press and draw. At present, the *komuz* has become so popular it can be considered a folk instrument in Dagestan. The *gaval* is a double-headed drum while the *töp* is a tambourine with jingles. The Dagestani *tiplipitom* is identical to the Georgian pottery kettledrum called the *diplipito;* a bell is tied to the instrument to be hit from time to time with a drum beater.

211

263 Manufacture of Tadzhik folk instruments
Dushanbe, Tadzhik S.S.R., U.S.S.R.

Georgian *changi* harp

The *ashugs,* folk singers in *AZERBAIDZHAN,* recite and sing their songs to the accompaniment of a string instrument called the *saz* which has a highly arched pear-shaped body and a long neck. The flat soundboard has small soundholes which, however, may sometimes appear instead on the sides. The number of strings varies from four to eight, the strings being of three types — melody, key and accompaniment. The most common tuning is in fourths and fifths, the melody strings being tuned a fourth higher than the key strings while the accompaniment strings are a fifth higher. The development of the Azerbaidzhani classical musical style is directly tied up with the *tar,* a plucked chordophone differing from the *saz* in construction and shape. The body of the *tar* is shaped like the figure *S,* the belly being stretched with bull's percardium. There are usually 11 strings in three colour-coded groups: white yellow and black, arranged in double courses. The *tar,* together with the *kemanje* fiddle and the *djaff* tambourine form an instrumental ensemble capable of playing classical as well as folk repertoire.

ARMENIA, occupying the southern part of Transcaucasia, is known for its ancient plucked chordophone *pandira* used for song accompaniment. The popular instrument of the *gusans* (as folk musicians are called) is a kit (small long-bodied fiddle) *kjamani* whose shape is reminiscent of the Italian *sordine.* The remaining Armenian instruments are of Perso-Arabic origins, namely the *'ud* lute, *qanun* zither, *santir* dulcimer, *naquara* pottery drums and *daf* tambourine.

The major instrument of the *GEORGIANS* settled in the western and central Caucasus is the plucked *panduri.* Its popularity is so great that even other instruments of the string family have been named after it. It is shaped like the Dagestani *agach komuz;* the three gut strings are tuned in seconds or thirds, or the two top strings are in unison while the bottom one is tuned an eight higher. The *chonguri* is somewhat different to the *panduri* since its body is less elongated but more arched and its four strings are tuned in quart-sext accord with a doubled fifth. The plucked *chonguri* is played mainly by women, whose other major instrument is the *changi* harp with strings of twisted horsehair.

CHINA, JAPAN AND KOREA

Chinese philosophy assigns an important role to music which it conceives as an art of tones, words and movement. In Chinese music, matter is much more than a mere medium for sound-making. The longer the tone lasted and the better it was isolated, the deeper was it thought possible to penetrate into the very essence of matter. This was also one of the reasons why — quite in contrast to European music — the Chinese attached great importance to the idiophones.

This importance of the idiophones for ancient Chinese music has been attested to by discoveries of lithophones which show a great

Georgian *chonguri*

264 Dagestani drummers

degree of perfection despite the fact that they date several thousands years back. One of these instruments is the *s-ch'ing*, the origins of which are now dated as the 3rd or 4th millennium B.C. Originally the stones had been shaped irregularly, later they were L- shaped and an image of an instrument in this form appears on a brass bowl dating from the Period of Warring States (Chan Kuo 481-221 B.C.) and on a stone relief from the Shang period (1550—1028 B.C.). It also cannot be entirely ruled out that idiophones might have been used as a means of payment since the custom has survived in some remote parts of Southeast Asia till modern times.

A series of tuned suspended slabs of stone form the *pien ch'ing* shown on rock paintings in the famous cave temple of the Thousand Buddhas in the Tun Huang gorge, dating from the Chou period (1028—221 B.C.). The collections kept today in the Temple of Heaven complex in Peking, part of which is devoted to ancient Chinese musical instruments, contain also an 18th-century *pien-ch'ing* with 16 tuned jade stones. The *fang-sian* was sometimes a lithophone, sometimes a metallophone. It was formed by eight oblong bars suspended in a wooden frame. The instrument can be seen on paintings in the Tun Huang caves

265 Drum and guitar
Mural painting, cave temples of the Thousand Buddhas, Tun Huang,
Kansu province, Sui dynasty (581—618)

Chinese *sheng* mouth harmonica and sectional view of the pipes

266 Chinese bell

267 Chinese musical instruments, *top left: p'ai-pan* clapper, vertical *siao* flutes, *kuan* shawm, *kung-hou* harp, *sheng* mouth harmonica *hsing-erh* cymbals, *p'ai-pan* clapper, small *bangu* drums, *ti* flute, *chang-ku* and *po-fu* drums
Mural painting, cave temples of the Thousand Buddhas, Tun Huang,
Kansu province, T'ang dynasty, 8th century

dating from the Sui dynasty (A.D. 581—618). At that time the *fang-sian* was a popular folk instrument. Nowadays lithophones are used only in temple services.

The ancient Chinese instrumentation also included various metallophones, bells, gongs and cymbals. The *yün-luo* (luo = gong) gong chimes is of Mongolian origin. It is composed of 10 to 24 bronze bowls. Naturally, a very common type of material used for the construction of idiophones was wood. A xylophone of a very peculiar construction is the *chu,* a wooden tub fitted with a swivel hammer beating three times into the bottom of the tub prior to each verse of the Confucian hymn. A block of hardwood beaten with a cylindrical bar is called the *pang'-c.* The *p'ai-pan* is commonly used in folk ensembles as well as in opera for rhythm accentuation. The instrument consists of three or more wooden plates, each having two little holes in its upper part, and joined together by a cord. The *mu-yü* is a type of wooden bell without a clapper, but with carved ornaments reminiscent of fish fins. This is why the instrument is called 'wooden fish'. A very ancient instrument is the *yü* scraper (*yü* = tiger) carved from wood to resemble a crouching tiger on a base.

268 Chinese *yün-luo* chime

Chinese *pien ch'ing* lithophone

Chinese *p'ai-siao* panpipe

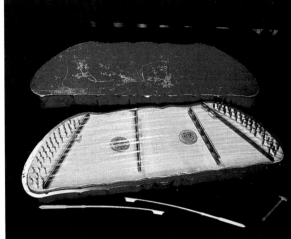

270 *Lu-sheng* mouth harmonica and *yang-ch'in* dulcimer

271 *Yang-ch'in* dulcimer

Of the winds, one of the oldest Chinese instruments is the *p'ai siao* panpipe with 12 to 24 stopped bamboo pipes in a flat wooden box, often brightly painted. The side-blown *ti* flute was very common in the music of the 2nd and 1st century B.C., and was an inspiration for the painters of the Tun Huang period as well as for sculptors who carved the images of musicians playing flutes into the face of cliffs in the Szechwan province. The *ti* used nowadays is about 61—63 cm long, with nine holes, the first hole being covered with a very fine cane or reed membrane, the other six holes fingered. The last two holes serve for wind escape and a string is inserted through them and tied so allowing the instrument to be hung. The tube is reinforced with rings of wound thread, painted with black lacquer.

The ancient anthology of Chinese poetry *Shih Ching* also mentions an aerophone called the *sheng,* sometimes erroneously labelled the mouth organ, although the instrument has nothing in common with an organ. In fact, the set of bamboo tubes of varying length does not have the same function as the pipes of a regular organ. A much better name for the *sheng* would be mouth harmonica, and actually it was the sheng which provided the idea on the basis of which the Western mouth harmonica was developed. The *sheng* usually consists of 17 bamboo tubes: 13 are cut obliquely with a free reed fixed in the notch. The length of the tubes is carefully dimensioned to amplify sufficiently the sound of the vibrating reeds.

The oldest instruments among the Chinese string family are two types of zither common in various shapes and versions to all nations of East and Southeast Asia. They are the *se* and the *ku-ch'in,* and the two have much in common in many aspects. The *se* is mentioned in Chou period literature (13th—12th century B.C.). Today, a 25-string *ta-se* and a 16-string *siao-se* are used. One of the popular motives of Chinese art has always been a poet playing or giving instruction in playing the *ku-ch'in,* in shape quite similar to the *se.* The ku-ch'in is mentioned in

219

272 Chinese *suo-na* shawm

273 Chinese *sheng* mouth harmonica

274 Chinese *ti* and *chettö* flutes

220

275 Chinese *ku-ch'in* zither

tales dating from the 6th century B.C. All dimensions seem to have a symbolic cosmological meaning: the length represents the 366 days of the year; the width symbolizes the six directions, i.e. north, south, east, west, zenith and nadir; the thickness in the centre symbolizes the four seasons; the head is wider than the base meaning that the noble is higher than the humble which is lower; the belly is arched like heaven while the back is flat like the earth. The tuning depends on the mode of the performed piece.

From the 3rd century China had more frequent contacts with her western neighbours which contributed to the import of musical instruments from India and Central Asia. It was probably at this time that the *p'i-p'a* lute reached China from Central Asia, and the *p'i-p'a* soon became the most common solo instrument not only in China but also in Korea, Vietnam, Cambodia and Japan. The instrument has an arched back tapering gradually into the neck topped with a pegboard. The four strings are tuned in the mode of the performed piece. According to an ancient Chinese legend, in the times of empress Wu (A.D. 684—705) a man from the land of Shin discovered in an old tomb an instrument round like the moon and called it *yueh-ch'in* or 'the instrument of the moon'. The body is circular, with low ribs, a short neck and a sickle-shaped head. The fixed scale is determined by nine frets, three inlaid in the fingerboard and six in the bellyboard.

The only Chinese bowed instrument is the *erh-hu* (*erh* = two; *hu*,

276 Chinese guitar

abbr. of *hu-ch'in* = fiddle). The small hexagonal or octagonal body is made of hard wood. The belly is covered with snake skin. The neck is formed by a bamboo stick running through the resonator, and the two strings are tuned a fifth apart. The player plays it while sitting and rests the spike on his knee. The bow hair is wound through the strings and the left fingers lightly touch (but never press since there is no fingerboard) both strings simultaneously.

Of the great variety of drums, the *ku* is mentioned in literature of the Yin period (18th-12th century B.C.) The *po-fu* drum is carried suspended on a cord round the neck and is beaten with both hands. Naturally, drums were also important military instruments. The Tun Huang frescoes show that drums were not only to frighten the enemy with their great sound but were also used to direct combat and relay orders. Drums have also played an important role in the Chinese theatre and an entire drum language was developed comparable perhaps only to the famous African talking drums. The drums used in the Chinese theatre consist of the *tan-p'i-ku* drums and the *hsing-erh* cymbals, supplemented with the *tatchang-ku* bass and *siao-tan-ku* tenor drums, bells and other instruments. A typical feature of them is the manner in which the membrane is attached to the head since in China it is usually nailed to the body. Of course, this renders any tuning impossible in contrast to the drums of India the membranes of which are usually tensioned by means of leather thong lacing. (The nailing of the skin down to the drum body and other phenomena in Oriental music so incomprehensible to the European can be perhaps best explained by the belief that drums are endowed with magical power which is thought to be enhanced by the nails.) Folk and professional instrumental ensembles use a low-bodied barrel drum called the *chang-ku,* beaten with two drumsticks. The *yao-ku* is similar, but has a higher body and two metal rings by means of which the drum is carried suspended around the drummer's shoulders. A small, low, yet massive-bodied drum is called the *tien-ku* with the skin nailed from the top to the head. Quite common is the *pan-chu* which has a thick wooden shell in the shape of

277 Chinese *p'i-p'a* lute

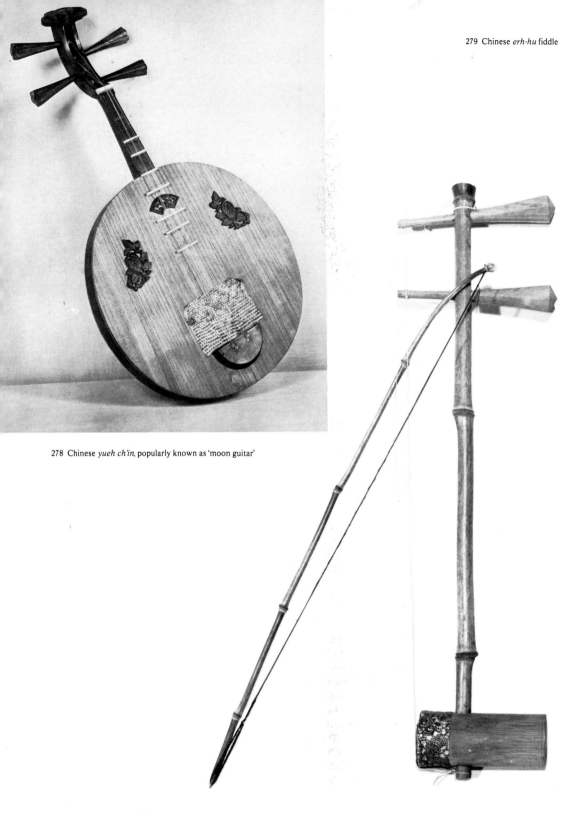

279 Chinese *erh-hu* fiddle

278 Chinese *yueh ch'in*, popularly known as 'moon guitar'

280 Chinese *ku* drum

281 Chinese *yao-ku* drums

282 Chinese folk music ensemble: *chang-ku* drum, *lo* gong, *hsing-erh* cymbals, *suo-na* shawm, *sheng* mouth harmonica

Japanese *shoko* gong

an inverted goblet and a small hole in the bottom. The drum rests on a three-legged stand and is played by the leader of the ensemble with two sticks.

During the reign of the Manchu dynasty (1664—1912) Chinese music absorbed new influences which sometimes were not in accord with the Chinese philosophy of music. The Manchu rulers recognised and supported especially the most ancient musical styles and rejected many of the instruments of the T'ang period. The 19th century saw the arrival of European instruments in China, and their use caused many disputes. Some categorically refused anything European while others considered the native Chinese instruments obsolete. Today there are many instrumental ensembles in China using both Chinese and European instruments.

Like many other nations, the *JAPANESE* have been fond of the art of music ever since the most ancient times. Clay figurines (*haniwa*) from the 2nd — 3rd centuries and the first literary records attest to the existence of ancient magical and shamanistic musical instruments considered old even then. Among the instruments of the period is the *yamato-goto* zither, called also the *wagon*, with a long arched body. When Buddhism was universally accepted in Japan in the 6th century, masked dance rituals became very important. They were called *gagaku*

283 Tibetan drum, rattle and cross flute

and the same name was applied to the drums accompanying the rituals. Following the Chinese example, music in Japan was also under the direct auspices of the Imperial court, and the name *gagaku* signifies the status which the classical court music enjoyed since it means *noble music,* and even today it holds a predominant position in Japan. Contemporary *gagaku* musicians play one wind and one string instrument plus one of the European symphonic orchestra. The winds play the same role in the *gagaku* as the strings in the symphonic orchestra. The main melody instrument is a short double reed of Chinese origin called the *hichiriki.* Its short (18 cm) tube is made from specially prepared bamboo and is reinforced with cherry tree bark. The seven finger holes on the overside and two on the underside allow generation of tonal intervals even smaller than quartertones by means of a special fingering technique. The shrill sound of the instrument is well described in the delightful *Makura no soshi* (Pillow-Book) by Sei Shonagon, a leading lady writer of the period around A.D. 1000. 'The terrible sound of the *hichiriki* is like the noisy cicadas in the autumn.' Other melody instruments of the *gagaku* are three side-blown *fue* flutes. The shortest

284 Tibetan large *rag-dung* trumpets

Japanese *da-daiko* drum   285 Large Japanese court *gagaku* drum

with six holes is called the *koma-fue*, the middle-sized one with seven holes is the *kagura-fue*, while the longest is called the *ryuteki* or *yoko-fue*. The *sho* mouth harmonica corresponds to the Chinese *sheng*. The reeds are tuned with extreme precision with wax droplets and a special agent is applied to prevent condensation of humidity, which is also the reason why the *sho* is kept warm with a glowing charcoal fire in a pottery bowl when the instrument has a pause during a piece.

The task of the *shoko* gongs (which come in three sizes and are suspended in a circular frame with a base) is to break down the phrasing with individual strokes accentuating the drums. The leader, who sets the tempi, holds a small drum called the *kakko* whose two heads are tensioned with rope lacing. A larger drum called the *taiko*, beaten only on one side with two beaters, is suspended from a stand in front of the player. The huge *da-daiko* drum is used in the *bugaku* dances. It stands on a separate platform surrounded with a handrail and is decorated with brightly coloured curtains.

The modern *gagaku* uses only three stringed instruments: zithers

229

called *wagon* and *gaku-so* and the *gaku-biwa* lute. The two zithers are versions of the Chinese *ku-ch'in* and *ku-chêng* zithers. The *biwa* also clearly reveals its Chinese origin, the instrument reached Japan in the 9th century. Its pear-shaped body is belted above the bridge with a leather strap about 15 cm wide. There are two crescent-shaped soundholes in the centre of the soundboard. The four strings are tuned in a, e, a, c¹ and are sounded with a special plectrum striking technique.

The instrumental orientation of the *gagaku* music found a continuation in the *koto* music; *koto, samisen* and *shakuhachi* laid the foundation for the *Edo* period music. The major instrument of the *koto* music is a 13-string zither called the *koto*. Since the instrument lacks fingering marks, playing is usually limited to the plucking of unstopped strings

286 Japanese *shakuhachi* flute

287 Japanese *san-no-tsuzumi* drum

230

288 Japanese *koto* zither

Korean *kayagum* zither

289 Japanese *samisen* lute

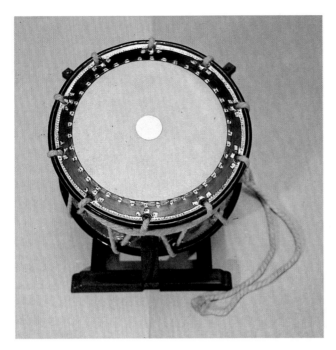

290 Japanese *sime-daiko* drum

291 Japanese *san-no-tsuzumi* drum

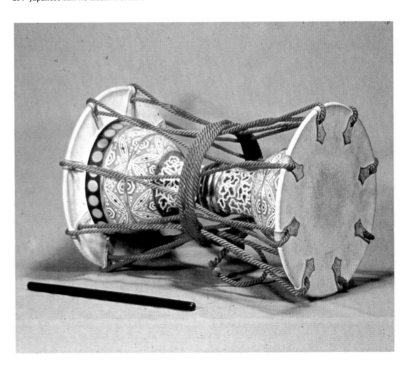

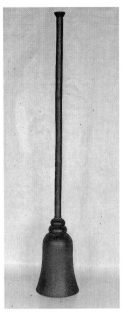

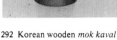
292 Korean wooden *mok kaval* trumpet

293 Korean *tjango* drum

supported by two frets common for all the strings. However, each string has an individual movable bridge and is sounded with plectra shaped like elongated fingernails and worn on the fingers. The major instrument of the *Tokugawa* period (1603—1868) is the *samisen,* a guitar-like instrument. The instrument originated in China and a whole range of sizes is made today to match the voice compass of the singer. The resonator is formed by a rectangular wooden frame. The three strings are tuned in various ways and are sounded with a *baci* plectrum made of white wood. A somewhat rarer plucked chordophone is a four string 'lune guitar' of Chinese origin called the *gogen.*

Shakuhachi music owes its existence to the end-blown flute of the same name. As with the overwhelming majority of Japanese instruments, this bamboo flute also originated in China. It has five finger holes producing the tone scale d, f, g, a, d¹, but the application of the so-called *mari-kari* technique makes it possible to play a far greater number of tones. The *mari-kari* is based on a combination of partial closing of the finger holes and different embouchure.

Typical instruments are to be found also in the *kabuki* theatre music, usually various types of bells, gongs, jingles, xylophones and drums producing a varied kaleidoscope of sounds.

Archeological findings of vessel flutes of burnt clay as well as tomb paintings of musicians with end-blown flutes dating from the beginning of the 1 st millennium A.D. prove that musical traditions in *KOREA* go very far back into the past. Many Korean musicians also used to perform in the *gagaku* ensembles at the Japanese court, and in this way influenced to a certain extent Japanese music. A great many instruments are quite similar to their Japanese and Chinese counterparts, e.g. the *ö* scraper is identical to the Chinese *yü* while the Chinese gong chimes *yün-luo* had an identical counterpart in the Korean *una,* including the same number of gongs. The Korean *sheng* is identical to the Chinese *sheng* mouth harmonica, etc.

Mural pantings from the Koguryo period (1st century B.C. — 7th century A.D.) show musicians playing end-blown flutes called *tchun-so,* sometimes reaching up to 1 m in length. An important position among the winds is enjoyed by a bamboo fipple flute called the *pchiri* with eight finger holes and a very piercing sound quality.

The most popular Korean instrument is the 13-string bowed *kayagum* zither. Very similar in look is a ten-spring bowed zither called the *djunadjan.* The *yangum* dulcimer used to be so small that it was first played in the palm of the left hand but its dimensions gradually grew so that today it has a flat trapezoidal body and a great number of metal strings.

However, the Koreans consider a double goblet (hourglass) drum called the *tjang* to be their true national instrument. It is somewhat smaller than the similar Japanese *san-no-tsuzumi.* Records of the *tjang* go as far back as the Koguryo period when it used to be played in a huge orchestral body consisting of more than 200 musicians. This ensemble is considered by the Koreans to have been the first large polyphonic orchestral body in the history of music. Today, the *tjango* drum has a colourfully painted body and rope laced skins. The left head is played with the hand, the right with a bamboo stick. The tone pitch of both heads can be adjusted and the skins are usually tuned a fifth apart.

294 Japanese *gagaku* orchestra, *left-to-right: fue* flutes, *hichiriki* shawm, *sho* mouth harmonicas and *san-no-tsuzumi* drum

295 Drum and gong chime
Basrelief, Angkor Wat Temple, Cambodia, 9th century

Laotian *khen* mouth harmonica

SOUTHEAST ASIA

Music played in Cambodia, Laos, Thailand, Burma and Vietnam differs from other Oriental music in its tonal systems. The main instruments of Southeast Asian music are various metallophones: xylophones, drums and winds. Classical instrumental ensembles of these countries originally never featured bowed string instruments which seem to have arrived in Southeast Asia only in the 12th century. Ever since the 16th century there have existed two large classical ensembles in *CAMBODIA*, the *peyphat* which acquired its name from its leading wind, the double reed *pey* thought to be the sweetest-sounding instrument of Southeast Asia. The rest of the *peyphat* ensemble are various xylophones, gong chimes and drums.

The importance of the *khong* gong chimes reaches well beyond the borders of Cambodia and the instrument is common throughout Southeast Asia. The *khong* can be seen on the reliefs in the Angkor Wat Temple, Cambodia (built 1112−1152). The instrument consists of 16 bronze gongs in a semi-circular wooden frame. The player sits within the semi-circle, beating the gongs with two elephant hide-covered beaters. The *roneat-ek* xylophone, sometimes mistaken for a typical Cambodian instrument, originated in India and reached Cambodia only in the 19th century via Siam. There are three types of the *roneat-ek*, all with a cradle or boat-shaped resonator on a base. A pair of large barrel drums is also used in the *peyphat* orchestra. The drums are called *skor-thom*, have water buffalo hide heads and are supported with a base and tipped slightly towards the player.

The major Cambodian chordophone is the *chapei* lute, identical to the Vietnamese *dan day*. The resonator body is trapezoidal or round,

Burmese *turr* fiddle

and is usually open on the bottom to compensate for the great discrepancy between the length of the strings and the small volume of the resonator. The neck of the *chapei* found in the Kompong Cham province is so long that the player is barely able to finger the strings up below the sickle-shaped head. The two double courses are tuned a fifth apart.

LAOTIAN music has been shaped by its Vietnamese and Cambodian models. The only truly indigenous instrument is the *khen* mouth harmonica, a simpler counterpart of the Chinese *sheng,* made also from bamboo pipes forming a raft 1−3 m in length. The other important wind instrument apart from the *khen* is an end-blown flute called the *kluy* which is identical to the Vietnamese *klui* and Cambodian *khloy.* The instrumentation of a Laotian ensemble is almost identical to that of the Cambodian and Thai orchestras.

The basis of *THAI* instrumental music is the so-called *piphet* orchestra consisting of the *pi nai* shawm and percussion instruments divided further into melody (xylophones, gong chimes) and rhythm (drums and metallophones with indefinite pitch) sections. The tube of the *pi nai* is slightly flared at both ends and has six finger holes. The sound is enchanting, especially if the *pi nai* accompanies a tune of the *ghong vong yai* xylophone. Another type of xylophone, the *ranad ek,* richly decorated with carvings, mother-of-pearl and ivory, is identical to the Cambodian *roneat-ek.* Other Thai instruments also resemble instruments native to Cambodia and China.

In view of its geographical position and history, it is surprising how little Burma has been influenced by the music of either India or China.

296 Thai *pi nai* shawm

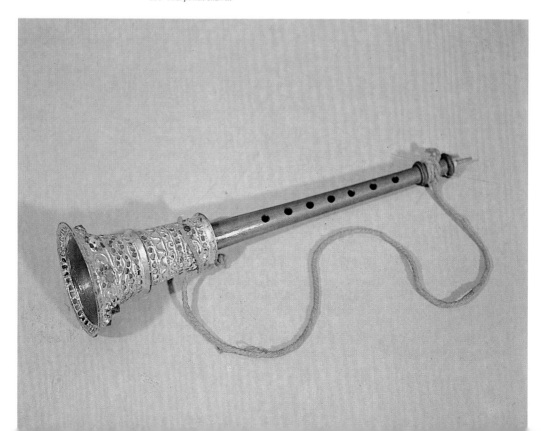

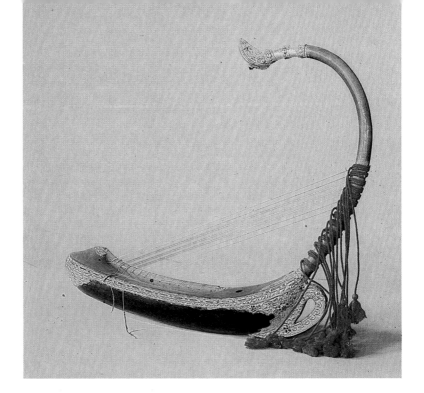

297 Burmese *saung* harp

Vietnamese *sa ram* drum

Musical instruments, however, do reveal certain Vietnamese influences: the *hne* shawm slightly resembles the Vietnamese *cai-ken,* while the bamboo *waleko* clappers are called *cai-sinh* in Vietnam. However, the king of the Burmese instruments is the drum set called the *patvaing.* The instrument looks like a huge richly ornamented crown more than 1 metre high, decorated with gold and precious stones. Inside the crown circle the drummer is seated, beating the rhythm with the sticks on up to 21 graduated drums suspended within the circular frame. Another circular frame instrument, or rather a set, is the *tjivuaing* gong chimes played usually together with the *patvaing.* The player sitting on a low seat strikes 12—18 small gongs with a compass of up to two octaves. A typical Burmese instrument is a bowed harp called the *paung* with 13 silk strings tensioned with cotton-woven cords, and the *rabob,* a kind of fiddle.

Ancient pictorial and literary sources prove the existence of a great many musical instruments in *VIETNAM.* In the 16th and 17th centuries there were numerous temple and secular instrumental orchestras, among them also ensembles formed only by winds and drums. As unique for Vietnam as the *patvaing* for Burma is the *dan bau,* a single-string instrument with a surprisingly simple but ingenious design. The instrument, a sort of compound bow, is formed by a narrow long wooden resonator with one string leading into a wooden funnel attached by a bamboo lever by means of which the pitch of the single string is changed.

The Vietnamese long-necked lute called the *dan day* with high bone frets is identical to the Cambodian *cha-pei.* Various bowed instruments

237

of different shapes and sizes are usually of a Chinese origin and many have even retained their original Chinese names.

The rhythm of an instrumental orchestra is supported by drums and xylophones. Among the most commonly used instruments of this type are the *phach* clappers and a drum called the *trong-ban*. Indigenous to North Vietnam provinces is a set of bamboo tube chimes called the *dan-to-rung*. The tubes are tied together and suspended horizontally in a semi-circle. The *than la, tin canh* and *chieng gong* resemble the gongs of the Indonesian *gamelan*. However, in Vietnam gongs are not grouped in gong chimes with the exception of the three-gong *tam-am-la*, and the playing technique also differs from that of the *gamelan* practice. While the classical *gamelan* is formed by gongs and gong chimes played usually by one man, in Vietnam each musician holds his single gong striking it with the beater when his turn comes. The gong chimes is formed by 7 to 14 musicians, and the instrument as well as the repertoire are passed from fathers to sons.

Vietnamese *dan bau* monochord

298 Cambodian musical instruments *left-to-right:* drums, *pey* shawm, *chapei* lute, *tro-khmer* fiddle

299 Laotian musical instruments *left-to-right: khong vong yai* gong chime, *rang nat* sylophone and a pair of *skorthom* drums; in the background: *se u* and *se i* bowed chordophones

300 Laotian musical instruments: vertical flute, small cymbals and goblet drums

301 Burmese *patvaing* drum set

THE INDONESIAN ARCHIPELAGO AND OCEANIA

Besides a variety of traditional and contemporary folk music styles, there are also artistically highly developed forms of classical music in *INDONESIA*. The majority of these musical forms are inseparably tied to a complex of theatrical and poetic forms developed by the so-called Indo-Javanese culture which bloomed 1000 years ago in Java, leaving its impact also on southern Sumatra, Bali, Madura, Lombok and other islands of the Indonesian archipelago. During the first stages of development, the Indo-Javanese culture was strongly influenced by cultural imports from India, Siam, Cambodia and China. However, once on Indonesian soil, they immediately provided fresh stimulation for a qualitatively new kind of art whose vitality and possibilities of further improvement were to be tested in the centuries to come.

It is probably Indonesia where the European will be most struck by the proverbial 'enchanting spell' of Oriental music, as expressed by the world-famous *gamelan* music (gamelan meaning literally an instrumental ensemble). The *gamelan* is composed of 14—17 instruments and a singer, it is divided into several distinct instrumental sections, each having a special function of its own to fulfil. The tune is carried by the ringing tones of metallophones called *sarons* developed from xylophones more than 1000 years ago. There are 12 slightly arched

Indonesian *saron* metallophone

bronze bars, five in the pentatonic *slendro* scale and seven in the heptatonic *pelog* are suspended in a wooden resonator, very often in the shape of a crouching dragon. The instrument is precisely tuned and the pitch of the bars is raised by filing away material at the ends; to lower the pitch material must be filed off in the centre. The highest pitched bar is the *saron panerus* or *peking* while the lowest is the *saron barung.*

The main theme is elaborated on by gong chimes called the *bonang* which is formed by small bowl gongs resting on a string lattice stretched in a low frame. Fourteen are tuned in the *pelog* and ten in the *slendro* scales. Against the basic melody rises the sound of the *sulino,* a type of end-blown flute and of the *rabob,* a spike fiddle of Perso-Arabic origin. Both the *sulino* and the *rabob* lend the gamelan music its heterophonic character. The key tones are accentuated by the *slentem gantung* of the *gender panembung,* chimes of bronze bars suspended over individual bamboo tube resonators. The *gender* has a compass of one octave. The main movements of each piece of music are concluded with strokes on large gongs called the *gong gedá* while individual phrases are concluded by another metallophone called the *gong kemondong* consisting of two rectangular metal bars suspended on crossed strings above a wooden resonator box. The player of the latter also handles bronze cymbals called the *gong ketuk* producing a dull sound.

The sound of the gongs which are actually the most important instruments of the South-Asian music is brightened by the gentle tinkle of

302 Gong chime. Indonesia, Kalimantan

303 Drums
Solomon Islands

other metallophones, the *gender barung* and *gender panerus*. These instruments are formed by freely suspended bars tuned in unison with their individual bamboo tube resonators. The *gender panerus* with its high pitch compass tinkles like chimes and its clear bronze sound provides a fine contrast to the dull voice of the *gambong kaye*, a trough xylophone. The latter consists of 18–20 wooden bars, slightly arched and suspended over a rectangular wooden tub or cradle-shaped resonator in a similar manner as in the Japanese *mokkin*. Xylophones that had already reached this stage of development can be seen on reliefs in the Panataron Temple, Java, dating from the 14th century.

Gamelan instrumentation is supplemented with the *tjempelung* dulcimer, a relative of the Chinese *se*, played with two beaters, and with the *bedug*, a drum suspended on a chain. The *gamelan* concord is characterized by a unique combination of the solo vocal part and the orchestral sound. The art of *gamelan* still draws huge audiences and has even been becoming more popular outside Indonesia. Of course, the *pelog* and *slendro* scales still represent a serious barrier between the European and the traditional Indonesian tuning but many modern composers have recognized the *gamelan* as a rich source of melody invention capable of enriching the arsenal of contemporary symphonic theory.

Another folk instrument has recently become extremely popular throughout the entire Indonesian archipelago, namely the *anklung*, a highly-refined rattle formed by several bamboo tubes tuned in chords

Javanese *rebab* spike fiddle

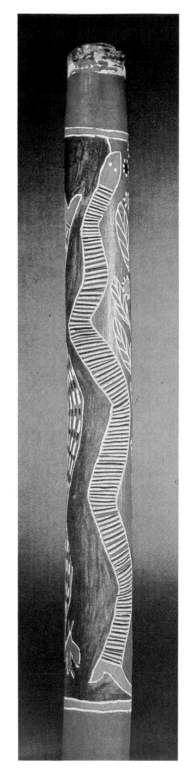

304 *Didgeridoo*
Australian aboriginal instrument

305 *Anklung*
Indonesia, Java

and inserted freely in a slit bottom bar of a bamboo frame. When the tubes strike the cross-bar of the frame, they produce a pleasant, hollow, slightly dull sound similar somewhat to that of cowbells. *Angklungs* are made in different sizes and pitch and a group of these instruments can have a compass of two octaves.

Under the geographical name of *OCEANIA* this publication includes not only the archipelagos and isolated islands in the central and western Pacific (Melanesia, Micronesia and Polynesia) but also Australia and New Zealand. However, the geographical borders are not identical with the borders of various musical cultures and the entire area deserves a thorough investigation as to its musical cultures.

The most primitive forms of musical expression are found in those cultures which regard sounds as the voices of spirits. One of the instruments of the Australian aborigines is a hollowed trunk called the *ubar* and beaten with frayed ends of short palm tree boughs. On Tahiti and the Windward Islands, a singleheaded drum called the *pahu* is used, with a body made from a hollowed tree trunk. In Maori, however, the word *pahu* signifies a slit drum suspended from a huge rafter construction and serving as a signalling-device. Another type of slit drum which is sounded by the friction of the hand is the *nunut* on New Ireland.

Hollow pieces of wood, beaten with a stick, or stamping tubes, are called *tohérá* on Tahiti. The *ipu,* a stamping instrument made from a large gourd to which a smaller one is attached, is common in the Hawaiian Islands. The player beats the gourds on the ground, the fingers simultaneously striking the gourds as well. Apart from the most primitive idiophones such as the Hawaiian *pulai,* or the Maori *tetera* and the *singing chips,* the majority of musical instruments in this region of the world are merely simple wood and gourd clappers, rattles, jew's harps, bull-roarers, slit drums and other idiophones.

Of the wind instruments, the most typical Australian aborigine instrument is the *didgeridoo,* a primitive wooden trumpet made of a hollowed bamboo stick or tree branch about 120—140 cm long. The player produces a dark grunting sound by blowing into the trumpet in regular intervals. Besides *panpipes, vessel flutes* made of gourds are quite common throughout Oceania as well as *fipple* and *nose flutes.* The bamboo *jew's harp* is called the *niau kani* in Hawaii and the *roria* in New Zealand. Chordophones are practically limited to the *ukeke* musical bow used in Hawaii for communication with the spirits. Melanesia is one of the rare locations where *reed tube zithers* have also been discovered. The small guitar known as the *ukulele* was brought to Hawaii by Portuguese workers—in Portugal it used to be called the *machete.*

306 Slit drum
New Guinea

AMERICA

LATIN AMERICA

In 1964 an archaeological expedition discovered a settlement near Paracas, Peru—a settlement which must have been inhabited as early as 9000 years ago. Stone bowls, polished beads, necklaces and stone mirrors all attested to a relative sophistication in the ancient inhabitants of the settlement. Among other artefacts, a wooden flute was discovered in very good condition due to the extreme dryness of the sand bed in which it was found. *PERUVIAN* music had reached a high level of development about 2500 years ago and its contemporary *panpipes, whistles* and *flutes with finger holes* could produce complex tunes.

Instruments dating from the pre-Columbian era have been discovered in *Mexico: scrapers, rattles, jingles, bells, tubular* and *vessel flutes, shell horns* and *trumpets.* There were also many discoveries of statuettes and clay figurines of musicians, dancers and shamans with masks and anklet jingles, worn by the original inhabitants of *MEXICO,* the

307 Mayan rattles
Detail, fresco, Bonampak, Mexico, 662—830

Aztec *teponextli* slit drum

308 Cuban *cha-cha* rattles

Aztecs, Chorotega and Zapotecs for festivities and rituals. Mural paintigs in Bonampak, a centre of Mayan culture, show processions of musicians with various instruments, mainly drums which prove that music had been an integral part of all rites. The American Indians even had their own god of music: the Aztecs called him *Macuilxochitl* (Five Blossoms) or *Xochipilli* (the Blossom Prince).

A sacred instrument played only at festive occasions was a slit drum called the *teponextli*, hollowed from a single piece of wood. It was usually elaborately carved to resemble an alligator, puma or ocelot. On the bottom of the drum was a hole; the slit was H-shaped, forming two tongue-like protrusions which after having been cut to different thickness on the underside gave two different pitch tones when beaten with wooden sticks. The *teponaxtli* was either suspended or rested on a base. A single-membrane drum called the *huehuetl* was cut from a tree trunk and covered with jaguar or deer skin and tensioned either

247

309 *Silbador* whistling pot
Colùmbia, pre-Conquest period

with ropes or nailed down. The murals in Bonampak and illuminations in the Becker Codex show the *ayotl,* a scraper made from the shell of a giant tortoise.

After the Conquest, the Spaniards attempted to exterminate indigenous music as well as its instruments. At the beginning of the 17th century, for instance, the Archibishop of Lima ordered all Indian instruments destroyed and burned and the Jesuit Arriaga bragged of destroying 603 large and 3 418 small instruments in one campaign.

In Latin American folk music, one of the youngest folk music styles to develop, a considerable role was played by the fact that there are many similarities between Latin American Indian music and Spanish folk music, and some similarities can be found even among musical instruments, especially in the percussion family *(castanets—maracas, tambourine—pandareta,* etc.). Another very important factor in the development of the Latin American folk music was the heritage of the African tradition. The unique ability to absorb rapidly the musical folklore of the nation amongst whom they had been transplanted enabled the millions of black African slaves accept the foreign musical culture and superimpose on it their own artistic traditions.

Folk music in *MEXICO* still uses many Indian instruments like the *raspador* scraper, the *sonajas* rattle, the *chililihtli,* a burnt clay sideblown flute, or a rifle-shaped shawm called the *chirimia,* and sounded

Mexican flute

by suction rather than by blowing. However, the central position in folk music of Mexico and all other Latin American countries belongs to the *guitar* and its many variations used in various countries of the continent. A simple folk guitar is called the *charango*, in Cuba a three-string *tres* is commonly played while the four-string version is called the *cuatro*. The *tiple* is a high-pitched guitar, while the *violao* is a Brazilian guitar.

Besides the *Spanish guitar*, another European import was the *harp* which soon became a part of the folk instrumentation in Latin America. Today, village Indians still make their simple harps and some of them are genuine virtuosi on the instrument. However, in contrast to the original European harps the Latin American folk versions of the instrument have markedly broad resonators with round sound holes, and are not played sitting but standing.

In *CUBA*, the largest of the Caribbean islands, the original Indian music was soon expelled by that of the black African slaves who played instruments brought over from their homelands. The unique feeling of the Cubans for rhythm can transform almost any conceivable object into a musical instrument, be it baking sheet, a pair of metal spoons, a hoe without its handle, or even a ploughshare. A pair of wooden sticks about 18 cm long and clashed together, called *claves*, can be found throughout Central and South America. This concussion idiophone is played in the following way: the left hand holds one stick, the bent fingers and the cupped palm forming a resonator, while the

310 Mexican flute and small drum

311 Peruvian panpipe

right beats with the other stick held perpendicularly on the former in different spots, producing a metallic sound differing in pitch according to the exact spot struck.

A very important place in Afro-cuban instrumentation is held by various rattles. The *güiro* is a dried gourd with a cord net stretched over it, the gourd filled with dried nuts or beads (the *güiro* is also the name of a scraper, while the rattle described here is also called the *cabaca*). *Maracas* are also made of dried gourds, although contemporary dancers use plastic *maracas* filled with steel shot.

Apart from the primitive vessel flute called the *botija*, Cuban folk music uses no other wind instrument. The *botija* has an earthenware vessel with a narrow mouth and a small hole on the side serving as a mouth hole. The player can change the pitch somewhat by moving his right hand along the vessel mouth.

On the other hand, the variety of Cuban drums is immense since the drums have a predominant position in Cuban folk music. Indeed, there are many bands composed entirely of drums. Folk dances are accompanied by the *joca*, a single-headed drum that was originally from the Congo. Many ensembles use the *conga*, a barrel-shaped single-headed drum made of staves and reinforced with steel hoops. The *bongoes* are a pair of conical drums of different size and pitch joined by a short wooden bar. The player holds the bongos between his knees, playing them with bare hands and fingers. The *congas* are played with hands only, too, and the native drummers are genuine virtuosi capable of playing complex and intricate rhythm patterns and can even produce a *glissando* on their instruments.

Although the *marimba* had been originally brought over the ocean from the African continent, today the instrument is considered a Latin American folk instrument, especially in *GUATEMALA,* where it has

312 Horn and drum. Argentina

313 Drum. Chile

Mexican harp

been the national instrument for several hundred years. The largest *marimba* type, called sometimes the *xylorimba,* consists of 137 chromatically tuned wooden blocks with the compass up to 11 octaves. Under each bar there is an accoustically-tuned resonator with a small membrane-covered hole for tone prolongation. The bars are beaten with various types of beaters of different weight and hardness of the rubberized head allowing the player to produce all kinds of sound effects.

Although the *flutes* discovered in *PERU* date more than 9000 years back, the instrument has nevertheless remained still the most typical in the instrumentation of Peruvian Indian music. The flute, an end-blown cane tube called the *quena,* is identical to the Bolivian *kena* which had been adapted to the diatonic scale under Spanish influence. The primitive wooden or clay *aylliquepa* trumpet is a descendant of the original clay trumpets of the early Peruvian civization. Two types of drums predominate in contemporary Peruvian folk music: the barrel-shaped double-headed *tynia* and the single-headed *huancar.*

251

314 Drums, panpipes and horns
Bolivia

315 Drums and flute
Panama

Air duct of the *slibador* whistling pot

The typical wind instrument of the *BOLIVIAN* Indians is the panpipe which comes in various sizes. The huge *bajón* panpipe can be up to 2 m long. A popular instrument of the *mestizo* population is the *charango* guitar made from armadillo carapace.

The instrumentation of the largest South American country, *BRAZIL* is markedly dominated by rhythmic instruments aptly called 'ritmadores' or 'rhythm makers'. The rhythm pulsing in Brazilian folk music has often been compared to heartbeat without which there is no life. Similarly, without rhythm there would be no Brazilian music.

The terminology of Brazilian musical instrumentation has not yet been standardized and identical types of instruments are named differently in various areas while one name can often signify two entirely different instrument types. Add the names of the innumerable instrument versions and the terminological chaos is complete. For example, a rattle made of tin sheet and shaped like a fir cone is called the *xero* in Pernambuco but the *adja* in Bahía. A type of *maraca* rattle with an outside network of dried seeds or beads is called the *caboca* but also the *afoxe*. *Ganza* is the name of a rattle but in Bahía the name signifies the *reco-reco* scraper (also called the *güiro*), elsewhere it is the name of a bamboo notched stick.

Some Indian tribes in very remote areas still use early primitive instruments like the nonmetallic *ike* trumpet (the Bororo tribe) or *nose flutes* common in the Amazon River basin. Almost all Indian tribes use various kinds of *bull-roarers* called the *yelo* in Brazil but known as the *palo roncador* in Columbia and Venezuela. It is a thin wooden plate tied to a string and rotated in the air. The plate also rotates around its axis and the combination of the two motions produces a humming noise similar to the wailing of the wind. The smaller the plate and the faster it is spun, the higher the pitch.

316 Mexican folk instruments, *left-to-right:* rattles and small drums, marimba, double bass and guitar

Bullroarer of the Bororo tribe
Indians, Brazil

317 Single hand flute and drum, clappers
North America

Instruments of the Brazilian blacks do not differ much from those of their Cuban and Haitian brothers, but some have different names. The *agogó* is a double bell made of steel sheet and is similar to modern cowbells. In Pernambuco large *ingome* drums are used while the *batá* and *carimbá* membrane drums come in many variations and shapes. A small frame drum is called the *pandeiro.*

However, a really national instrument of Brazil is a guitar of Portuguese origins called the *violao,* with five or six double courses. The tuning differs from region to region and according to the type of the piece performed.

The *guitar* is also the most common instrument in *CHILE* where instrumentation in the past had been always under strong Spanish influences. An instrument of a unique construction, used by the Araucan Indian minority numbering some 100,000 people, is a double musical bow called the *künkülkawe* and sounded with another bow.

In *ARGENTINA,* the guitar is again the most common native instrument. Guitars accompany the Argentinean *pampa* dances in extremely fast and terse styles. The Patagonian Indians make a musical bow called the *kohlo* from a horse rib and horsehair. The *kohlo* is plucked with condor feathers, producing a gentle but barely audible sound.

Musical bow of the Patagonian Indians

The most recent folk instrument to have been invented in Latin America is the *steel drum* made first from ordinary oil barrels in *TRINIDAD* in the 1940's. Empty barrels are cut to the size, tempered, tuned and grouped in bands which now enjoy immense popularity in the Caribbean and elsewhere. The most common steel drum consorts are called *ping pong* (giving 25 tone pitches), *second pan, rhythm, guitar, cello* and *bass* (5 pitches).

The mutual influence of various Latin American musical cultures on each other has not terminated yet and so far no systemized terminology of musical instruments has been produced. However, Latin American instruments enjoy a great popularity in Europe and North America, thanks to various Latin American dance orchestras and jazz. Composers of contemporary serious music in Europe and America have also been enriching their scores with the unusual sounds of Latin American instruments.

NORTH AMERICA

No precise picture of the ancient indigenous instrumentation of North America can be made on the basis of the musical instruments found

318 Drum and wind instruments,
Baniva tribe, Venezuela

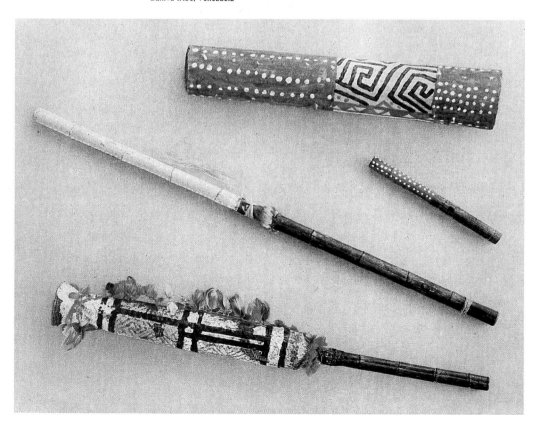

255

319 Sheet metal bells
Ivory Coast

among the North American Indian tribes today. However, it can be safely presumed that their music and instruments of the past could not have differed much from those of the Indian populations of Central and South America. Pod-, seed- or pebble-filled leather-bag *rattles* are still used there to accompany dances. Rarely also *whistles* without finger holes are found, the airstream brought into the blow hole by means of a special mouthpiece. Singing is usually accompanied with a *single-headed drum* similar to the *tambourine,* held in the left hand while the right marks the rhythm with a beater. Drums are also made from hollowed tree trunks and covered with skin on one end. There are also some *double-headed drums* to be found, e.g. war drums, and drums

320 *Sansas*
The Cameroons and South Africa

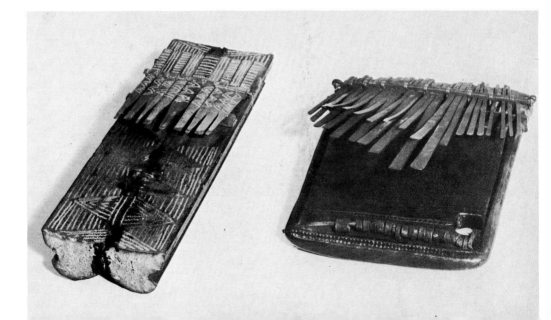

Nigerian gourd rattle

filled with water *(peyote drums)*. Unique and rare are the primitive *fiddles* of the Apache tribe, made from a hollowed-out cactus plant.

The colonists of North America naturally brought the instruments of their Old World homelands. This was especially true of the string instruments like the *banjo, guitar,* and the *Appalachian dulcimer,* a long board plucker zither similar to the French *bûche.* The instrument has three metal strings, one carrying the tune, while the other two are drones.

Apart from these instruments and their variants like the *dobro,* a guitar with a circular metal resonator, as well as all kinds of folk and home-made fiddles, various types of *bumbasses* and other primitive single string bass instruments can be found in the U.S. reflecting the rich musical invention of both the blacks and the whites who had all started with their own national traditions only to fuse the individual elements in the proverbial melting pot of the American culture, enriching the treasury of North American musical folklore with new musical forms.

AFRICA

Africa offers a huge variety of musical instruments ranging from simple *scrapers, rattles, stamping pits* and millet stalk *whistles* to most

321 *Marimbas* (balaphones)
Zaire

257

Apunga horn, Guinea-Bissau

complex *xylophones* and *harps*. Of course, not every tribe uses the same musical instruments. For instance, the Kindiga tribesmen of East Africa have no other instrument but the simplest *gourd rattle,* although the performers also whistle and clap their hands. A most common primitive instrument found also elsewhere in the world is the *bull-roarer,* called *burubush* by the Hottentots, *seburuburu* by the Ghwana and *adys-oro* by the Nigerian Ibo tribe.

Some native African instruments permit solo harmonization although harmony in African music serves only as an embellishment or variation of the given theme. The most sophisticated of these instruments is the *sansa,* or *mbira,* as it is called by the tribes speaking one of the Bantu dialects, *omposhawa* (Ashanti), *usimbi* (along the Zambezi River), *dimba, ekende, ibeka, pokido* (the Congo) or *ambira* (Mozambique), etc. It consists of a number of split cane metal tongues over a wooden resonator, the tongues supported with a lateral bar. The

322 Lyre. Kenya

Namibian musical bow

323 Angle harp

East African scraper

other ends are free to be plucked by the thumbs—hence the name of *thumb* or *Kaffir piano.* Lyrical pieces composed for the *sansa,* including usually a vocal part, rank among the most refined in African music.

The *xylophone* has a great variety of names among different tribes (*akadinda* or *entaala* in Uganda, *ambira* in Ethiopia, *bala* in Mali and Guinea, *balafo* in Sudan, *kalanba, ilimba, baza, dimba* in the Congo, *mbila* in South Africa) is of Malayan origin. Xylophones consist of tuned wooden bars supported in their nodal point of vibrations. The bars are struck with beaters. Xylophones of some Bantu tribes from southern Africa have a resonator under each bar made of a carefully selected dried gourd. The air volume in the gourd amplifies the vibration of the bar. A hole is cut in the gourd and covered with the

259

324 Senegalese drums

protective skin of spider eggs, the skin vibrating in concord with the bar lending the tone a sharper tone colour.

Although the wind family is not so numerous in Africa as elsewhere, bamboo cross flutes can be found in the former Portuguese colonies and in South Africa where the instrument is called the *naka ya lethlake.* A long end-blown flute with six finger holes made from bamboo is played by Ethiopian shepherds of the Tana Lake district. The long straight metal trumpet common in some Ethiopian towns is a descendant of a Perso-Arabic cultural import. One of the indigenous African aerophones is the side-blown *apunga* horn used in the Congo.

There are certain similarities to be found between the melodic features of African music and the music of American Indians, like the imitation bird songs, beast cries or humming and wailing of the wind. Probably they are connected with the immediate expression of human emotions like sighing, crying, laughing, etc. This can be also traced in the design and construction of musical instruments, most markedly so in the *musical bow* called the *amzad* or *to* in North Equatorial Africa,

zhezhilava in Malagassy or *hunga, mtangala, ndimbga, qubo, hade,* etc, in South Equatorial Africa. When fully stretched, the string of a South African bushman's bow produces partial tones amplified by the mouth cavity of the player. This fact proves that originally musical instruments developed from objects of everyday use and also that partial tones were known and used in the earliest stages of the development of the human race. The musical bow of the Hottentot tribe called the *gora,* unsuitable for hunting or war, consists of a bow stick and a string extended with a quill, the tip of the flat quill being fastened to the stick. The other end of the string is normally attached to the bow. The player inserts the quill in his mouth without touching it with his teeth and breathing heavily, vibrates the feather and the string which produces some overtones.

In Sudan, Uganda and some other parts of East Africa a bowl-shaped plucked lyre is widely used, called the *kissumba* or *kissar* in Sudan, *obukane* in Kenya and *gezarke* in Nubia and resembling the ancient Greek *lyre.* It has a bowl-shaped resonator of either wood or

Angolan harp-lute

325 Vertical flute
Ethiopia

gourd covered with hide and two bamboo arms joined at the top with a yoke. Besides this instrument various folk types of bow harps can be found in Africa. Lutes called *wambi* (*ndöna* in the Congo, *angra okwena* in East Africa and *ubo* in Nigeria) have box-like wooden resonators with six elastic thin plates keeping the liana creeper strings permanently tensioned.

Perhaps no other instrument has played such an important role in the history of mankind as the drum, an instrument which can be traced as far back as the Stone Age. Today there exist several hundred variants of the drum in the world, with even more names. Idiophone and membranophone drums of the African music can even carry a tune and

262

express a whole scale of various tonal colours corresponding to the finest variation of mood. The pitch of some African drums can be changed within a compass of a whole octave by altering the tension of their heads. Indeed, African drums not only 'sing', they can even 'talk'. It seems that the term musical instrument is not really adequate for some African drums.

The ability of some drums to 'talk' is caused by the fact that some African languages are of tonal semantic character. Any auxiliary speech parts like suffixes, prefixes, etc., are almost entirely lacking in these languages and precise meanings are conveyed by the same monosyllabic stem words differing only in tonal qualities. The tonal semantic languages communicate by several tone pitches: high, middle and low. This aspect of the language brings music and speech closer together. The tribes living in Ghana, Togo or the Cameroons communicate at very long distances by means of these 'talking' drums.

Drum making in Africa has always been a trade secret passed from fathers to sons. There are 'male' drums sounding lower and 'female' drums sounding a third or fourth higher. The drum 'language' has many fixed phrases and expressions for various phenomena and occasions of daily life birth, death, marriage, etc. Chieftains and important tribesmen have their own drum names which are inherited. The *ombutu* and *öngalabi* are only two examples of the great variety of Ugandan talking

326 Kettledrums
The Congo

Drum from Dahomey

327 Large *bagana* lyre, small *kerar* lyre and *nagarit* drum
Ethiopian oil painting

drums used to convey invitations, to announce harvest time, to greet tribal leaders and guests of honour.

The Yoruba in Nigeria have retained an ancient religious cult based on worship of mythical ancestors. There are about 400 of the latter and each has a special drum motive assigned only to him. An important role is played by the 'talking' drums in folk dance ensembles. When a member of the royal family in Uganda performs a dance, the *miagaro* is played, dances of Ghanaian tribal leaders are accompanied by the *bombaa* and the *mointsim,* while the *ompe, boadze, osevenji* and *moses* are played in West Africa. However, every drum band has a chief drum which sets the pace and tone for the entire band. It 'talks' to the dancer and the singers, 'calling' the tunes and step variations. In Ghana, Nigeria, Guinea and Tanzania there are even special schools teaching the traditional art of playing the 'talking' drums.

The use of friction drums is often connected with magical fertility rites. These drums have a hole made in the membrane through which runs a stick or rope. Sometimes the stick is pressed into the membrane without piercing it and fixed in this position from within the vessel. The membrane is then vibrated, usually by rubbing the stick, rope or stalk with resined hands. Typical examples of the African friction drum are the *ingungu* and the *moshupiane,* both from South Africa.

Ethiopian instruments have been strongly influenced by Arabic -Islamic culture. Its music uses several instruments of the accompaniment of the Koptic liturgical chant, e.g. the *tenasin,* a *sistrum* quite like its ancient Egyptian counterpart. The huge *bagana* lyre resembles the ancient Egyptian and Greek lyres. The *bagana* is large and square-shaped and considered an instrument of the aristocracy. It is thought to be a copy of David's harp. The *kerar* lyre is bowl-shaped and regarded as truly a folk instrument. Very important in secular as well as liturgical music is the *naqarit* kettle drum and a large barrel-shaped drum called the *kabaro* draped with expensive textiles.

ARABIA

The diversity of Arabic music and its instruments is shown in a famous tale from the *Thousand and One Nights* in which a princess ordered her slave to bring some musical instruments, and the maid 'returned

Egyptian spike fiddle

328 Arabic clarinet *arghul al kebir*
Egypt

265

329 Arabic *zamr* shawm
Syria

presently with a Damascene lute, a Persian harp, a Tartar pipe and an Egyptian psaltery.' The deepest imprint on the music of all Arabic nations had been left by the musical culture of Persia which greatly influenced the further development of Arabic musical theory, instrument design and construction.

The Arabs do not have many idiophones, and the few they do have are mainly metallophones. An example of the latter is the *snug,* in fact three small cymbals. Two are held in the right hand and are struck with the third one held in the left. The *quaraqit* are metal plate-shaped castanets.

The common instrument of Arab and Turkish professional musicians is the *nay* flute (Arabic *nay* = wind instrument). This is very difficult to play since the tube is open at both ends and the mouthpiece has no fipple or notch; it is made in seven different tunings. One of the important wind instruments of Northwest Africa is a cane flute called the *kashbah.* In the traditional design common among the Bedouins, the *kashbah* has three finger holes. A short recorder-like fipple flute called the *nira* is played in the towns of northern Morocco, similar to the Algerian *gawaq.*

The Arabic *zamr* shawm has a conical tube with a flared bell and 7—8 fingerholes. The double reed of split cane is held entirely in the mouth, which acts as a wind reservoire allowing the player to produce

Algerian *rebab*

tones more evenly and flowingly. The Tunisian and Algerian versions of the *zamr* more closely resemble the Egyptian *zummarah,* which is a double clarinet with two equally long tubes and six fingerholes. During play the musician always covers the two same-lettered fingerholes at the same time. A similar instrument fitted with split cane reeds is also played in Morocco where it goes under the name of the *sghanin.* The double clarinet called the *arghul,* the traditional instrument of the FELLAHIN, is an ancient Egyptian instrument. It is made in three sizes ranging from 40 to 140 cm in length, the two pipes firmly lashed together and the mouthpiece formed by two simple pipes with an idioglottal reed each. However, only the shorter of the two pipes has finger holes, the longer pipe being only a drone. The Arabic *bagpipe* is actually nothing but an *arghul* fitted with a bag. The Saudi bagpipe, called

330 Double *mezeud* shawm
Tunisia

267

331 Arabic *mezúd* bagpipe. Tunisia

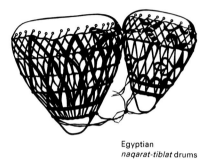

Egyptian
naqarat-tiblat drums

332 Arabic *qanun* zither. Egypt

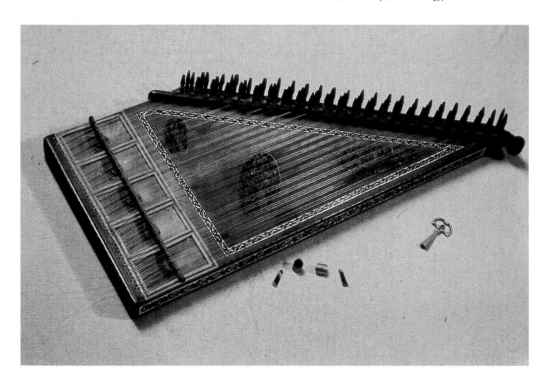

Tunisian drum

the *zukra,* has a bag with fur on the outside whereas the Tunisian *mezúd* has a hairless skin bag.

In the festive processions in Fez and during the month of *Ramadan* the single rhytmically repeated tone of the *nefir,* a straight brass trumpet, can be heard. The *shah nefir* is a Persian circular horn. The *karna,* an Iraqi long straight trumpet, is used for fanfares.

However, the best known instrument of the Arabic world, admired by theorists and performers alike, is the *'ud* lute. (Arabic countries west of Egypt prefer to call the instrument the *quitra,* a derivation of the ancient Greek *kithara.*) A decisive role in the development of the *'ud* is said to have been played by the famous Abdul Hassan Ibn Haffi Ziryab, who is credited with having added the fifth (lowest) string and introducing a new tuning in d, e, a, d¹, a¹. Under the influence of the Ottoman Turk culture which mixed with the original Arab tradition when the Turks conquered Arabia in the 16th century, the *'ud* used in Iraq even acquired a sixth string. The modern version of the *'ud* is almond-shaped, with an elaborately carved rosette soundhole, inlaid with mother-of-pearl, and a distinctly separated neck. The strings of this short-necked lute play melody only, never chords, and are plucked with a plectrum.

333 Arabic *rayta* shawm and *bendir* tambourine Algeria

334 Turkish *dillidüdük* flute

Turkish *deblek* drum

Apart from the *'ud*, in the Islamic. Near East there also appeared another short-necked lute made from a single piece of wood, covered with skin and having a sickle-shaped head. The instrument originated in Persia and spread eastward to Sulawesi, southward to Madagascar and via Moor-dominated Spain it reached Europe, appearing eventually as far as Central Europe where it became known as the *koboz*. However, in the Near East the original plucking technique was later replaced by bowing, and two versions of this fiddle appeared under a new name of the *rebab*. One had a narrow arched body with curved or lobed sides, indigenous to Northwest Africa. The other version, basically Egyptian, had a trapezoidal body. Both versions had two low pitched strings. A close relative of the *rebab* is a three-string Moroccan chordophone with a tortoiseshell body called the *genbri*.

Like other originally Arabic instruments, the *qanun* board zither (Greek *kanon* = rule) also reached Europe via Spain and later was renamed the *psaltery*. (This trapezoidal plucked chordophone played a great role in European medieval music.) The modern Arab *qanun* has a flat, oblong resonator box. The soundboard is formed partly by thin wood going from the stringboard almost to the bridge with three decorative rosettes, and partly by leather stretching over the entire right-hand side of the instrument including the bridge. There are 26 metallic treble courses stretched parallel across the stringboard from the left rectangular end and over the bridge on the right-hand side to the pegs inserted in the oblique right edge of the box. The strings are plucked with plectra worn on both index fingers. A similar instrument is the Persian *santir* (Greek *psalterion*), a dulcimer (beaten zither) shaped as a symmetrical trapezoid and with 18 four-courses beaten with two light beaters. In medieval times the *santir* (the Indian version of which is called the *santoor*) reached Central and Southeast Europe via Spain. Today, its modernized version is known in the folk music of Hungary, Slovakia, Moravia and other regions of Central Europe as the *cimbalom*.

Three types of drums are played in Arabic Islamic music: frame, goblet and kettledrums. The small *tar* tambourine with jingle discs is held with the membrane facing the right hand beating alternate strokes

335 Tunisian fiddle *rabab*

336 *Santir* dulcimer
Iran

on the rim and the skin. The right beats the main rhythm pattern while the left provides the secondary figures. The *darabukke* is a pottery goblet drum whose 'stem' is held under the left arm. The membrane is beaten with two kinds of strokes: light and muted beaten with the left hand and full and strong with the right. The *darabukke* is very popular in folk ensembles although it is also used in classical Arabic music. The

337 *Zurna* shawm
Iran

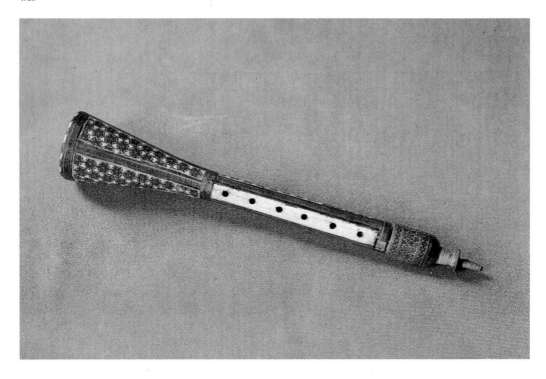

338 Tuareg woman with drum
Algeria

naqqarat tbilat is a pair of small kettledrums with wood or pottery bodies laced together and beaten with two light sticks.

An interesting offshoot of the Perso-Arabic musical culture is the folk music of Turkey. From the 16th century onward, Turkish music was influenced by, and to a certain extent also influenced, Arabic music. The original home of the Turks had been the plains of Central Asia where some Mongolian tribes still use the ancient type of drum — called the *bar* in Turkey—in their shamanistic rites. An instrument called the *lyra* is still played in Trabzon (Trebizond), although it is not a lyre but a version of the Turkish *kemanje* spike fiddle. Other Turkish instruments are similar to their Arabic counterparts: a cylidrical shawm called the *düdük*, the conical flared *zurna* shawm, the *tulúmi* bagpipe, the *'ud,* the *qanun,* the *daf* and *dumbelek* drums, etc.

339 *Ei-chek* fiddle
Iran

340 *Mizmar* shawm
Egypt

EUROPE

SCANDINAVIA

In Europe indigenous folk music has become comparatively unimportant, in contrast to the situation in most other parts of the world. Indeed, any original instrumental folk music is hard to find in modern Europe. However, distinct regional traits can still be perceived.

The sober character of Scandinavian musical intonation is expressed in a wide use of stringed instruments. An instrument called the *kantele*, a descendant of the medieval *psaltery*, is used in *FINLAND* in playing

341 Norwegian Hardanger fiddle, the *Hardangerfelen*

342 Finnish *kantele* zither

rune songs. Its wing-shaped resonator box supports up to 30 strings. A four-string bowed chordophone called the *kanteleharpe* or *jouhikko* with a highly arched chiselled back and a flat belly is a Celtic import to Finland via Sweden. The instrument has no proper fingerboard, but a round hole is provided on the left side through which the player stops the strings with his fingers. The instrument is laid on the left thigh and the bottom end is rested against the right knee. The reed flutes known as the *lira* and the *luddu* and wooden trumpets known as the *tjurju* and the *torvi* were originally shepherds' instruments.

Polish large trumpet

Czech hurdy-gurdy and detail of its tangent mechanism

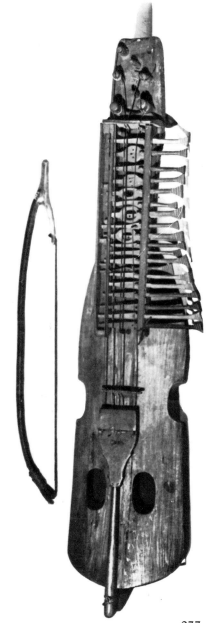

343 Swedish *nyckelharpa*

277

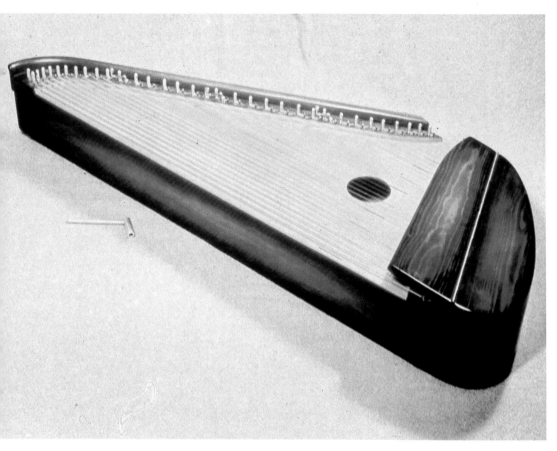

344 Finnish *kantele* zither

A relative of the *jouhikko* is the Swedish *stråkharpa*. Its shape resembles the medieval *srowd* (*crot*, Welsh *crwth*), the Icelandic *fidla* and the Estonian *tallharpha*. Another ancient relic is the *nyckelharpa*, a bowed fiddle with strings stopped by keys, in Germany it was known as the *Schlüsselfiedel* (keyed fiddle). Actually, it is nothing but a later version of the medieval hurdy-gurdy from which it has retained only the tangent mechanism since the strings are sounded with a bow. The *hummel* zither with a helmet-shaped body and metal frets on the side of the soundboard is identical with the Norwegian *langleik*, Danish *humle*, and Dutch *hommel*. The drone strings are tuned in the tonic and the subdominant scale. In the 1830's a bowed zither was invented in Sweden called the *psalmodicon*. It was used mainly in church music and for musical instruction in schools.

Itinerant folk musicians in *NORWAY* used to play the so-called *hardangerfelen*. Till this day the Hardanger fiddle has remained so popular that it has almost entirely driven most other Norwegian folk instruments into oblivion. The instrument is usually richly decorated, with an

345 Norwegian *langleik* zither

Swedish *stråkharpa*

elaborately carved scroll and four stopped and four sympathetic strings. Another ancient Norwegian instrument is the *langleik* zither with an elongated or sometimes helmet-shaped body and 4—14 diatonically tuned strings plucked with a plectrum. Of the wind instruments, the ancient long horn called the *lur* has survived, and is made of wood or birch bark. A small shepherd horn called the *prillar* is made of ox or male goat horn.

THE U.S.S.R.

The development of folk art and music in what is now the U.S.S.R. has been greatly influenced by the lively cultural interchange between the

346 Lithuanian wooden *skrabalas* bell chime

347 Russian *gusli*

various peoples who settled there. A typical relic of a once very rich musical heritage are the *lozhki,* regular wooden or metal spoons with elongated handles and decorated with jingle bells. The *lozhki* are held between the fingers of the right hand and the convex sides of the spoons are beaten against each other. Accompaniment players sometimes manage four or five *lozhki* pairs simultaneously. In the Tula Region, an ancient cog rattle called the *treshchotka* is still played by women at wedding celebrations.

However, the most common and popular instrument of the entire Soviet Union has been the *concertina* and lately the *accordion.* The instrument arrived in Russia in the 1840's and the subsequent efforts of Russian instrument-makers to modify it to suit the requirements of Russian folk music gave birth to numerous variants. The Saratov concertina (*saratovskaya*) is a single-row diatonic instrument, and in contrast to the other major type, the Livny version (*livienskaya*), the *saratovskaya* produces different tones on the press and on the draw. However, more common are double-row concertinas; for instance, the Cherepov type (*cherepovskaya*) was made in several sizes. The later transfer of semitones to the right hand keyboard then gave birth to the chro-

348 Estonian *kannel* zither

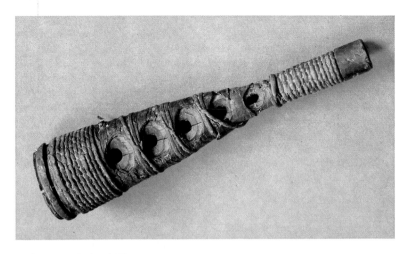

349 Russian shepherd *rozhok* horn
18th century

matic concertina; the most sophisticated model from the turn of this
century was named the *bayan* after the legendary singer. Usually the
bayan has 52 buttons in three rows on the right hand side; the bass
keybord has 100 bass buttons in five rows, the first and second containing the fundamental and auxiliary basses from G to F sharp, the third
to fifth rows operating major and minor triads and dominant and diminished sevenths of any tone in the chromatic scale. After the Second
World War the *accordion* also became very popular, and the original
bayan right-hand buttons were replaced by piano keys.

350 Russian *sopel* whistle flute with case

The only ancient wind instrument to survive in Central Russia is the *kuvikli* panpipe, which has five graduated pipes. However, these are not lashed together but held separately in the hands during play. One of the oldest wind instruments among the eastern Slavs was the *sopel*, identical to the Ukrainian *sopilka* and the Byelorussian *dudka*. Another archaic instrument is a double flute called the *svirel*, but known as the the *podvoynaya svirel* (double whistle) in Byelorussia. Its two pipes are not lashed together and form an acute angle in the hands of the player. The Ukrainian double flute (the *dvodentsivka*) is constructed from a single piece of wood and has one common beak-like mouthpiece. The *zhaleyka* is common in northern Russia and Byelorussia, while in the southern parts of Russia the *double zhaleyka* can be found.

Bagpipes exist only in the Ukraine but two variants of the instrument are known there: one with a single chanter only, the other with a chanter and a parallel drone. The *rozhok* (a mouthpiece horn instrument

Ukrainian *bandura*

351 Ukrainian *bandura*

352 Polish *zhlobozaki* fiddle

353 Polish *koza* bagpipe

354 Russian earthenware *svistilki* whistles

355 Russian *zhaleika* flutes

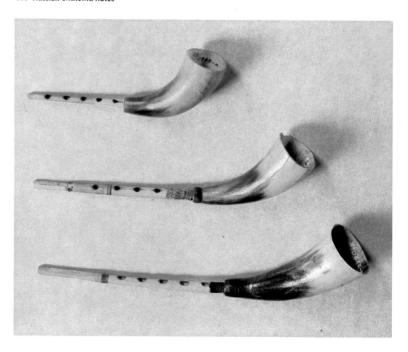

with fingerholes) was made world-famous in the 1880's by Nikolai Kondratiev and his *rozhki* players. The members of the ensemble played exclusively by ear and the task of the band leader was to control the correct division of voices.

Historical records prove the *gusli* was once the most popular of Russian stringed instruments. It was a kind of board zither which had developed from the medieval *psaltery* by having acquired more strings and an enlarged resonator box. The *wing gusli* is indeed shaped like a wing and has 12—14 diatonically tuned strings. The construction of the *rectangular gusli* is more complicated since the instrument has up to 80 chromatically tuned strings. In 1914 a *keyboard gusli* was invented. It was a sort of *autoharp,* the keys lifting the desired dampers, so that one hand selected the chords, while the other plucked the released strings with a plectrum made of tough leather. Other plucked chordophones include flat-backed lutes such as the *domra, bandura* and *balalaika,* all coming in consorts ranging from descant to contrabass versions. The *bandura* is the most common Ukrainian folk instrument. The descendant of the old *domra* is the famous *balalaika* with its typical triangular body. In the Smolensk Region a hurdy-gurdy has survived called the *lira* (*relya* in the Ukraine). It has one melody and two drone strings. The construction of the hurdy-gurdy has been improved several times since the First World War. An ingenious instrument is the nine-string *relya* tuned in diminished thirds and equipped with an accordion-like action. The wheel has been substituted by an endless, adjustable pressure belt bow made of plastic.

356 Russian *saratovskaya* concertina

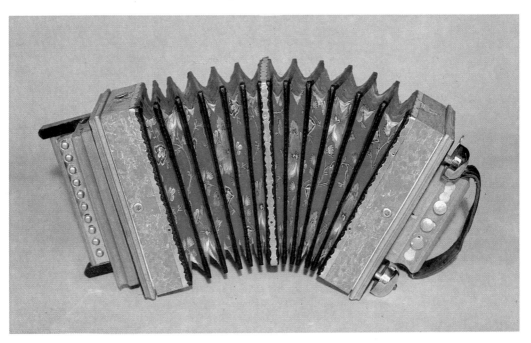

357 Slovak flute

The ancient musical culture of the Lithuanian, Latvian and Estonian nations goes as far back as the pre-Christian era, and reached the peak of its development in the 15th century when Lithuania spread from the Baltic to the Black Sea. The most typical of the small number of indigenous idiophones is a set of wooden bell chimes called the *skrabalas* in Lithuanian and the *koka zvana* in Latvian. The instrument consists of bells suspended in a common frame and sounded with wooden mallets. Only the *kraatspill* scraper and stamping stick has survived in Estonia. The instrument is scraped against, or stamped on, the floor when the mood at the village dance is at its highest.

The Lithuanian *skuducisi* (skuduchisi) flute is related to the Russian *kuvikli*. It is used in five to seven member consort ensembles with each player handling two or three instruments. The *ozguris* is a Lithuanian horn with three to five fingerholes, and is identical to the Latvian *azar-*

358 Russian *novorzhevskaya* concertina

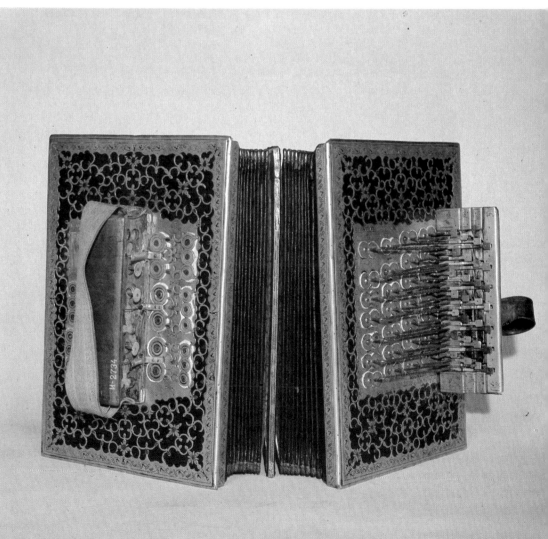

359 Bohemian bagpipe
19th century

ags and the Estonian *sarvu.* A wooden trumpet called the *trimitas* which was once common throughout Scandinavia has survived only in Lithuania. The *torupill* bagpipe with a bag made of a cow's stomach, one chanter and one drone is still quite popular in Estonia.

The main folk instrument of all Baltic nations of the U.S.S.R. is a psaltery or board zither type of plucked chordophone called the *kankles* in Lithuania, the *kokle* in Latvia and the *kannel* in Estonia. The instrument is played on the knee, the strings being plucked with the fingers of the right hand while the left hand stops the strings.

CENTRAL EUROPE

Central Europe has more idiophones (rattles, cog rattles, clappers, bells, etc.) than other parts of Europe and also a greater variety of bowed chordophones, while flutes and mouthpiece aerophones predominate among the winds. Reed instruments are somewhat less common. There is a great variety of bagpipes, however, and recently the accordion has also become a popular folk instrument.

360 Moravian dulcimer

POLAND is a bagpipe country. But although a great variety of bag-pipes are to be found in Poland, all are basically of the bellows action type, consisting of a small goatskin bag placed under the right armpit, the left pressing the air-filled bag supplying the wind to the chanter and the drone. Both pipes are ended with a cow horn and brass combination bell.

The *koziol* bagpipe is large, and the *koziol ślubny* (betrothal bagpipe) is played during wedding ceremonies together with the small *mazanki* fiddle which has three strings tuned a fifth apart, all however sounding a fifth higher than the regular violin. Some ancient flute types such as the *fujarka* have also survived in Polish folk music, and horns (*rogi*) are still played in some parts of Poland.

Folk music in *CZECHOSLOVAKIA* is flourishing, especially in Slovakia where there has been developed a type of instrumental folk music whose unique character has no counterpart elsewhere in Central Europe. Common throughout Slovakia is a shepherd fipple flute *pastierska píšťala)* decorated with pokerwork ornaments. The *koncovka*

361 Ukrainian *gusli*

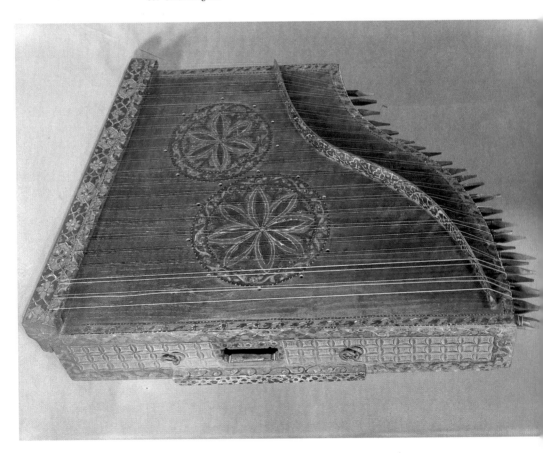

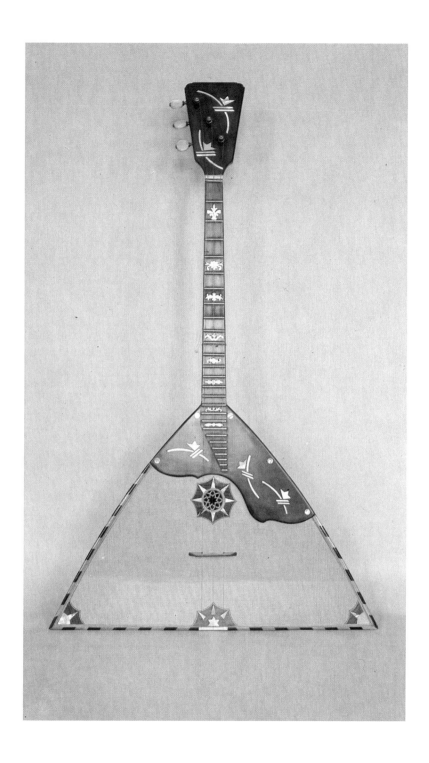

362 Russian *balalaika*

363 Rumanian shepherd *buciume* trumpets

Slovak *dvoyachka* double flute

(end flute) is an end-blown flute with a slightly tapering bore and no fingerholes. A progression of partial tones can be obtained by different manners of stopping the end hole with the left index finger.

A unique instrument among the family of European winds is the *fujara* (fuyara), an end-blown bass flute with the pipe 140—200 cm long. The upper end of the stopped tube is connected with a leather joint to another, narrow tube about 40—80 cm long, fitted with a short mouthpipe. In the bottom part of the main pipe there are three widely-spaced fingerholes. Only about half of the tones of the three-octave compass can be effectively used since the lower tones are too weak. A unique sound effect is the so-called start blow-off, a signal which the player produces to get ready to start his tune. First a murmuring sound will be heard and then a melody will slide progressively down from the upper register down to the fundamental key tone producing minute ornamental tunes.

The Slovak bagpipe called the *gajdy* (gaydy) appears today in two versions. The *goral gajdy* (mountaineer bagpipe) is typically fitted with a single chanter, the other type having two chanters. The bag is either kid or lamb skin turned inside out. Both the chanter and the drone are

365 Moravian cog rattle and clapper

decorated with metal inlays and ended with a bell made of ox horn and brass sheet.

The *forgólant,* a four string hurdy-gurdy is still played in *HUNGARY.* Quite popular also is a rectangular *zither* with two double fingered courses and eight drone strings. After 1800, the *cimbalom* dulcimer became the Hungarian national instrument, although it had already been known in the folk music of other European nations, especially in Bohemia. Half of the strings are divided by bridges in the 2:3 ratio so that the divided strings are tuned in fifths. The modern *pedál cimbalom* was built in 1874 by a Budapest instrument-maker of Czech origin, József Schunda who was also the author of the first *cimbalom* instruc-

367 Yugoslavian *zurla* shawm

Bulgarian *gadulka*

368 Bulgarian *gadulkas* and *tanbura*

tion book (1876). However, the Hungarians have yet another national instrument. It is the *tarogato* wooden shawm (double reed) with a flaring bell and modern keywork mechanism. J. V. Schunda, the inventor of the modern *cimbalom*, built also a single reed *tárogató*.

RUMANIAN folk musicians called *lautari* accompany their songs with the *cobza*, a short-necked lute with a body glued together from wide maple staves and a flat spruce soundboard with several ornamentally-arranged sound slits. The top of its body tapers into a backbent pegboard. The four double and treble courses tuned in fifths are reversed, i.e. the lowest strings are on the right hand side of the body. The *nai* (from Arabic *nay*) is a panpipe with 8—24 pipes of different length but identical diameter joined by a bent collar. The player moves the panpipe to and fro at his lips producing clear rapid trill sounds. In shepherd music various cane fipple flutes are still being used as well as the *fluier*, a wooden flute with six fingerholes. The name of the *bucium*,

369 Slovak *fuyaras*

370 Slovak bagpipe

a long wooden trumpet with a pipe-bent foot evokes echoes of the ancient Roman *buccina*.

Every region of *BULGARIA* has its own musical instruments, usually of Perso-Arabic origins. The instruments reached Bulgaria via Turkey which ruled Bulgaria for centuries. A typical instrument of southwestern Bulharia is the four-string plucked *tanbura* with its highly arched belly and a long neck with metal frets. The *gadulka,* a folk fiddle with a pear-shaped body progressing gradually into a short neck with no

Yugoslavian *dvoynitsa* double flute

371 Yugoslavian *gusle*

fingerboard, is popular in western Bulgaria. The *gadulka* is held vertically, resting on the knee, the fingernails of the left hand slightly touching the strings to produce flageolet tones. The *kaval* flute common
to Thrace can perform surprisingly intricate tunes. The *tupan* bass
drum is identical to the *tupans* of Macedonia, Albania and southern
Serbia.

SOUTHEASTERN AND SOUTHERN EUROPE

Folk instruments of southeastern and eastern Europe reveal the influences of the cultures of previous conquerors. Indiophones are mainly
various types of clappers, scrapers, xylophones and metallophones. The
frames of some drums testify to the Arabic origins of these instruments.
Predominant among the winds are single reed clarinet types which

302

Greek lira

seem to express best the main features of Mediterranean instrumental music.

A famous folk instrument of *YUGOSLAVIA* is the *gusle* fiddle with a body made from a single piece of wood and covered in skin. The short neck with the single huge peg is topped by an elaborately sculptured head. The single string is made of twisted horsehair and is stretched over a high bridge. The player holds the *gusle* between his knees, fingering the string from the side without fully stopping it. A glissando effect can be produced by a special sliding motion of the fingers. Recently, the gusle has been replaced in many regions of Serbia by the *tambura* and the *accordion*. The *lirica* is the oldest Mediterranean string instrument, and is common along the coast of Dalmatia.

An instrument unique to *GREECE* is an iron clapper shaped like tongs and called a *massá*. It is used for rhythmic accompaniment. The major members of the lute family are a bass lute with five strings called an *outi,* the four-string *laghouti,* and the recently-popular *bouzouki.* Among the representatives of the bowed strings are various *liras,* usually pear-shaped and with three strings tuned in fifths. The *lira* can be played either sitting, in which case the instrument is held vertical and slightly tilted back, or standing or walking when it is rested in midriff.

The relics of a once rich treasury of folk instruments in *ITALY* are *bagpipes, shawms* and *flutes.* A relatively great number of wind instruments have been preserved in Sicily. A quite peculiar instrument is a terracotta whistling pot held by the handle and blown into the mouth producing a humming sound. A somewhat similar sound is produced by the *caccarella* friction drum. However, one of the most typical instruments of Italian folk music is the *launeddas* of the Abruzzi shepherds.

372 Greek *outi* lute and *liraki* fiddle

373 Hungarian *forgólant* hurdy-gurdy

374 Greek (Mytilenian) *darabukke* drum

375 Basque flute-and-tabor combination: *txistu* and *tamboril*

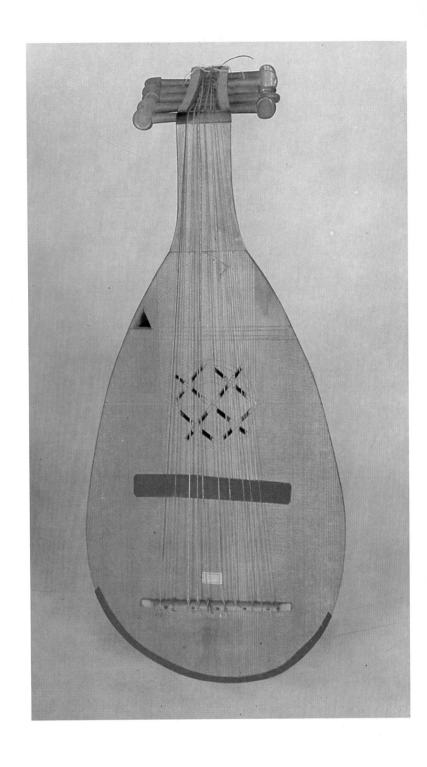

376 Rumanian *cobza*

377 Hungarian zither

This multiple clarinet consists of three cane pipes of different length. Two are lashed together, the shorter having four square fingerholes, the longer being a drone which can be extended with additional foot joints. The reed cut in a small mouthpipe is shaped like a swallow's tail. The third and shortest pipe is separated from the other two and has five to six fingerholes. The *tricballac* or *tricca-ballaca* is a set of wooden clappers consisting of three mallets with handles pivoting in a common yoke. The centre mallet is fixed while the side mallets are fitted with jingle discs, pivot and strike the centre mallet. The *sceta vajasse* scraper is formed by two sticks, one smooth, the other serrated or

378 German *hackbrett* dulcimer

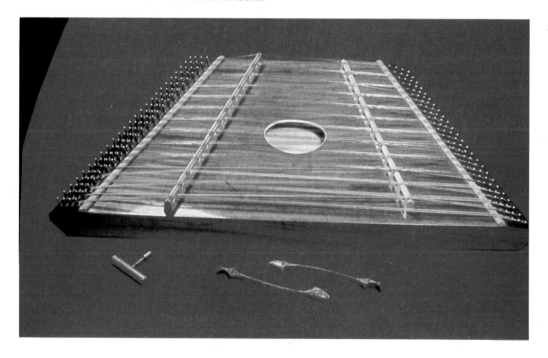

notched. The smooth stick is held under the chin rather like a violin while the right hand uses the serrated stick with jungle discs as a sort of a bow. Another type of idiophone is the *nacchara* of Naples, actually two wood plates shaped like castanets.

WESTERN EUROPE

Because of industrialization and urbanization, musical folklore has almost entirely died out in some countries of western Europe. In *GERMANY*, the traditional basis of instrumental music had been destroyed

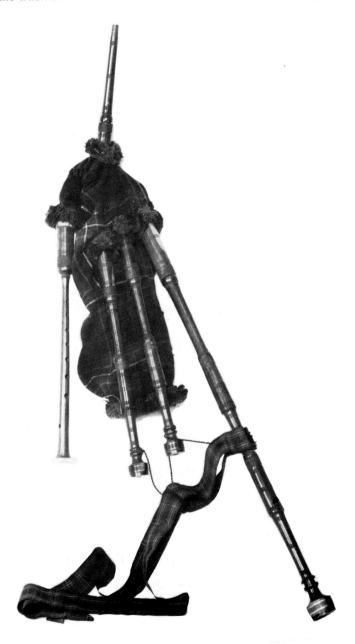

379 Scottish bagpipe

380 Irish harp

Italian *piffero* shawm

already by the Reformation which allowed only choir singing. Only occasionally, during Church holidays, were some traditional customs still observed, with the accompaniment of simple sound-making instruments such as the *cog rattle,* a friction drum called the *Rommelpot* or a friction idiophone called the *Waldteufel* (known as the *ronker* in Flanders, *bourdon* in France and *hoo'r* in England).

In contrast to Germany, the rich heritage of folk instruments in *FRANCE* can perhaps be compared only to the treasury of the Balkan nations. In southern France two types of double-headed drums are found which are played simultaneously with a fipple flute with three

309

fingerholes. The player plays the flute with his left hand while the right beats the drum. The Provencal *tabor (tambour)* drum has a long cylindrical body; the fipple flute is called the *galoubet*. The Catalonian drum of this pipe and tabor combination is small and the pipe is called *flaviol*. This 'one hand' pipe called *chiruba* in the Soule region and *llauto* in the Ossau, is in Gascony paired with the *tambourin de Béarn* (stringed drum) whose strings are struck with a beater. In Provence, both types of friction drums will be found: the *pinnate* with a clay body, a membrane and a rubbing stick, and the *cigale* sounded by rotation. A double reed shepherd shawm called the *gralla* can be found in the Roussilon, Landes and Vendée regions. Brittany has two types of bagpipe: the small *biniou koz* with a chanter and a drone with both single and double reeds and the large *biniou bras* with three drones.

The majority of stringed instruments still retain their archaic shapes. The *épinette des Vosges* zither is a descendant of the medieval psaltery and is similar to the German *Scheitholt*, Dutch *Noordsche Balk* and Danish *humle*. The four strings are stopped with a wooden block and plucked with a plectrum, the stopping technique being quite similar to that used for the bottle-neck steel guitar. Very popular in the Massif Central, Landes und Upper Brittany regions is the *vielle hurdy-gurdy* with a bulbous lute-shaped body and a carved pegboard representing a girl's head.

The *bagpipe*, once an instrument very common in Flanders as shown in the paintings of Brueghel, has not survived in the Low Countries but has become a truly national instrument in *IRELAND* and *SCOTLAND*. The Irish *piob mór* is a warpipe and a slight modification of the traditional Scottish *highland pipe:* the *piob villean* is similar to the English *small pipe*. However, the truly national Irish instrument is the diatoni-

381 French hurdy-gurdies and bagpipe
La Bourrée Bourbonnaise folk group

382 A Basque national instrument: the *alboka*

cally tuned *Irish harp* which developed from a small Old Norse harp and whose shape has remained practically unchanged for more than 1000 years. The instrument is quite difficult to play since every string has to be dampened after having been sounded before the next string can be plucked.

A unique branch of western European folklore is *BASQUE* folk music, for which a peculiar shepherd *alboka* hornpipe is a typical instrument. It has two cane or wooden pipes joined with a semicircular segment serving also as a handle. Both pipes have horn bells at the end and protective mouthhorns with reeds fitted inside. One pipe has three and the other five fingerholes. The instrument is somewhat similar to the ancient and now obsolete Welsh hornpipe called the *pibcorn* and the Scottish *stock-and-horn.* The Basque version of the pipe-and-tabor is the *txistu* flute with the *tamboril* drum. The pair is an important member of the *SPANISH cobla* band accompanied also by the *tiple* and *tenora* shawms and the *gaita* bagpipe. However, modern *cobla* instrumentation uses also modern instruments and a double bass. In *PORTUGAL* several instruments can still be found whose names remind us of the times of the Arab conquest. The local flute is called the *alaud,* there is a square tambourine called the *aduf* and a primitive fiddle known as the *rebeca.*

As elsewhere, the original folk instruments of the western European nations are being driven out by the *accordion* and the *concertina,* which are very popular in France and England. The Basque version of the latter instrument is called the *trikitixa,* and it is used together with a tambourine called the *panderoyotzale* to accompany singing.

Spanish *verimbao* jew's harp

311

III. MECHANICAL MUSICAL INSTRUMENTS

Man has always experimented with the mechanization of not only instrument-playing techniques but also the construction of instruments which could be played entirely automatically. The result of these attempts were various mechanical musical instruments *(automatophones)*, whose playing is controlled by a barrel or a punched paper roller. The barrel system is based on the fact that pins and bridges on

383 *Carillon*
Dome of the Royal Palace, Amsterdam, 1664

Mechanical *carillon*
1 Bells 2 Hammers 3 Tracker
system 4 Pegged cylinder

384 Barrel organ
J. Riemer's Sons, Chrastava, Bohemia, late 19th century

the surface of a barrel can—at a low speed of rotation—perform certain mechanical actions, which, when coupled with a simple lever system, will operate the vibrator part of the mechanism. In fact, the paper roller with its punched holes represents a sort of 'notation' of the piece and when coupled with a pneumatic action permits almost a true reproduction.

The first automatophones to appear were the 13th-century bell chimes called *carillons* and coupled with tower clocks. There are, for instance, only a few Dutch towns whose church or town hall towers lack a carillon. However, from the musical point of view the carillon as an automatophone is only of minor importance, although in the 16th century there appeared first carillons which did not just automatically

play a simple pre-set tune or sequence but were operable by means of a keyboard. Once a spring-operated clockwork mechanism had been invented, small chimes were mounted in *chiming clocks.* Cheap wooden clocks with glass bell chimes used to be traditional product of the German Black Forest (Schwarzwald) region. These clocks had 8—16 glass bells and could play short simple folk tunes. Since the 16th century, miniature chimes were also mounted in pocket watches.

Long before and even after the arrival of Edison's phonograph, music boxes were the only household mechanical music-makers. Where the first music box was made and by whom has still not been established with any degree of certainty. However, music boxes first appeared at the beginning of the 19th century as a product of Swiss watchmakers. The sound producing part of the instrument was a steel comb with as many reeds or tongues as required for the piece. The comb reeds were plucked by a spiked (or studded) cylinder rotated either manually by means of a crank or mechanically by clockwork. The whole mechanism was mounted in a wooden box which served as a resonator. The character of the instrument mechanism which had much in common with

385—386 Music box
František Řebíček, Prague, first half of the 19th century

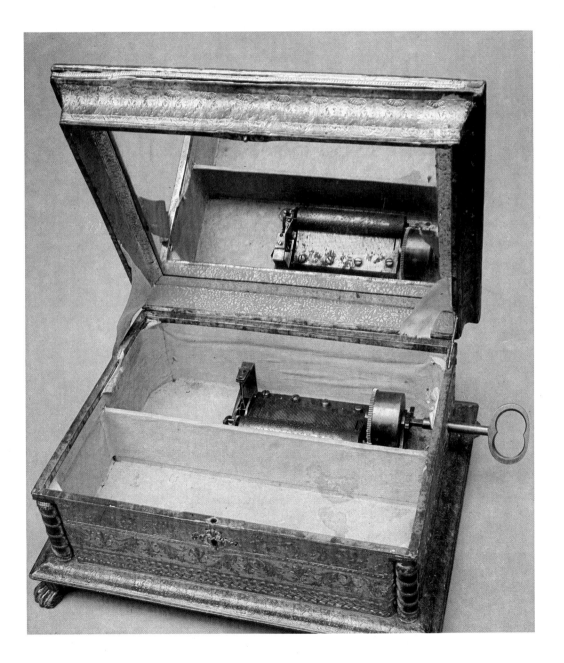

the clockwork was highly suitable for large-scale production and the Swiss watchmakers therefore soon established the production of music boxes on mass scale, and till today Switzerland has practically retained a monopoly for music box production. The shortcomings of the novelty, i.e. the inability to perform more tunes than could be coded in the cylinder were later overcome by cheap interchangeable discs, the latter having also paved the way for *polyphones* with special reed plucking mechanisms. Music box manufacture is still carried on in Switzerland and some polyphones are still made in the United States.

However, the sound of mouthpiece instruments still could not be reproduced mechanically and only the invention of the free reed made the imitation of brass sounds possible. A free reed automatophone called the *melodica* was patented in 1822 by Wilhelm Vollner of Germany. Most common types of free reed automatophones employed interchangeable cardboard or metal discs. In shape and size these instruments resemble old phonographs or victrolas without the typical horn. The instruments were manufactured and marketed under various tradenames such as the *Intona, Ariston, Manopan, Mignon,* etc.

387 Barrel organ with movable figurines
Late 19th century

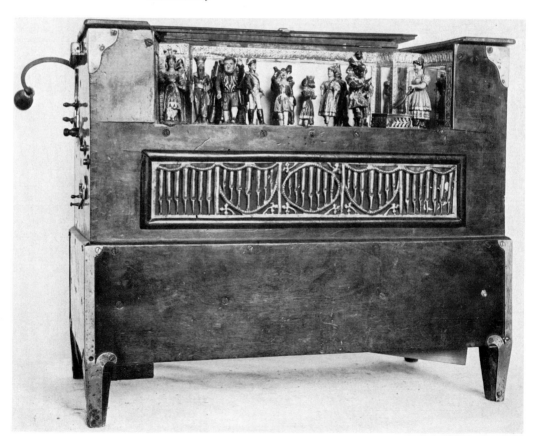

388 Orchestrion
Gossling, Hilversum, early 20th century

Manopan
1 Free reed 2 Flap valve
3 Wind 4 Spring 5 Pin (stud)
6 Perforated carton

389 Barrel organ with cylinder
Bacigalupo, early 20th century

The birthplace of organ automatophones was medieval Italy, but in the 16th century the knowledge of their construction reached Germany and England. Small pipe mechanisms coupled with a clockwork and called *flute-playing clocks* were extremely popular during the Rococo period. The mechanism was actuated at regular intervals by clockwork housed in luxuriously decorated cases. Haydn, Mozart and Beethoven as well as others wrote scores for the cylinder of the music clock.

Another instrument featuring mechanically-operated pipes was the *barrel organ*. However, the existence of a genuine crank-operated barrel organ can be safely dated no earlier than the early 18th century. Nevertheless, the construction and external design of the instrument were already on such a sophisticated level that the instrument practically remained unchanged even in later periods. The original miniature *bird organ* was later improved and enlarged, the case being divided into two parts. The upper case housed the cylinder, the tracker action and the bellows while the lower case housed the pipes. To encompass all the pipes in the limited space of the box required great ingenuity but at the beginning of the 1860's there appeared barrel organs with vertical rather than horizontal pipes and apart from the original flues reed pipes were also adopted. This type of *barrel organ* was called the *Wiener Werkl* since it was a Viennese speciality. Barrel organs were usually built by builders of regular organs since the instrument re-

390 Free reed *Ariston*
Leipzig, early 20th century

Music box
1 Steel tongues 2 Studded cylinder (barrel)

391 *Polyphon*
Leipzig, early 20th century

placed the organ in country churches, especially in France and England.

The growth of modern technology awoke a great interest in mechanization in all spheres of human activity. No wonder then that there were also efforts to perfect the sound of automatophones, and to enrich their poor and monotonous performance by the imitation of a greater variety of instruments and indeed of an entire orchestra. Such instruments were called *orchestrions,* and one of the versions of this instrument called the *panharmonicon* and invented by Johann Nepomuk Mälzel was honoured by none other than Beethoven who wrote

392 *Organetto* (barrel piano)
A. Martin, Madrid, ca. 1910

393 *Manopan* with pneumatic traction and free reeds. Early 20th century

Barrel organ
1 Pipes 2 Tracker bars
3 Spring 4 Flap valve 5 Wind
6 Studded barrel

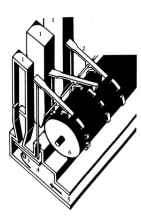

a piece called *Wellington's Victory at Vitoria* (1823) for the instrument. Improved orchestrions tried to copy the sound of an entire orchestra as truly as possible, but, as ingenious as the orchestrion mechanism was, the instrument never reached the level of sophistication of the later *pianola* since the only thing that the orchestrion did solve perfectly was the problem of rhythm. The dynamic possibilities still remained very poor and the instrument could be played either in low volume with only one stop engaged or loudly with all the stops. The main aim was to have the instrument playing loudly enough, and consequently least care was paid to the quality of the sound so that the orchestrions never rose above the level of mere barrel organ music.

On the other hand, the history of string automatophones is not as rich as that of the carillons and barrel organs since mechanical means of sounding the chordophones were much more difficult to find. *Spinets* with keys pressed by pegs of a cylinder were described by Mersenne as a German invention. Mechanical spinets housed in artistically decorated cases were a speciality of Samuel Bidermann of Augsburg in the 16th and 17th centuries. Finally, at the end of the 19th century, after a pause of almost two centuries, Charles Kendall of the U.S. devised an automatophonic *banjo* whose strings were plucked

394—395 Automatic spinet and a view of the playing mechanism
S. Bidermann, Augsburg, ca. 1620

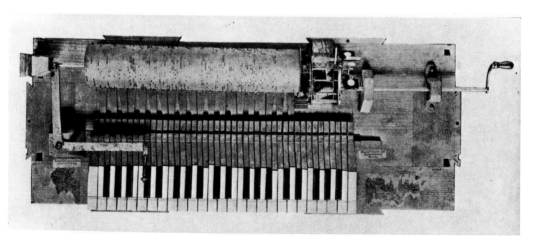

with tiny mechanical 'fingers'. At the same time a patent was registered in Germany for an automatic zither called the *chordephon* whose 44 strings were sounded by a metal disc.

No less difficult to achieve was the mechanical sounding of the bowed instruments which is precisely the reason why the bowed strings had resisted all attempt at automation for such a long time. From the very beginning, it was quite clear that the bow was unsuitable for automation and designers therefore concentrated on designs of an endless rotating bow. The efforts were crowned with a practical success in 1908 when the first automatophonic violin was made in the U.S. under the name of the *virtuoson*. It was merely a regular violin in a case with

396 Orchestrion, internal view
Popper, Leipzig, 1929

397 Orchestrion
Bruder Bros., Hannover, ca. 1925

a system of levers actuated by electromagnets which replaced the left fingers of the violinist's hand. Since the traditional bow was replaced with a wheel, the resulting impression was that of several violins playing simultaneously. However, of all violin automatophones only two models ever became practical, and both only in a combination with a pianola. The most successful and best-sounding was the *Phoniliszt-Violina* with three violins and a pianola, a product of the Hupfeld Company of Leipzig.

Long before the epoch-making invention of the hammer action piano at the beginning of the 18th century, there had already existed stringed automatophones. All *harp-playing instruments* were based on this simple mechanism and even the famous street corner hand-cranked *barrel piano (organetto)* from the beginning of the 20th century was also operated by means of a cylinder. However, none of the attempts to improve the musical performance of these mechanical *player pianos* met with any success and not even the improvement of the barrel helped much. The first kind of instrument was made in France in 1863, the *pianola* being a registered trade mark patented in 1897 by an American engineer E.S. Votey, but the instrument was perfected only

325

later and eventually became the most sophisticated mechanical musical instrument in the 1930's.

The *pianola* or *player piano* had 88 mechanical fingers instead of the mere ten which a musician has at his disposal, and thanks to the perforated paper roll the 'fingers' could be employed with disregard to the possibilities of the human hand. This meant, for instance, that basses could be held without a pedal, or arpeggios and perfect trills played, or harmonization arranged whether possible with human hands or not. Moreover, the tempo, dynamics and damper selection could also be controlled by buttons and levers.

For a long time the *player piano* was considered an automatophone reproducing simply pieces composed for the regular piano. The tendency not to regard it as a mere automatophone but as a new musical instrument in its own right for which compositions must be modified and even written was accepted only when the instrument was already being rapidly pushed into oblivion by music machines. And so the player piano faded as did all other automatophones — and equally as unjustly, too — after the new music machines had made their victorious appearance.

Mechanical stringed instruments
1 String 2 Hammer 3 Spring
4 Barrel

IV. ELECTRIC AND ELECTRONIC MUSICAL INSTRUMENTS

The first attempts to utilize electricity to power musical instruments date from as early as the 18th century. Indeed, a remarkable device must have been an electric mutation orchestrion by the Czech inventor, Prokop Diviš; the instrument was called the *Denis d'or*. However, neither the records of its construction nor of the principle on which it had been based has survived. Some 30 years later, in 1761, Jean Bap-

399—400 Electrophonic guitars, ca. 1955

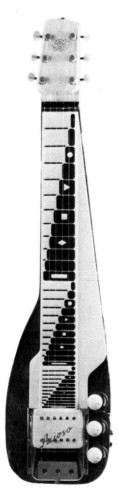

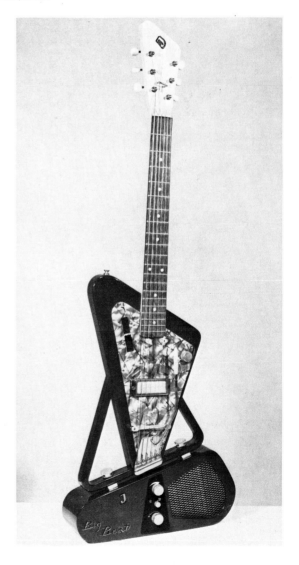

401—402 Modern electrophonic guitars

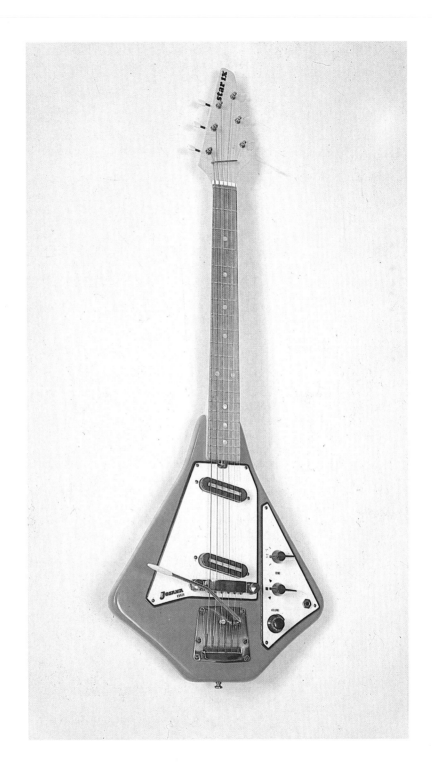

Kurbelsphärophon of Jörg Mager

tiste Delaborde of Paris invented his unsuccessful *clavecin electrique* or electric harpsichord.

The first instrument to generate sound electrically was the *telharmonium* of an American engineer Thaddeus Cahill, who invented it in 1906. His machine employed rotary generators and telephone receivers, but despite its huge popular appeal the instrument soon faded away since it was too bulky and complex to be practical.

A new stage of development of electric musical instruments producing new timbres and promising great aspirations took place from 1920 to 1927. According to their principles of design, these instruments could be divided into two groups. The first utilized the interference of two high inaudible A.C. frequencies known also as radio whistles. This unpleasant feature of ancient wireless receivers was now deliberately produced by a generator and modified to the desired sharpness, timbre, volume and duration. A representative of this group is the *thereminvox* of the Soviet physicist Lev Sergeevich Theremin. One of the high frequencies was stable while the other was adjustable by hand through the proximity of the hand to a metal rod projecting from the instrument. The player waved his hand in the air as if producing the tones from ether. This is why electronic music was in the past often generally termed 'etheric music', 'air music' or 'sphere music'. The second group were A.C. machines working with 16 Hz — 20 kHz frequencies. A typical representative of this group would be Bertrand's *dinaphone* which employed two valves and a rotary capacitor.

The first successful results were soon to be followed in the 1930's by a whole number of new electric instruments. Maurice Martenot designed a keyboard monochord called *ondes Martenot* (Martenot waves) for which scores were written by composers of the stature of Darius Milhaud, André Jolivet and Jacques Ivert. Arthur Honegger used the instrument in his *Joan d'Arc.* The *sphärophone* and *electric organ* of Jörg Mager could produce not only a sliding glissando but also innumerable new tone colours. Mager was also the inventor of the *calleidophone, electrophone* and *partiturophone;* Rimski-Korsakov (a grandson of the famous Russian composer) together with Kreitser and Ivanov designed the *emeritone;* Friedrich Trautwein fathered the *trautonium,* for which Paul Hindemith, Richard Strauss and other famous composers wrote music; there was the *mixturtrautonium* of Oscar Sala, the *hellertion* of Helberger and Lertes, Langer's and Halmagyi's *emicon,* and so on.

During the period between the two World Wars other instruments were also invented based on the principle of the selenophone (Spielman's *superpiano*) or a compromise between mechanical and electric-tone generation (Nernst's piano). Just before the outbreak of the Second World War the Telefunken Company of Germany developed a monophone instrument by uniting the systems of two different electric instruments.

However, all these instruments shared one common shortcoming: they were extremely difficult to operate and made great requirements on the musical hearing and feeling of the performer. Nevertheless a genuine boom in the field of electric instruments came after the Second World War, based on the progress achieved during the 1930's and 1940's. New and more sophisticated instruments were introduced. Tl first were electrophonic instruments in which an electromagnetic pick-up changes the mechanical vibrations of the string into electric oscillations (electrified guitars, double basses, violins, pianos and even saxophones); the second group is constituted of purely electronic instruments where the tone is generated in electrical circuitry. Pitch, volume and timbre have their counterpart in electric wave frequency, amplitude and harmonic spectrum. The tone is changed into audible frequencies with an electro-acoustic divider. The instruments can be monophonic (*melodica, bassophone, electronium, clavioline,* etc.) or polyphonic which employ either rotary electric generators replacing the vibration of an elastic body by a serrated wheel as in the *Hammond* or *pipeless organs,* or the instrument generates the tone frequency without any acoustic-mechanical vibration as in the *consonanta organ, piano organ, ionica,* etc.

The great advantage of electronic musical instruments is that they

403 *Emeriton*
Rimski-Korsakov, Kreitser, Ivanov, ca. 1925

404 Crystal trombone
Bachet Bros., Paris

405 Electric percussion instrument
Bachet Bros., Paris

employ no moving parts. What the designers of the electronic orga_
had in mind was the construction of an instrument which would be
capable of replacing fully the regular pipe organ. The sound of the pipe
organ can be exactly copied with electronic staggered frequency res-
ponse generators producing tones rich in higher harmonies. At first
most engineers in the field of electronic musical instruments tried to
replace electrically both the sound and the playing techniques of the
traditional instruments. This is still the case with all types of electronic
organs, but the present development seems to imply that the future
mission of electronic instruments is not merely to copy classical musical instruments, but instead to develop new possibilities in music making.

If there is any branch of modern technology of a truly miraculous
character, it is electronics. Thanks to its limitless possibilities a new

406 Electronic organ
Model *Eminent*

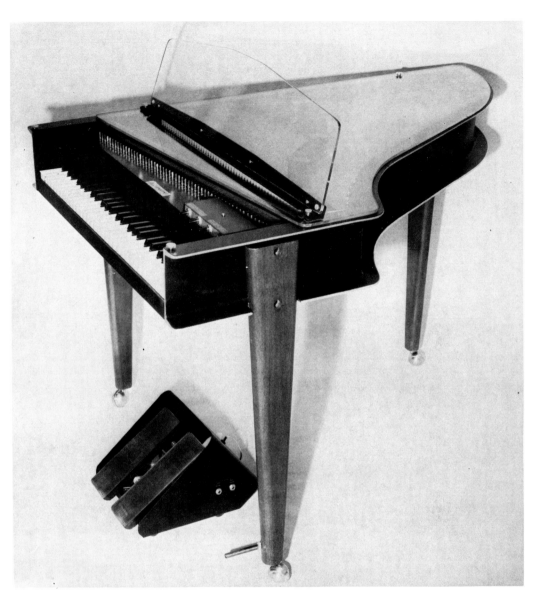

407 Baldwin electric harpsichord

generation of electronic musical instruments have recently been developed, with a much greater operational reliability stemming from the latest trends in miniaturization and the revolutionary technique of computerization.

The *synthesizers* owe their existence to the sophisticated LSI (Large Scale Integration) circuitry. These instruments are equipped with programme control which means that the attack and decay characteristics of any conceivable instrument can be produced, mixed and modified by

Ondes Martenot of Maurice Martenot

408—409 Electronic organs
Model *Vermona*, German Democratic Republic

410 Electronic musical instrument
Bell Telephone System, U.S.A.

the computer memory which has been incorporated in the instrument.

The first types of electronic instruments coupled with a synthesizer appeared in the late 1960's — the most important being the Moog synthesizer. Another development, the Phoenix model Hammond organ, incorporates a multiple derivation divider replacing more than 2000 transistors, i.e. 12 tuning discs. The instrument also features an automatic rhythm unit which can produce any rhythmical pattern. A group of computer music experts at the University of Utah designed an instrument which — when used in conjunction with a computer — can play complex concertos, fugues, sonatinas, etc. as programmed from the notation. The process can be also reversed, i.e. the composition can be recorded and the computer will make a print-out notation. This instrument called *musicational organ* will perhaps play a great role in the field of music instruction, since it can be easily adapted for teaching the fundamentals of music. The core of the instrument is an electronic organ coupled with a small digital computer, printer and display. When a composition is to be loaded into the computer memo-

411 Synthesizer
Model *Mark II*, U.S.A., American composer Milton Babitt

ry, it will be expressed in numerals, letters and symbols on the input typewriter. Once the score is loaded, a couple of pushbuttons are pressed and the instrument will offer an instant replay of the composition. Entire orchestral scores can be stored in the memory and a computer command will make the instrument play any selected individual part or the entire score.

The history of musical instruments has always been characterized by a certain logic of historical development. An invention is usually preceded by the conditions necessary to put the invention into practice. For instance, when attempting to simulate the sound of the traditional pipe organ with electronic gear, and to replace the organ with electric instruments in liturgical music, designers at first clashed with the accepted musical tastes. Later, when electronic instruments had already won their place in the sphere of popular entertainment music and especially rock music, electronic instruments were accepted also by serious creative music.

Today, the modern orchestra and its instruments bear little likeness

Thereminvox of L. S. Theremin

to their ancient ancestors, and the gap between traditional acoustic instruments and their electronic relatives is even greater. Electronic musical instruments help to develop conditions for a new sphere of musical art, electronic music. True, it still finds its greatest use only as radio, TV and film music and as a new art it has made only the very first creative steps. However, recently an entirely new world of sound has been penetrated by man, a treshold has been reached of a new experience where nothing resembles the cornerstones of the entire structure of music as known by the endless past generations nor the exterior and interior structure of its musical instruments. It will require still greater efforts before the electronic musical instruments enter the realm of genuine artistic expression. The far-reaching impact of this fundamental revolution in music still cannot be foreseen. The new electronic musical instruments permit the creation of endless sound colours, and in conjunction with computers open the new realm of electronic music machines. It seems that the music-machine relationship constitutes an integral part of the much broader problems of the future development of the arts as such. Still, one thing remains sure and that is that computer technology has not said its last word in music.

412 Synthesizer
Model *Moog 55.* U.S.A.

413 Electronic music score
Leo Kirchner: Quartet No. 3

TUNING AND NOTATION OF THE MOST COMMON EUROPEAN MUSICAL INSTRUMENTS

Note: Empty notes designate the sounded compass, full notes the notated compass. Where only empty notes appear, the sounded and notated compasses are identical. Notes given in square brackets designate extended tonal compass which can be achieved on some instruments of the type.

I. IDIOPHONES

II. AEROPHONES

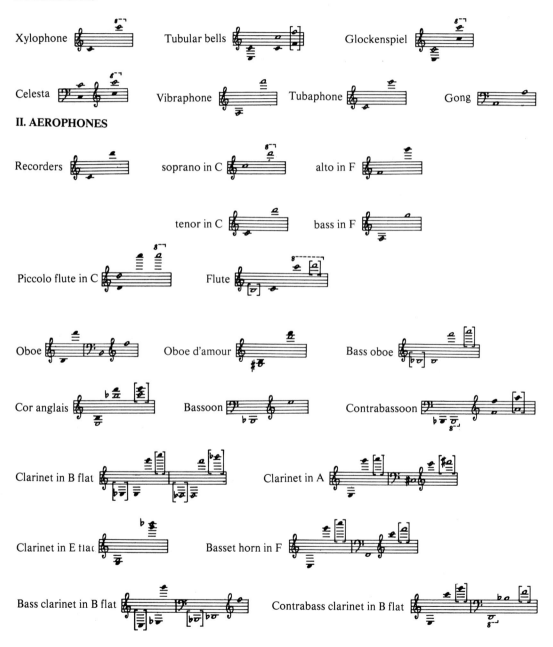

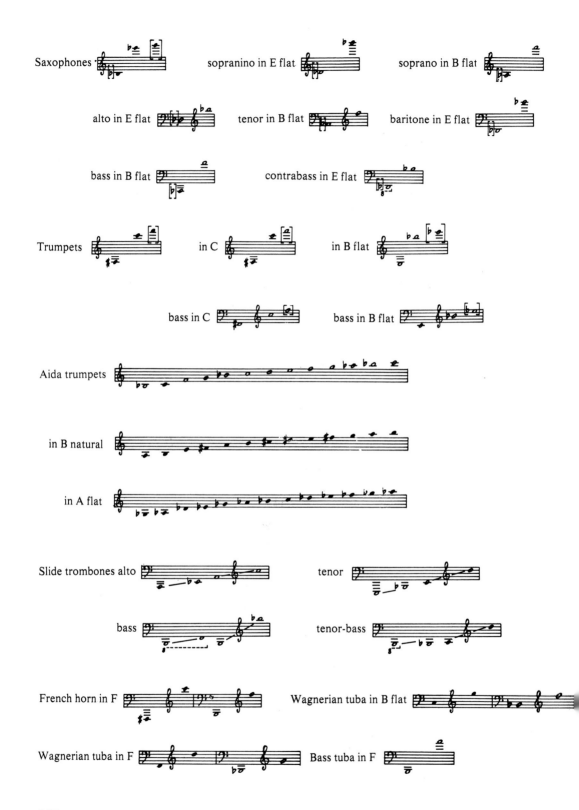

Contrabass tuba in B flat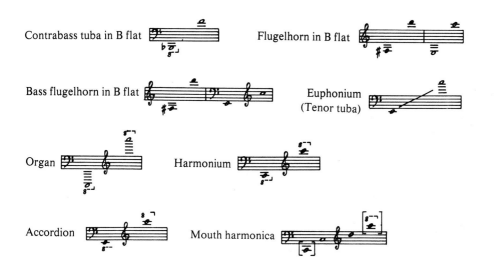

Flugelhorn in B flat

Bass flugelhorn in B flat

Euphonium
(Tenor tuba)

Organ

Harmonium

Accordion

Mouth harmonica

III. CHORDOPHONES

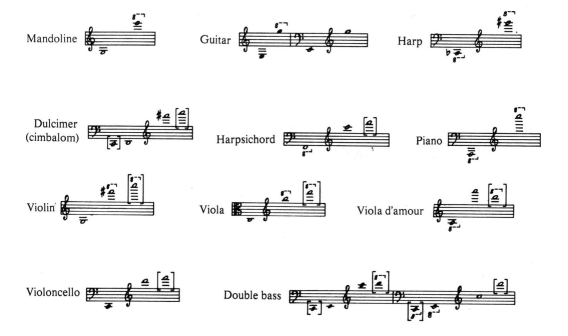

Mandoline   Guitar   Harp

Dulcimer
(cimbalom)   Harpsichord   Piano

Violin   Viola   Viola d'amour

Violoncello   Double bass

IV. MEMBRANOPHONES

Smaller timpani

Larger timpani

GLOSSARY OF TERMS

AEROPHONE a wind instrument.

AMPLITUDE the maximum displacement of a sound wave determined by its peak-to-peak distance.

ARCHAEOORGANOLOGY science on pre-historic musical instruments.

ARPEGGIO sounding of the notes of a chord in rapid succession rather than simultaneously.

ARS NOVA a musical art which originated in Florence in the Middle Ages, utilizing new secular and folk elements.

AUTOPHONE see *Idiophone*.

BARREL the funnel-shaped resonator of the woodwinds.

BELL the funnel-shaped metal resonator of the brass family instruments.

BOURDON a drone, sustained pipe or string bass.

CAPOSTATO a fixture used with plucked chordophones to shorten all fingerboard strings simultaneously.

CHORDOPHONE a stringed instrument.

CHROMATIC SCALE a series of 12 semitones within one octave of the tempered tuning.

CONTINUO (Italian *basso continuo*, continued bass), also called thorough bass, a type of Baroque instrumental music with accompaniment chords designated by numbers written above the bass score, developed from the practice of Italian organists in the late 16th century.

COUNTERPOINT the art of adding a related but independent melody or melodies to a basic melody, in accordance with the fixed rules of harmony.

COURSE two or more strings tuned usually in unisono or an octave apart.

CROOK a metal tube, usually *S*-shaped and made of brass, fitted in the top joint of a woodwind instrument and serving as a mouth tube, facilitating easy blowing and holding of the instrument.

CROSS-FINGERING a technique used on old aerophones to produce semitones which are not the natural tones of a diatonic scale. Such a semitone (e.g. G sharp) would be formed by uncovering the fingerhole of the next tone in the scale (i.e. A) while keeping the hole of the basic tone (i.e. G) covered. Cross-fingering is rarely used on modern instruments.

DIATONIC SCALE a series of tones progressing in full tones and semitones.

DIMINUTION shortening of the note values in mensural notation in the sense of alla breve (also called division in 16th century English practice).

EMBOUCHURE a combination of technique and sensitivity to control the labial muscles used for the generation of tones on wind instruments, particularly the mouthpiece instruments. In the case of the reeds, the function of the lips is practically limited to the control of the sound-producing device (the reed) while in the case of flutes the lips merely direct the wind properly against the blow-hole edge.

ETHNOMUSICOLOGY the scientific study of folk music.

ETHNOORGANOLOGY the scientific study of folk instruments.

FLAGEOLET TECHNIQUE a technique of playing the bowed chordophones consisting of touching lightly the strings in certain places to produce soft partial tones.

FORMANT a rumble, noise or din generated when a musical instrument is played (e.g. when a beater strikes the xylophone bar) and influencing the overall character of the sound colour of the instrument.

FREQUENCY the number of cycles of oscillation per second, determining the tone pitch.

GENERATOR a part of a musical instrument causing the oscillation of its vibrator.

GLISSANDO a gliding effect produced by sounding a series of adjacent tones in rapid succession.

HETEROPHONIC sounding differently; heterophony occurs when musical instruments each perform the same tune but each with its own variant although the basic theme remains common for all the instruments.

IDIOPHONE a musical instrument in which the entire material of which the instrument is composed is sounded.

IMPROVISATION a performance without preparation, made up on the spur of the moment according to the player's disposition, abilities, mood, etc.

INSTRUMENTATION a set of musical instruments, or an arrangement of music for a combined number of instruments.

INTERVAL the difference in pitch of two tones.

LINGUAPHONE a reed instrument with a vibrator in the form of a thin flexible strip called the reed.

MEMBRANOPHONE a musical instrument in which a membrane is sounded.

METALLOPHONE a musical instrument with a metal vibrator.

MODE a progression of tones arranged in a scale from which a tune is formed.

MONOXYLIC made of a single piece of wood.

MOTIF the smallest musical element in music design from which a composition grows.

MOUTHPIECE the most important part of mouthpiece wind instruments, consisting of two parts: the cup, against which the lips are rested, and the stem fitted into the tube proper of the instrument. The two parts of the mouthpiece are separated by a 'sluice' which is actually the narrowest part of the instrument bore.

MUSICAL MACHINE any device like a record-player, tape-recorder, juke-box, etc. Whereas musical instruments produce music, these devices merely reproduce it.

MUTE a device used for diminishing the sound of a musical instrument.

NODAL POINT any part of the vibrator that cannot move because it is fixed, e.g. the ends of a string, the periphery of a membrane, the fixed points of idiophones or the stopped ends of pipes.

OBBLIGATO a necessary, indispensable part as opposed to the non-obbligato voice which can be entirely left out from the concord.

ORGAN DRONE a sustained bass tone while other voices progress in harmonically logic progressions disregarding the drone.

ORGANOGRAPHY the description of musical instruments.

OVERBLOWING 1. the generation of certain partial tones instead of the fundamental tone when playing a wind instrument.
2. an enlargement of the tonal compass of the basic scale into a higher pitch (usually an octave or duodecim) by the means of the overblowing key on reed instruments.

PARTIAL TONES (also called harmonics) tones sounding together with the fundamental tone. Their frequencies are exact multiples of the frequency of the pure fundamental tone (1:2:3:4 ... etc.), so that besides the fundamental tone of a musical instrument its octave, duodecim, etc., are also sounded.

PEDAL TONES a term for natural deep fundamental tones of the mouthpiece instruments.

PIPE, FLUE a pipe equipped with a sharp edge called the lip (upper lip) struck by the wind and causing the pipe to sound.

PIPE, REED a pipe equipped with a tone-producing reed or tongue.

PIPE, STOPPED a pipe with an octave lower than an unstopped (open) pipe of the same footage (speaking length).

PIPE, UNSTOPPED a pipe which sounds an octave higher than a stopped pipe of the same footage (speaking length).

PIROUETTE a metal disc on shawms and oboes against which the player's lips are rested.

PLECTRUM a small, thin and flexible piece of wood, horn, ivory, metal, plastic, etc., used for striking of the strings of plucked chordophones.

POLYCHORDIC having a large number of strings.

POLYPHONIC having several melodies; a composition combining a number of individual but harmonizing voices or melodies.

REED, BEATING is slightly larger than the aperture or opening; it vibrates due to the wind stream and alternately closes and opens the wind passage.

REED, FREE is fixed at one end, closing perfectly the aperture in a metal frame and vibrating through it, rather than against it. The wind causes the reed to vibrate periodically, producing wind pulses of identical frequency.

RESONATOR that part of a musical instrument which amplifies the sound.

SQUEAK unintended overblowing.

SYMPATHETIC STRING a string appearing on some chordophones besides the regular fingered strings and sounded by the vibrations of the latter rather than directly by the musician.

TANGENT a metal blade fitted to the rear end of a clavichord's key bars and sounding one of the strings, respectively sounding and shortening it in fretted clavichords.

THOROUGH BASS see *Continuo*.

TONALITY the relation of the harmony of a musical movement to the prescribed key. On the basis of tonality, the composition may often be dated, or its author or his nationality determined.

TONIC the keynote of a composition.

VIBRATOR the vibrating part of a musical instrument whose function is to generate sound waves.

IMPORTANT WORLD COLLECTIONS OF MUSICAL INSTRUMENTS AND THEIR CATALOGUES

AUSTRIA
Vienna: Kunsthistorisches Museum — Sammlung alter Musikinstrumente
  Schlosser, J. *Die Sammlung alter Musikinstrumente*, Vienna 1920
  Luithlen, V. *Katalog der Sammlung alter Musikinstrumente*, Vienna 1968
BELGIUM
Brussels: Musée des Instruments Musicaux
  Musée Instrumental du Conservatoire Royal de Musique
  Mahillon, V. Ch. *Catalogue descriptif et analytique du Musée Instrumental...*, Ghent 1893—1933
CZECHOSLOVAKIA
Prague: Národní muzeum (National Museum)—Muzeum české hudby (Museum of Czech Music)
  Buchner, A. *Průvodce výstavou České hudební nástroje minulosti* (A Guide to the Exhibition of Czech Musical Instruments of the Past), Prague 1950
DENMARK
Copenhagen: Musikhistorisk Museum
  Hammerich, A. *Musikhistorisk Museum zu Kopenhagen. Beschreibender Katalog*, Copenhagen 1911
  Private collection of Carl Claudius
  Claudius, C. *Samling af Gamle Musikinstrumenter*, Copenhagen 1931
FRANCE
Paris: Musée Instrumental du Conservatoire National Supérieur de Musique
  Chouquet, G. *Le Musée du Conservatoire National de Musique. Catalogue raisonné des instruments de cette collection*, Paris 1875
  Pillaut, L. *Le Musée du Conservatoire National de Musique. Suppléments au Catalogue*, Paris 1884—1903
  Musée National du Louvre (Musical instruments of the Ancient East)
  Musée Guimet (Musical instruments of the Eastern Asia)
GERMAN DEMOCRATIC REPUBLIC
Eisenach: Bachhause zu Eisenach
  Buhle, E. *Sammlung alter Musikinstrumente*, Leipzig 1913
Halle an der Saale: Händel Museum
  Sasse, K. *Musikinstrumentenausstellung*, Halle 1958 *Musikinstrumentensammlung. Besaitete Tasteninstrumente*, Halle 1966
Leipzig: Musikinstrumenten-Museum der Karl-Marx-Universität
  Rubardt, P. *Führer durch das Musikinstrumenten-Museum der Karl-Marx-Universität Leipzig*, Leipzig 1955
Markneukirchen: Musikinstrumenten-Museum
  Jordan, H. *Führer durch das Musikinstrumenten-Museum, Markneukirchen*, Markneukirchen 1975
GERMAN FEDERAL REPUBLIC
Bamberg: Musikhistorisches Museum Neupert
  Führer durch das Musikhistorische Museum Neupert, 1938
Berlin: Staatliches Institut für Musikforschung. Musikinstrumenten-Museum
  Berner, A. *Das Musikinstrumenten-Museum, Berlin 1968*
Munich: Bayerisches Nationalmuseum
  Bierdimpfl, K.A. *Die Sammlung der Musikinstrumente des baier. Nationalmuseums*, Munich 1883
  Münchner Stadtmuseum—Musikinstrumentensammlung
Nuremberg: Germanisches Nationalmuseum
GREAT BRITAIN
London: Victoria and Albert Museum
  Catalogue of Musical Instruments: Vol. I. Russell R.,
    Keyboard Instruments, London 1968;
    Vol. II. Baines, A.
    Non-Keyboard Instruments, London 1968
  British Museum (Contains precious bequests of private collectors, musical instruments of ancient and oriental nations.)
  Horniman Museum
  Jankins, J. *Musical Instruments*, London 1958
HUNGARY
Budapest: Magyar Nemzeti Múzeum
  Gábry, G. *Alte Musikinstrumente*, Budapest 1969
INDIA
Calcutta: Indian Museum
  Meerwarth, A. M. *A Guide to the Collection of Musical Instruments Exhibited in the Ethnographical Gallery of the Indian Museum Calcutta*, Calcutta 1917
ITALY
Cremona: Museo Civico (Contains commemorative objects of famous Cremona violin-makers from the Cozio di Salabue Collection)
Milan: Museo degli Strumenti Musicali, Castello Sforzesco
  Gallini, N. *Museo civico di antichi strumenti musicali*, Milan 1958

Naples: Museo Nazionale (Antique musical instruments)
Rome: Museo dell'Accademia di Santa Cecilia
THE NETHERLANDS
The Hague: Haags Gemeentemuseum
  Ligtvost, A.W. *Exotische en oude europese muziekinstr. in de muziekafdeling van het haagse gemeentemuseum*, The Hague 1955
Leiden: Rijksmuseum van Oudheden
Utrecht: National Museum van Speeldoos tot Pierment (Special collections of mechanical musical instruments)
SPAIN
Barcelona: Museo de Musica
SWEDEN
Stockholm: Musikhistoriska Museet
  Svanberg, J. *Musikhistoriska Museet i Stockholm—Instrumentsamling*, Stockholm 1902
SWITZERLAND
Greifensee: Sammlung historischer Blechblasinstrumente und Trommel
U.S.A.
Boston: Museum of Fine Arts
  Bessaraboff, N. *Ancient European Musical Instruments*, Boston 1941
Los Angeles: University of Southern California, School of Music
  Norvell, P.J. *A History and a Catalogue of the Albert Gale Collection of Musical Instruments*, 1952
Morristown: Yesteryear Museum (Special museum of mechanical musical instruments)
New York: Metropolitan Museum of Art—Crosby Brown Collection
  Catalogue of the Crosby Brown Collection of Musical Instruments of All Nations, New York 1904—05
Scarsdale: Museum of Music (Special museum of mechanical musical instruments)
  Graham, L. *A Pictorial Outline of the History of Mechanical Music*, New York 1967
U.S.S.R.
Leningrad: Institut teatra, muzyki i kinematografii
  Blagodatov, G.I. *Katalog muzykalnych instrumentov*, Leningrad 1972
Moscow: Gosudarstvennyj centralnyj muzej muzykalnoj kultury im. M.I. Glinky
  Kulikov, V.M. *Muzykalnye instrumenty narodov Sovetskogo soyuza v fondach Gosudarstvennogo centralnogo muzeya muzykalnoj kultury M.I. Glinky*, Moscow 1977

SELECTED BIBLIOGRAPHY

The first genuinely scientific literature on musical instruments appeared at the beginning of the 16th century but any more intensive research aiming at a deeper and more thorough understanding of the problems of organology from the physical and technical, musical and aesthetic or cultural and historical viewpoints dates from only as late as the last quarter of the 19th century.

The presented list is therefore primarily a selected bibliography of monographs on the individual instruments or of works dealing with distinct periods in the development of the latter. The list does not include individual studies and articles scattered in various periodicals.

General Bibliography

Agricola, M. *Musica Instrumentalis Deutsch.* Wittenberg, 1528—1545 facsimile Leipzig 1896

Alton, R. *Violin and Cello,* London 1964

Arakelian, S. *Die Geige,* Frankfurt 1968

Avgerinos, G. *Lexikon der Pauke,* Frankfurt 1964 *Handbuch der Schlag- und Effektinstrumente,* Frankfurt 1967

Bacher, J. *Die Viola da Gamba,* Kassel 1932

Bahnert-Herzberg-Schramm. *Metallblasinstrumente,* Leipzig 1958

Baines, A. *Woodwind Instruments and their History,* London 1957 *Musical Instruments through the Ages,* London 1963 *European and American Musical Instruments,* London 1966

Baron, E.G. *Historisch-theoretische und praktische Untersuchung des Instruments der Lauten,* Nürnberg 1727; facsimile Amsterdam 1965

Bate, P. *The Oboe,* London 1956 *The Trumpet and Trombone,* London 1966 *The Flute,* London 1975

Bedos de Celles, F. *L'Art du Facteur d'Orgues,* Paris 1776; facsimile Kassel 1934

Bohn, H. *Musikleben in Altertum und frühen Mittelalter,* Stuttgart 1954

Bermudo, J. *Declaración de Instrumentos musicales,* Osuna 1549; facsimile Kassel 1957

Beer, A. *Geigen: Originale, Kopien, Fälschungen, Verfälschungen,* Frankfurt 1967

Bessaraboff, N. *Ancient European Musical Instruments,* Boston 1941

Besseler, H. *Die Musik des Mittelalters und der Renaissance,* Potsdam 1931

Blades, J. *Percussion Instruments and their History,* London 1970

Boalch, D. *Makers of the Harpsichord and Clavichord,* London 1956

Bornefeld, H. *Das Positiv,* Kassel 1941

Bragard, R. and De Hen, F.J. *Musical Instruments in Art and History,* Rhode-Saint-Genèse 1967

Brandimeier, J. *Handbuch der Zither,* Munich 1963

Broholm, H., Larsen, W., Skjerne G. *The Lurs of the Bronze Age,* Copenhagen 1949

Brüchle B.—Janetzky K. *Kulturgeschichte des Horns,* Tutzing 1976

Buchner, A. *Extinct woodwind instruments of the sixteenth century,* Prague 1952 *Musical Instruments through the Ages,* Prague 1956 *Fiddling Angels at Karlštejn Castle,* Prague 1967 *Geigenverbesserer,* Kassel 1973

Buhle, E. *Die Musikalischen Instrumente in den Miniaturen des frühen Mittelalters, I. Die Blasinstrumente,* Leipzig 1903

Carse, A. *Musical Wind Instruments,* London 1939

Cervelli, L. *Contributi alla storia degli strumenti musicali in Italia. Rinascimento e Barocco,* Rome 1967

Closson, E. *Histoire du piano,* Brussels 1944

Daubeny, U. *Orchestral Wind Instruments, Ancient and Modern,* London 1920

Dolmetsch, N. *The Viola da Gamba,* London 1962

Dorf, R. *Electronic Musical Instruments,* New York 1954

Douglas, A. *The Electronic Musical Instrument Manual,* London 1957

Eichborn, H. *Die Trompete in alter und neuer Zeit,* Leipzig 1881

Eichelberger, H. *Das Akkordeon,* Leipzig 1964

Ellerhorst, W. *Handbuch der Orgelkunde.* Einsiedeln 1936

Euting, E. *Zur Geschichte der Blasinstrumente im 16. und 17. Jahrhundert,* Berlin 1899

Farga, F. *Geigen und Geiger,* Zürich 1940

Flood W.H. *The Story of the Bagpipe,* London and New York 1911 *The Story of the Harp,* London and New York 1905

Galpin, F.W. *The Music of the Sumerians ... the Babylonians and Assyrians,* Cambridge 1937

Girard, A. *Histoire et richesse de la Flute,* Paris 1953

Goehlinger, F.A. *Geschichte des Klavichords,* Basel 1910

Haacke, W. *Orgeln in aller Welt,* Stuttgart 1965

Hajdecki, A. *Die italienische Lira da Braccio,* Mostar 1892

Harrison, F. and Rimmer J. *European Musical Instruments,* London 1964

Heckel, W. *Der Fagott,* Leipzig 1931

Heinitz, W. *Instrumentenkunde.* Potsdam 1929

Henley, W. *Antonio Stradivari,* Brighton 1961 *Universal Dictionary of Violin and Bow Makers,* five volumes Brighton 1960

Hill, W.E. *Antonio Stradivari, his Life and Work,* London 1902

Hirt, F.J. *Meisterwerke des Klavierbaus,* Olten 1955

Hunt, E. *The Recorder and its Music,* London 1962

Jahnel, F. *Die Gitarre und ihr Bau,* Frankfurt 1963

Jansen, W. *The Bassoon, its History, Construction, Makers, Players and Music,* London 1978

Kinsky, G. *Katalog des Musikhistorischen Museums von Wilhelm Heyer in Köln,* Cologne 1912 *Geschichte der Musik in Bildern,* Leipzig 1929

Kirby, P.R. *The Kettle-Drums,* London 1930

Kool, J. *Das Saxophon,* Leipzig 1931

Langwill, L.G. *An Index of Musical Wind-Instrument Makers,* Edinburgh 1962 *The Bassoon and Contrabassoon,* London 1965

Lütgendorff, W. *Die Geigen- und Lautenmacher vom Mittelalter bis zur Gegenwart,* Frankfurt 1922

Marcuse, S. *Musical Instruments: A Comprehensive Dictionary,* New York 1964

Menke, W. *History of the Trumpet of Bach and Handel.* London 1934

Mersenne, M. *Harmonie universelle,* Paris 1636; facsimile London 1963

Morley-Pegge, R. *The French Horn,* London 1960

Neupert, H. *Das Cembalo,* Kassel 1956 *Vom Musikstab zum modernen Klavier,* Kassel 1960

Oeuvre collective *Das Akkordeon,* Leipzig 1964

Planyavsky, A. *Geschichte des Kontrabasses,* Tutzing 1970

Pohlmann, E. *Laute-Theorbe-Chitarrone,* Lilienthal-Bremen, 1977

Praetorius, M. *Syntagma Musicum,* Wolfenbüttel 1619; facsimile Kassel 1958

Rendall, F. *The Clarinet,* London 1957

Rensch, R. *The Harp,* New York 1950

Richmond S. *Clarinet and Saxophone Experience,* London 1977

Rühlmann, J. *Die Geschichte der Bogeninstrumente,* Brunswick 1882

Russell, R. *The Harpsichord and Clavichord,* London 1959

Sachs, C. *Reallexikon der Musikinstrumente,* Berlin 1913; *Sammlung alter Musikinstrumente bei der staatlichen Hochschule für Musik zu Berlin,* Berlin 1922; *Geist und Werden der Musikinstrumente,* Berlin 1929; *Handbuch der Musikinstrumentenkunde,* Leipzig 1930; *The History of Musical Instruments,* London 1942

Schultz, H. *Instrumentenkunde,* Leipzig 1931

Sharpe, A. P. *The Story of the Spanish Guitar,* London 1954

Smithers, Don L., *The Music and History of the Baroque trumpet before 1721,* London 1973

Stauder, W. *Alte Musikinstrumente,* Würzburg 1973

Straeten, W. van der *The History of the Violoncello, the Viol da Gamba, their Precursors,* London 1915 *The History of the Violin,* London 1933

Sumuer, W. K. *The Pianoforte,* London 1966

Vadding, M.—Merseburger, M. *Das Violoncello und seine Literatur,* Leipzig 1920

Virdung S. *Musica getutscht...,* Basel 1511; facsimile Kassel 1931

Winternitz, E. and Strunzi, L. *Die schönsten Musikinstrumente des Abendlandes,* Munich 1966

Bibliography on folk instruments

Alexandru, T. *Instrumentale muzicale ale poporului romin,* Bucharest 1956

Arbatsky, Y. *Beating the Tupan in the Central Balkans,* Chicago 1953

Aretz, I. *Instrumentos musicales de Venezuela,* Cumaná 1967

Atanassov, V. *Systematyka na Bulharskyte narodni muzykalny instrumenty,* Sofia 1977

Ayerstarán, L. *Música en el Uruguay,* Montevideo 1953

Baloch, N. A. *Musical Instruments of the Lower Indus Valley of Sind,* Hyderabad 1966

Bandopadhyaya, S. *The Music of India,* Bombay 1945

Bose, F. *Musikalische Völkerkunde,* Freiburg 1956

Brandel, R. *The Music of Central Africa,* The Hague 1961

Carrington, J. E. *Talking Drums of Africa,* London 1949

Collaer, P. *Ozeanien; Amerika (Musikgeschichte in Bildern),* Leipzig 1965, 1967

Daniélou, A. *La musique du Cambodge et du Laos,* Pondichéry 1957

Dhanit, Y. *Thai Musical Instruments,* Bangkok 1957

Farmer, H. G. *Studies in Oriental Musical Instruments,* Glasgow 1939,

Fischer, H. *Schallgeräte in Ozeanien,* Strasbourg 1958

Günther, R. *Musik in Rwanda,* Tervueren 1964

D'Harcourt, M. R. *La musique des Aymars sur les Hauts Plateaux Boliviens; La musique des Incas et ses survivances,* Paris 1925

Izikowitz, K. G. *Musical and Other Sound Instruments of the South American Indians,* Gothenburg 1935

Kaudera, W. *Musical Instruments in Celebes,* Gothenburg 1927

Kunst, J. A. *Hindoe-Javaansche Muziek-Instrumenten,* Weltevreden 1927

Kunz, L. *Die Volksmusikinstrumente der Tschechoslowakei,* Leipzig 1974

Laurenty, J. S. *Les chordofones du Congo Belge et du Ruanda-Urundi,* Tervueren 1960; *Les sanza du Congo,* Tervueren 1962

Leng, L. *Slovenské ľudové nástroje,* Bratislava 1967

Ling, J. *Nyckelharpan,* Stockholm 1967

Malm, W. P. *Japanese Music and Musical Instruments,* Rutland 1960

Martí, S. *Instrumentos musicales precortesianos,* Mexico City 1955

Oledzky, S. *Polskie instrumenty ludowe,* Cracow 1978

Ortiz, E. *Los instrumentos de la música Afrocubana,* Habana 1952—55

Reinhard, K. *Chinesische Musik,* Kassel 1956

Sárosi, B. *Die Volksmusikinstrumente Ungarns,* Leipzig 1966

Söderberg, B. *Les instruments de musique de Bas-Congo,* Stockholm 1956

Tran van Khê *La musique vietnamienne traditionnelle,* Paris 1962

Vega, C. *Los instrumentos musicales aborigines y criollos de la Argentina,* Buenos Aires 1943

Viertkov—Blagodatov—Jazovickaya *Atlas muzykalnych instrumentov narodov S.S.S.R.* Moscow 1963, second edition 1976

Walin, S. *Die schwedische Hummel,* Stockholm 1952

Williams, F. E. *Bull-roarers in the Papuan Gulf,* Port Moresby 1936

Wirz, P. *A Description of Musical Instruments from Central North-Eastern New Guinea,* Amsterdam 1952

Bibliography on mechanical musical instruments

Boston, C. N.—Langwill, L. G. *Church and Chamber Barrel-Organs,* Edinburgh 1967

Bowers, D. Q. *A Guidebook of Automatic Musical Instruments,* New York 1967—68; *Encyclopedia of Automatic Musical Instruments,* New York 1972

Buchner, A. *Mechanical Musical Instruments,* Prague 1958, facsimile New York 1979

Chapuis, A. *Automates, machines automatiques et machinisme,* Lausanne 1928; *Histoire de la boite à musique et de la musique mécanique,* Lausanne 1955

Chapuis, A.—Droz E. *Les automates,* Neuchâtel 1950

Clark, J. E. T. *Musical Boxes, A History and an Appreciation,* Birmingham 1948, 1952

Grew, S. *The Art of the Player-Piano,* London 1922

Hupfeld, L. *Dea-violina, die erste selbstspielende Violine,* Leipzig 1909

Mosoriak, R. *The Curious History of Music Boxes,* Chicago 1953

Newman, E. *The Piano-Player and its Music,* London 1920

INDEX OF NAMES

Abdul Hassan Ibn Haffi Ziryab 269
Abu-al Faraj al-Isfahani 42
Achilles 48.
Adlung, Jakob 110
Al Farabi (Alfarabius) 208
'Ala-ud Din, sultan of India 205
Albonesi, Afranio degli 93
Alexandre, père et fils 151, 155
Alphonso X, the Wise (Alfonso el Sabio), king of Leon and Castile 65
Amati, Nicóla 127, 133
Amír Chusrau 205
Anacreon 46
Andrea, Giovanni d' 100
Angermaier, Christoph 85
Aristotle 52
Arriaga 248
Ashurbanipal, king of Assyria 34, 35
Athenaus 43

Babitt, Milton 338
Bach, Johann Sebastian 101, 107, 135, 139, 141, 170, 178, 194
Bachet Bros 332, 333
Baldwin 335
Band, Heinrich 157
Barnia, Fedele 129
Baron, Ernest Gottlieb 108
Bauer, Jan 113
Beethoven, Ludwig van 319, 320
Bell Telephone System 337
Berlioz, Louis Hector 145, 146
Bermudo, Juan 76, 77
Bertrand 330
Besson, Fontaine 170, 182

Bidermann, Samuel 322, 323
Biest, Martin van der 110
Blühmel, F. 145
Boccherini, Luigi 121
Boehm, Theobald 161, 163, 164, 170, 171
Boethius, Anicius Manlius Severinus 58, 68
Brescia, Giovanni Maria da 111
Broadwood, John 130
Bruder Bros 325
Brueghel, Jan I ('Velvet Brueghel') 104, 310
Burgkmair, Hans 90
Burton, John 16
Buschmann, David 156, 157

Cahill, Thaddeus 330
Caldera and Bossi, Co. 192
Cambert 170
Casparini, Eugen 118
Červenka, A. 185
Červený, František Václav 8, 172, 181, 182
Champollion, Jean François 36
Charlemagne, king of the Franks 61
Charles VII, king of France 111
Charles the Bald 58—60
Cherubini, Luigi 164
Cicero, Marcus Tullius 50
Compenius, Essaias 89, 118
Constantine V (Copronymus), Byzantine emperor 69
Cousineau, Jacques-Georges 189
Cristofori, Bartolommeo 126, 128, 130
Ctesibius of Alexandria 56

Dardanus 58
David, king of the Hebrews 55, 69, 71, 265

Debain, Alexandre François 151
Debussy, Claude Achille 168, 171
Delaborde, Jean Baptiste 327, 330
Denner, Johann Christoph 116
Diodorus Siculus 28, 49
Diviš, Prokop 327
Dohnal, Joseph 169
Dolmetsch, Arnold 126
Domenichino (Zampieri, Domenico) 133
Donati 169
Dräger, Hans-Heinz 16
Dubois 194
Duiffopruggar 110
Dvořák, Antonín 170
Dyck, Sir Anthony van 75

Eberle, Jan Oldřich 142
Edison, Thomas Alva 314
Edlinger, Tomáš 124
Emmeram, Saint 61
Enescu, George 190
Ehe 103
Erard, Sebastian 189, 192
Eschenbach, C. F. 119
Esterházy, Nicholas, duke 142

Fétis, François Joseph 93
Flavius Vegetius Renatus 55
Frank, Johann Jobst 134
Franklin, Benjamin 149, 150
Fugger, family 108
Fürst, B. 116

Galli, Domenico 146
Gärtner, Anton 121

Genghis Khan 207
Gewaert, François Auguste 15
Girard, Philippe de 192
Glier, G. F. 119
Gluck, Christoph Willibald von 102, 161
Gossec, François-Joseph 163
Gossling 317
Goutrot 116
Grauwels, Hans 110
Gregory I, Saint, pope 69
Greenway, H. 185
Grenié, Gabriel Joseph 151
Grocheo, Johannes de 77
Grünewald, Matthias 100
Guarneri, Guiseppe (del Gesù) 133
Gudea, Lagash king 30
Gurlitt, Willibald 183

Haeckl, Anton 150
Haiden, Hans 192
Halliday 174
Hammond 331, 337
Hammurabi, king of Babylonia 31, 34
Handel, Georg Frederick 164, 178
Hass 103
Häusler, Josef 159
Haydn, Franz Joseph 142, 319
Hebenstreit, Pantaleon 128
Heckel W. 162, 167, 171
Helberger 330
Helst, Bartholomeus van der 109
Hero of Alexandria 55, 57
Herz, Henry 192
Hickmann, Hans 14, 17, 38, 41, 42
Hieronymus, Saint 58
Hieronymus de Moravia 15
Hildebrand, Zacharias 121
Hindemith, Paul 330
Hlaváček 186
Hollar, Václav 98
Homer 26, 44, 47
Honegger, Arthur 330
Horace 53
Hörlein, Karl Adam 194
Hornbostel, Erich M. von 15—17
Hotteterre, J. 6
Hotteterre, Louis 15
Hulinzký, Thomas 143
Hupfeld, Co. 325, 326
Hutchinson, Carleen 194

Ibn Sina (Avicenna) 208
Indy, Vincent d' 170
Isidore of Seville, Saint 79
Ivanov 330, 331
Ivert, Jacques 330

Jan of Středa, archbishop of Prague 79
Jantarski, Georgi 23, 25
John of Luxembourg, king of Bohemia 64
Joinville 79
Jolivet, André 330
Jordan 103
Josephus Flavius 42

Kaufmann, Angelica 148
Kendall, Charles 322
Kirchner, Leo 340
Knittlinger 159
Kotykiewicz 155
Kreitser 330, 331
Kühmeyer 192
Kunhuta, abbess 74
Kupecký, Jan 114
Kurfürst, Pavel 16, 17

Ladislav Pohrobek (Ladislaus the
    Posthumous), king of Bohemia and of
    Hungary 111
La Hire, Laurent de 94
Lanino, Bernardino 108
Lastman, Peter 112
Lefèbvre, Charles 190
Lehmann, Johann 12, 17
Lichtenstein, Ulrich von 64

Lídl 174, 180
Light, Edward 124, 135
Lionel 194
Louis IX, king of France 79
Louis XIV, king of France 12
Lyon, Gustave 190

Machaut, Guillaume de 64, 79, 125
Maestro del Cassone Adimari 82
Mager, Jörg 330
Mahillon, Victor Charles 15
Mahler, Gustav 178, 180
Majer, J.F.B.C. 85
Mälzel, Johann Nepomuk 320
Mantoya de Cardone, Johannes 107
Marcus Aurelius, emperor of Rome 53
Marius, Jean 128
Martenot, Maurice 330, 339

Martin, A. 321
Mason and Hamlin, Co. 156
Mauzaisse, Jean-Baptiste 137
Maximilian I, emperor of the Holy Roman
    Empire 90
Maximilian of Bavaria, duke 85, 191
Megaw, John Vincent Stanley 18
Meidling, Anton 95
Memling, Hans 76, 77, 103
Mendelssohn, Felix 102
Mersenne, Martin 84, 322
Michelangelo 135
Milhaud, Darius 330
Montagu, Jeremy 16
Moog, Robert 337, 339
Moritz 180
Mott, Isaac 192
Mozart, Wolfgang Amadeus 319
Muris, Johannes de 14
Mustel, Auguste 164

Nencheftkal, king of ancient Egypt 36
Nernst 330
Neuschel, Hans 103
Norlind, Tobias 17

Ongaro, Ignazio 126
Ott, Ondřej 108
Otto, Jacob Augustus 121

Pace, G. M. 132
Paganini, Nicolo 121
Pape, Jean Henri 190
Paul, Jean 150
Pentorisi, Murano da 97
Pepin the Short, king of the Franks 69
Pepoli, Hercule 141
Périnet, E. F. 173
Petzmeyer, Johann 191
Pfalz, Severin 159
Philo of Alexandria 56
Pitman 177
Pittrich 194
Plesbler, Francesco 134
Pollux, 32, 43
Popper 324
Praetorius, Michael 15, 77, 81, 84, 90, 93, 96
Pythagoras 69

Queisser 194
Quintus Ennius 54

Ramis 171
Ramses III, king of ancient Egypt 37
Raphael 135
Ravel, Maurice 168
Řebíček, František 315
Remigius, Saint, abbot 64
Richardson, Arthur 194
Rieger and Kloss 178, 182
Riemer, J.'s Sons 313
Rimski-Korsakov 330, 331
Ritter, Hermann 194
Röllig, Karl Leopold 190

Rossini, Gioacchino Antonio 102
Ruckers, Johannes 110, 138

Sachs, Curt 15—18
Sala, Oscar 330
Salò, Casparo da 110
Sattler 179
Sauer, Leopold 165
Sax, Adolphe 170, 182
Schaeffner, André 16
Schlegel, J. 115
Schlosser, J. 88
Schnitzer, A. 86, 103
Schönberg, Arnold 178
Schott, Martin 108
Schröter, Gottfried 128
Schubert, Franz 121, 150
Schunda, József V. 298, 299
Schweitzer, Albert 183
Sellas, Georgius 130
Seufert, Josef 168
Sieber, H. 122
Silbermann, Andreas 121
Silbermann, Gottfried 121, 130
Slocombe, Shirley 144
Solomon, king of Israel 41
Sousa, John Philip 182
Speer, Daniel 98
Spielman 330
Špork, František, count 116
Sprenger, Eugen 194
Stamic, Jan 117
Stein, A. 122
Stein, Johann Andreas 130
Stelzner, A. 183, 194
Stodart, R. 122
Stölzel, H. 145
Stradivari, Antonio 59, 133, 137, 144
Strauss, Richard 146, 171, 330
Streicher, Johannes 133, 192
Šudré 182

Tagore, Rabindranath 201
Theremin, Lev Sergeevich 330, 336
Thureau-Dangin, F. 30
Tiefenbrunner, Georg 161
Tieffenbrucker, Vendelin 102, 111
Tielke, Joachim 145
Tournieres, Robert 6
Trajan 27, 54
Trasuntinus, Vitus de 103
Trautwein, Friedrich 330
Tutankhamen, king of ancient Egypt 38, 39

Veleslavín, Daniel Adam of 110
Venantius Honorius Clementianus
    Fortunatus 28
Verdi, Giuseppe 178, 184
Vespasianus, Titus Flavius Sabinus, Roman
    emperor 42, 43
Vigna, Amendolo 52
Virchi, Girolamo de 91
Virdung, Sebastian 92
Vitruvius 57
Voboam, Jean 127
Vollner, Wilhelm 316
Votey, E. S. 325
Vuillaume, J. B. 183, 194

Wagner, Richard 102, 179, 182, 194
Walther, Johann Gottfried 117
Weber, Carl Maria von 121
Weidinger, A. 174
Wellington 322
Wenceslaus IV, king of Bohemia 79
Wheatstone, Charles 156
Wieprecht, Wilhelm Friedrich 180
Wild, Johann 148
Willer, Jan Michael 122
Winterhoff, H. E. 166
Wolfenbüttel, duke of 118

Zampieri, Domenico see Domenichino
Zídek, Pavel, of Prague 110
Zoffany, John 150

INDEX OF TOPICS

Accordion 13, 153, 156, 157, 183, 211, 281, 283, 291, 303, 311
Adulf (tambourine) 311
Agach-komuz (temur) (plucked chordophone) 211
Agogo (double bell) 254
Aida trumpet 170, 178, 342
Akakinda (xylophone) 259
Alaud (flute) 311
Alboka (hornpipe) 311
Alto aulos 47
Alto cornet 179
Alto saxophone 166
Alto viol 193
Alto viola d'amore 141
Ambira (xylophone) 259
American organ (cottage organ) 156
Angle harp 34, 35, 38–40
Angra okwena (lute) 262
Anklet jingles 246
Anklung (rattle) 242, 244
Anvil 69, 168
Appalachian dulcimer 257
Apunga (horn) 258, 260
Arched harp 38
Archlute 108
Archzittern 131
Arghul al kebir (double clarinet) 265, 267
Aulos 44–48, 49, 50, 52, 53
Automatic spinet 323
Automatic zither 324
Automatophonic banjo 322
Automatophonic violin 324
Autophone 15
Aylliquepa (trumpet) 251
Ayotl (scraper) 248
Azarags 289, 291
Bach (piccolo) trumpet 101, 178
Bagana (lyre) 264, 265
Bagpipe 14, 59, 62, 68, 69, 80, 85, 94, 122, 201, 267–269, 273, 284, 285, 290–292, 294, 297, 301, 303, 308, 310, 311
Bajón (panpipe) 253
Bala (xylophone) 259
Balafo (xylophone) 259
Balalaika 293
Baldwin electric harpsichord 335
Bandonion 157
Bandura 284
Bangu (drums) 216
Banjo 13, 184, 257
Bansari (flute) 205
Bansora (flute) 205
Barbiton 46, 50
Baritone 194
Baritone horn 180
Baritone oboe 171
Baroxyton 182
Barrel drum 39, 203, 235, 250, 251, 265
Barrel organ 313, 316, 318, 319, 322
Barrel piano (organetto) 321, 325
Bass (steel drum) 255
Bass cittern 99, 122
Bass clarinet 170, 341
Bass cornett 102, 103, 150, 154, 180
Bass drum 13, 196, 302
Bass flugelhorn 180, 343
Bass horn 28, 103, 171, 180
Bass lute 108, 303
Bass oboe 171, 341
Bass bombard 84, 85, 93
Bass recorder 93, 94
Bass sordone 86, 87
Bass trombone 178, 179
Bass trumpet 178
Bass tuba 103, 180, 181, 193, 342
Bass viol (barytone, viola di bordone) 101, 141, 145
Bass viola da gamba 145
Basset horn 341
Basso di camera 139
Bassoon 13, 84, 88, 94, 96, 116, 117, 160, 162, 167, 171, 172, 341

Bassophone 331
Batá (membrane drum) 254
Baya (drum) 207
Bayan (concertina) 283
Bayan (drum) 203
Baza (xylophone) 259
Bazaree (nose flute) 201
Beaten zither 271
Beater 211, 238, 242, 251, 256, 259, 310
Bedug (drum) 242
Belfry bell 61
Bell 78, 146, 163, 211, 217, 223, 233, 246, 256, 291
Bell chimes 280, 289, 313, 314
Bellarmonic 148
Bendir (tambourine) 269
Bin 202
Biniou bras (bagpipe) 310
Biniou koz (bagpipe) 310
Bird organ 319
Black cornett 90, 96, 98, 102, 104
Bladder pipe 62, 67, 90
Board zither 190, 213, 268, 270, 271, 273, 282, 291
Bohemian flute 64
Bohemian wing (ala bohemica) 72, 73, 75
Bombaa (drum) 264
Bombaix (drum) 264
Bombard 83, 84, 94, 112, 116
Bombardo sopranino 84
Bombardon 181
Bombardone 84
Bongoes (drums) 13, 197, 250
Botija (vessel flute) 250
Bouzouki (lute) 303
Bow harp 32, 237, 262
Bowed piano 192
Bowed zither 164, 191, 234, 278
Brass instruments 8, 51, 54, 96, 98, 101, 103, 116, 142, 145, 172–174, 180–182
Brass wind instruments 172–174
Buccina 53, 55, 67, 301
Bucium (trumpet) 294, 299, 301
Bull-roarer 245, 253, 254, 258
Bumbass 257
Burubush (serburu, adys-oro) (bull-roarer) 258
Button accordion 186
Cabaca (rattle) 250
Caboca (afoxe) (rattle) 253
Caccarella (friction drum) 303
Cai-ken 237
Calleidophone 330
Carillon 73, 312, 313, 322
Carimbá (membrane drum) 254
Carnyx (trumpet) 24, 26, 27
Castanets 159, 167, 248, 266, 308
Celesta 13, 164, 341
Cello 137, 255
Cetera 73, 74
Cha-cha (rattles) 247
Chagana 211
Chakan 93
Chalamelle (chalemie) 62
Chang (dulcimer) 209
Changi (harp) 212, 213
Chang-ku (drum) 216, 223, 226
Chapei (lute) 235–238
Charango (guitar) 249, 253
Cherepov double-row concertina (cherepovskaya) 281
Chettö (flute) 220
Chianuri (fiddle) 211
Chieng (gong) 238
Chililihtli (side-blown flute) 248
Chimes 61, 164, 217, 238, 241, 242
Chiming clock 314
Chinese cymbal 162
Chirimia (shawm) 248
Chitarra battente 108, 125
Chitarrone 94, 107, 108
Chitike (jingles) 200
Choir bassoon 96
Chonguri 213

Choor (flute) 208
Chord harmonica 159
Chromatic harp 185, 190
Chu (xylophone) 217
Cigale (friction drum) 310
Cimbalom (dulcimer) 13, 71, 207, 271, 298, 299
Circular horn 269
Cithern (cittern, citola, zitter) 91, 121, 122
Clappers 19, 38, 46, 59, 60, 68, 216, 217, 237, 238, 245, 254, 291, 296, 302, 303, 307
Clarina 116
Clarinet 13, 37, 115–117, 142, 161, 164, 170, 200, 201, 265, 302, 341
Clarinetto 116
Clavecin à maillets 128
Claves (sticks) 249
Clavichord (manicordium) 72, 78, 95, 99, 110, 126
Clavicylinder 148
Clavicytherium 79
Clavioline 331
Cobla (band) 311
Cobza (lute) 299, 306
Coelestine 148
Cog rattle 168, 281, 291, 296, 309
Compestating horn 179
Concertina 156, 186, 281, 283, 311
Congas (drums) 13, 196, 250
Consonanta organ 331
Contrabass clarinet 341
Contrabass trombone 179
Contrabass tuba 180, 181, 343
Contrabass violin 135
Contr'alto 194
Contreserpent 103
Cor de chasse (trompe de chasse) 116, 117
Cornet 85, 173, 179
Cornet à piston 173, 179, 187
Cornett 64, 67, 84, 85, 96, 98, 101, 116, 187
Cornon 182
Cornophone 180, 182
Cornu 53, 54, 55
Cowbell 244, 254
Crot 28
Crotals 168
Crowd (crot, crwth) 278
Crumhorn 85, 90, 93, 94, 116
Crystal trombone 332
Cuatro (guitar) 249
Curved trumpet 83
Cymbals 13, 34, 35, 40–42, 49, 57, 59, 61, 155, 161, 162, 196, 200, 216, 217, 222, 226, 239, 241, 266
Da-daiko (drum) 229
Daf (drum) 213, 273
Daina (drum) 203
Damar (rattle drum) 208
Dan bau 237, 238
Dan day (lute) 235, 237
Dan-to-rung (chimes) 238
Darabuka (goblet drum) 272, 305
Daulpaz (kettledrum) 208
Deblek (drum) 270
Decachord 59
Deff (drum) 42
Denis d'or (electric mutation orchestrion) 327
Dessus (bombard) 84
Dhola (drum) 199, 205
Didgeridoo 243, 245
Dilliüdük (flute) 270
Dimba (xylophone) 259
Dinaphone 330
Diplipito (kettledrum) 211
Diplokithara see harp-lute
Djaff (tambourine) 212
Djunadjan (bowed zither) 234
Dobro (guitar) 257
Doira (tambourine) 209, 211
Dombra (lute) 208
Double-action pedal harp 189
Double aulos 42, 52

Double bass 194, 253, 311, 343
Double bass viol (violone) 117, 135
Double bassoon (contrabassoon) 160, 171, 341
Double bell 254
Double-bladder shawm 65
Double clarinet 61, 201, 267
Double drum 28
Double English flageolet 155, 169
Double escapement piano 192
Double flute 29, 283–285
Double goblet drum see waisted drum
Double guitar 128
Double-headed drum 24 25, 79, 203, 211, 251, 256, 309
Double musical bow 254
Double-row concertina 281
Double shawm 34, 36, 39, 40, 52, 198, 201
Drum 8, 18, 28, 34, 42, 64, 69, 80, 184, 195–197, 200, 203, 204, 206–208, 211, 213–216, 222–227, 229, 230, 232–239, 242, 244, 247, 249–257, 260, 262–264, 268, 270, 271, 273, 302, 305, 310
Drum set 203, 237, 240
Drumstick 79, 205, 223
Dudaram (gong chimes) 208
Dudka 284
Düdük (shawm) 273
Dulcian 94, 96, 97, 101
Dulcimer 13, 71, 78, 110, 126, 128, 140, 209, 213, 219, 234, 242, 257, 271, 272, 291, 298, 307, 343
Dumbelek (drum) 273
Dumbrak 209
Dutar 209
Dvodentivka 284
Dvoyachka (double flute) 294
Dvoynitsa (double flute) 302
Echequier 125
Ei-chek (fiddle) 274
Electric harpsichord 330, 335
Electric organ 330
Electrified double bass 331
Electrified guitar 331
Electrified piano 331
Electrified saxophone 331
Electrified violin 331
Electronic organ 187, 334, 336, 337
Electronium 331
Electrophone 330
Electrophonic guitar 327, 328
Emeriton 330, 331
End-blown flute 230, 233, 234, 236, 241, 251, 260, 294
English flageolet 168
English horn 157, 171, 341
English violetta 142
Epinette des Vosges (zither) 310
Erh-hu (fiddle) 221, 224
Esrar (esraj) 140, 202, 205
Entaala (xylophone) 259
Euphone 148
Euphonium 172, 180, 343
Fang-sian 214
Fiddle 58, 59, 62, 63, 65, 67, 68, 69, 73, 75–78, 80, 108, 140, 202, 205–207, 209–213, 221, 222, 224, 236–238, 257, 270, 271, 285, 292, 301, 303, 311
Fidla 278
Fingerholed horn 61
Fipple flute 25, 245, 266, 292, 299, 309, 310
Fistule 64
Flageolet 25, 75, 190, 302
Flaios 64
Flavial (chiruba, llauto) (pipe) 310
Flexatone 159, 167
Flugelhorn 174, 175, 180
Fluier (flute) 299
Flute 6, 13, 17, 20, 21, 23, 26, 30, 31, 34, 37, 61, 62, 64, 65, 69, 115, 156, 161, 169, 170, 201, 207, 208, 216, 219, 230, 233, 234, 246, 249, 251, 252, 266, 270, 277, 284, 286, 288, 289, 291, 292, 295, 299, 302, 303, 305, 310, 311, 341
Flute-and-tabor 305
Flute de Behaigne (Bohemian flute) 64
Flûte douce 62
Flute-playing clock 319

Flute with fingerholes 246
Fonikon 182
Forgólant (hurdy-gurdy) 298, 304
Forminx 44
Four-sided harp 59
Frame drum 28, 32, 34, 35, 39, 42, 49, 197, 254, 271, 302
French horn 116–119, 150, 179, 342
Fretted clavichord 110
Friction drum 264, 303, 309, 310
Fue (side-blown flute) 228
Fujara (fuyara) (end-blown flute) 93, 294, 300
Fujarka (flute) 292
Gadulka (fiddle) 298, 299, 301, 302
Gagaku (drum) 228, 229
Gagaku (ensemble) 227, 229, 230, 234
Gaita (bagpipe) 311
Gajdy (gaydy) (bagpipe) 294
Gaku-biwa (lute) 228, 230
Gaku-so (zither) 230
Galatean salpinx 26
Galati (talking drum) 263
Galoubet (fipple flute) 64, 310
Gambong kayu (xylophone) 242
Ganza (rattle) 253
Gaul horn 26
Gaval (drum) 211
Gawaq (fipple flute) 266
Geigenwerk 192
Gender barung (metallophone) 242
Gender panembung (chimes) 241
Gender panerus (metallophone) 242
Gezarke (lyre) 261
Gidzhak 209
Gigue (jig fiddle) 59
Giraffe piano 168
Glass harmonica 148–151
Glockenspiel 13, 64, 78, 164, 173, 184, 341
Gogen ('lune guitar') 233
Gong 13, 20, 155, 163, 217, 223, 226, 229, 233–235, 238, 241, 341
Gong chimes 208, 217, 218, 234–239, 241
Gora (musical bow) 261
Goral gajdy (gaydy) (bagpipe) 294
Gourd rattle 257, 258
Gralla (shepherd shawm) 310
Grand harp 35
Gravicembalo col piano e forte 125
Great bass viol 109
Güiro 250, 253
Guitar 13, 34, 76, 77, 108, 118, 121, 124, 127, 129, 130, 214, 221, 222, 224, 233, 245, 249, 253–255, 257
Guitar (steel drum) 255
Gusle (fiddle) 302, 303
Gusli 281, 292
Hackbrett (dulcimer) 307
Halil 41, 42
Hammond (pipeless) organ 331, 337
Handbell 61, 78, 104, 208
Handäoline 156
Hardangerfele (fiddle) 275, 278
Harmonetta 160
Harmonica 159–161
Harmonium 13, 150, 151, 153, 155, 156, 164, 192, 343
Harmonium d'art 155
Harp 3, 14, 17, 25, 29, 32, 36, 37, 38, 39, 41, 42, 47, 59, 60, 63, 64, 69, 71, 72, 74, 76, 78, 92, 121, 137, 145, 181, 185, 189, 202, 212, 213, 216, 237, 249–251, 258, 265, 266, 309, 343
Harp cittern 102
Harp-lute (diplokithara) 124, 135, 262
Harp-playing clock 325
Harpsichord 13, 72, 98, 99, 103, 104, 110, 113, 121, 126, 133, 140, 141, 343
Harpsichord-spinet 138
Hazozra (trumpet) 41–43
Heckel clarinet 170
Heckelphone 171
Helicon 181
Hellertion 330
Hichikiri 228
High-hat cymbal 163
Highland pipe 310
Hne (shawm) 237

Home organ 158
Hook harp 159, 184
Horn 13, 22, 23, 26, 27, 38, 41, 49, 51, 60, 64, 65, 67, 80, 116, 174, 179, 201, 202, 206, 250, 252, 258, 280, 289, 292
Hornpipe 311
Hsing-erh 216, 222, 226
Huancar (single-headed drum) 251
Huehuetl (single-membrane drum) 247
Hummel (langleik humle, hommel) (zither) 278–280, 310
Hunga (mtangala, ndimbga, qubo, hade) (musical bow) 261
Hunting horn 104, 116 see also cor de chasse
Hurdy-gurdy 59, 63, 78, 79, 277, 278, 287, 298, 304, 310
Hydraulis (water organ) 42, 55–57
Iasti-balaban 211
Iba (rattle) see sistrum
Ike (trumpet) 253
Ilimba (xylophone) 259
Ingome (drum) 254
Ingungu (friction drum) 264
Iochin (dulcimer) 207
Ionica 331
Ipu (stamping instrument) 245
Irish harp 71, 311
Irish trumpet 28
Italian cymbal 163
Jazz drum kit 197
Jazz trumpet 178, 187
Jew's harp 208, 209, 245, 293
Jhanja (cymbals) 199, 200
Jig fiddle 59
Jingles 28, 39, 42, 61, 78, 80, 200, 201, 209, 211, 233, 246, 271, 307, 308
Joca (drum) 250
Kabak kamanje (fiddle) 271
Kabaro (drum) 265
Kagura-fue 229
Kakko (drum) 229
Kalamé 48
Kalamos 48
Kalanba (xylophone) 259
Kankles (kokle, kannel) (board zither) 282, 291
Kantele (zither) 275, 276, 278
Kanteleharpe (jouhikko) 277, 278
Karna (trumpet) 269
Karnay (trumpet) 209, 210
Kashbah (flute) 266
Kaval (flute) 295, 302
Kayagum (zither) 231
Kemanje (spike fiddle) 212
Kena (end-blown flute) 251
Kerar (lyre) 264, 265
Kettledrum 78–80, 111, 184, 194, 195, 203, 205, 208, 209, 211, 263, 265, 268, 271, 273
Keyboard harp 190
Keyboard monochord 330, 339
Keyed bugle 170
Keyed fiddle 278
Keyed trumpet 167, 174
Khen (mouth harmonica) 235, 236
Khnoue (trumpet) 38
Khong (gong chimes) 235, 239
Khong vong yai 236, 239
Kinnor 41, 42
Kissar (lyre) 261
Kissumba (lyre) 261
Kit (pocket violin) 139, 144
Kithara (cithara) 42, 44, 46, 47, 51, 52, 55, 60
Kitharic aulos 47
Kitharis 44
Kiyak 208
Kjamani 213
Kluy (klui, khloy) (end-blown flute) 236
Koboz (lute) 270
Kobyz (bowed instrument) 208, 209, 211
Kohlo (musical bow) 254
Koka zvana (bell chimes) 289
Komuz 210, 211
Koncovka (end-blown flute) 292, 294
Koto (zither) 230, 231
Koza (bagpipe) 285
Koziol (bagpipe) 292
Kraatspill (scraper) 289

350

Ku (drum) 222
Kuan (shawm) 216
Ku-chêng 230
Ku ch'in (zither) 207, 219, 230
Kung-hou (harp) 216
Künkülkawe (musical bow) 254
Kurtar (jingles) 200
Kurbelspärophon 330
Kuvikli (panpipe) 284, 289
Laghouti (lute) 303
Lap organ 156
Large trumpet 277
Launeddas (multiple clarinet) 303
Limba (flute) 207
Linguaphone 16
Lira (bowed string instrument) 77, 108
Lira (flute) 277
Lira (relya) (hurdy-gurdy) 287
Lira da braccio 100, 104, 111
Lira da gamba 111, 139
Liraki (fiddle) 303
Lirone perfetto 108
Lituus (trumpet) 49, 51, 53, 54, 55, 60
Livny concertina (livenskaya) 281
Lo (gong) 226
Lozhki 281
Luch'in (zither) 221
Luddu (flute) 277
Lu-sheng (mouth harmonica) 219
Lur 22, 26, 280
Lute 9, 32, 34—36, 38—41, 47, 59, 68, 74, 75,
  77, 78, 80, 92, 94, 98, 104, 106—108, 112, 113,
  121, 200, 205, 208, 211, 213, 221, 223, 230,
  231, 235, 237, 238, 262, 266, 269, 270, 273,
  274, 299, 303
Lyra (spike fiddle) 273
Lyre 25, 28—30, 32—35, 38—42, 44, 46, 47,
  50, 52, 124, 132, 258, 261, 264, 265, 273
Lyre-guitar 124, 132
Lyre harp 32, 33, 38
Machete (guitar) 245
Machine kettledrum 194
Magrefah 42
Makoma (compositions) 209
Mandira (cymbals) 200
Mandoline (Milanese, Neapolitan) 13, 134,
  343
Mandora 75, 78
Manopan 317, 322
Maraca (rattle) 248, 250, 253
Margaretum 79, 80
Marimba 250, 251, 253, 257
Massá (clapper) 303
Mathala 203
Mazanki (fiddle) 292
Mbila (xylophone) 259
Mechanical carillon 313
Mechanical spinet 322
Mellodeon 156
Melodica (automatophone) 316
Melodica (mouth organ) 159
Melodica (electronic musical
  instrument) 331
Melopiano 192
Mezúd (bagpipe) 268, 269
Miagaro (drum) 264
Mixturtrautonium 330
Mointsim (drum) 264
Mok kaval (trumpet) 233
Monochord 64, 69, 110, 238
Moog synthesizer 337, 338, 339
'Moon guitar' 221, 224
Morinchur (fiddle) 207, 210
Moses (drum) 264
Moshuk (bagpipe) 201
Moshupiane (friction drum) 264
Mouth harmonica (mouth organ) 157, 159,
  215, 216, 219, 220, 226, 229, 234—236, 343
Mridanga 203
Multiple clarinet 303, 307
Mundäoline 157
Musette (bagpipe) 122
Music box 314—316, 320
Music clock 319
Musical bow 20—27, 245, 254, 255, 259—261
Musicational organ 337
Nacchara 308

Nagarit (drum) 264
Nagasuaram (shawm) 199, 201
Nagora (kettledrums) 209, 211
Nai (panpipe) 299
Nai (side-blown flute) 209
Nail violin (nail harmonica) 148, 149
Naka ya lethlake (side-blown flute) 260
Naker (nacaire) (kettledrum) 79
Naquara (kettledrum) 205, 213
Naquarit (kettledrum) 265
Naqquara tbilat (kettledrums) 268, 273
Nay (flute) 37, 266, 299
Ndöna (lute) 262
Nefir (trumpet) 269
Nernst's piano 330
Niau kani (jew's harp) 245
Nira (fipple flute) 266
Noordsche Balk (zither) 310
Nose flute 245, 253
Novorzhev concertina
  (novorzhevskaya) 289
Nunut (slit drum) 245
Nyckelharpa (bowed fiddle) 277, 278
Ö (scraper) 234
Oboe 13, 37, 116, 150, 157, 162, 170, 341
Oboe d'amour 117, 170, 341
Oboe da caccia 171
Obukane (lyre) 261
Ocarina 155, 169, 190
Octave lute 104, 108
Octave virginal 110
Old Norse harp 311
Oliphant 61
Ombutu (talking drum) 263
Ondes Martenot (keyboard monochord) 330,
  336
Ophicleide 103, 174, 180
Orchestrion 317, 320, 322, 324, 325
Organ (pipe organ) 13, 14, 17, 21, 64, 65,
  88, 94, 113, 117, 118, 121, 122, 130, 151,
  176—178, 182—184, 186—189, 219, 319, 320,
  334, 338, 343
Orgue à percussion 155
Orpharion 122
Orphica 169, 190
Osevenji (drum) 264
Ottavina (virginal) 110
Outi (lute) 303
Ozguris (horn) 289
Pahu (slit drum) 244, 245
P'ai-pan (clapper) 216, 217
P'ai-siao (panpipe) 218, 219
Pandeiro (frame drum) 254
Panderoyotzale (tambourine) 311
Pandora 117, 122, 124
Pandorina 93, 126
Panharmonicon 320
Panpipe 20, 25, 28, 34, 47, 48, 52, 64, 85, 218,
  219, 245, 246, 249, 252, 253, 284, 299
Pantaleon (dulcimer) 128
Pardessus de viola 134
Partiturophone 330
Pastierska píšťala 292
Patvany (drum set) 237, 240
Paung (bowed harp) 237
Pchiri (flute) 234
Peaked harp 135
Pedál cimbalom 298
Pedal harp 136, 137, 184
Percussion instruments 14, 15, 146, 236, 248
Pey (shawm) 235, 238
Peyote (drum) 257
Peyphat (ensemble) 235
Phach (clappers) 238
Phagotum 93, 94, 96
Phonograph 314, 316
Phonoliszt-Violina 325, 326
Physharmonica 150, 153
Piano 13, 122, 126, 128, 133, 150, 157, 164,
  188, 189, 192, 193, 325, 326, 343
Piano accordion 157
Piano éolien 192
Piano harmonica 149
Pianola (player piano) 322, 325, 326
Pibcorn (Welsh hornpipe) 311
Piccolo bassoon 96
Piccolo cornet 179

Piccolo flute 156, 170, 341
Piccolo-heckelphone 164, 171
Pien ch'ing (lithophone) 214, 217
Pien-chung (gong chime) 218
Piffero (shawm) 309
Pi nai (shawm) 236
Ping pong (steel drum) 255
Pinnate (friction drum) 310
Piob mór (warpipe) 310
Piob villean (small pipe) 310
P'i-p'a (lute) 221, 223
Pipe 10, 20, 30, 41, 53, 64, 266, 310
Pipe and tabor combination 64, 65, 310, 311
Pipeless organ 331
Piphet (orchestra) 236
Po (bell) 215
Pocket violin (kit) 139, 144
Po-fu (drum) 216, 222
Pointed harp 135
Polyphone 316
Polyphonic 160
Portative (portable organ) 68, 69, 76, 78, 121
Positive (non-portable organ) 69, 89, 117
Postal horn 104
Prillar (shepherd horn) 280
Psalmodicon (bowed zither) 278
Psalterion 271
Psaltery 59, 63, 68, 69, 71—73, 77, 78, 110,
  266, 270, 275, 291, 310
Psaltery harp 32, 70—73, 74
Quanun (board zither) 213, 268, 270, 271, 273
Quaraquit (castanets) 266
Quart violin 135
Quarto bassoon 96
Quena (end-blown flute) 251
Quinterne 75
Quinto bassoon 96
Quinton 135, 139, 143
Rabab (fiddle) 271
Racket 85, 87, 88, 116
Rag-dung (trumpet) ·228
Ranasringa (horn) 27, 201, 202
Rang nat (xylophone) 239
Raspador (scraper) 248
Rattle 19, 34, 38, 61, 227, 242, 245—248, 250,
  253, 256, 257, 291
Rattle drum 208
Rauschpfeife 84, 90
Rayta (shawm) 269
Rebab (spike fiddle) 207, 209, 237, 241, 243,
  267, 270
Rebec 64, 75
Rebeca (fiddle) 311
Reco-reco (güiro) (scraper) 250, 253
Recorder 13, 85, 90, 93, 104, 108, 114, 133,
  266, 341
Reed tube zither 245
Rhythm (steel drum) 255
Robob (fiddle) 209
Rog (horn) 292
Rommelpot (friction drum) 309
Roneat-ek (xylophone) 235, 236
Roria (jew's harp) 245
Rote 28, 59, 67
Rozhok (shepherd horn) 283, 284
Ryuteki (yoko) fue 229
Sackbut 103
Salpinx 47, 49
Salterio tedesco (psaltery) 71
Sambuca 110
Samisen (guitar-like instrument) 230, 233
San-no-tsuzumi (drum) 230, 232, 234
Sansa (mbira, omposhawa, usimbi, dimba,
  ekende, ibeka, pokido, ambira) 256, 258,
  259
Santir (santoor) (dulcimer) 213, 271, 272
Sarangi (fiddle) 140, 202, 205, 206
Saratov concertina (saratovskaya) 281, 287
Sarinda 202, 207
Saron (metallophone) 240, 241
Saron barung (metallophone) 241
Saron panerus (peking) (metallophone) 241
Sarrusophone 167
Saung (harp) 237
Sax horn (baritone) 182, 191
Saxophone 13, 142, 162, 169, 170, 342
Sceta vajasse (scraper) 307

Scheitholt (zither) 310
Schlüsselfiedel (keyed fiddle) 278
Scraper 19, 21, 217, 234, 246, 248, 250, 253, 257, 289, 302, 307
Se (dulcimer) 219, 242
Sehem 38
Selslim 41, 42
Semipsaltery (micanon) 72
Serpent (bass cornett) 102, 103, 150, 154, 180
Sghanin (double clarinet) 267
Shah nefir (circular horn) 269
Shakuhachi (end-blown flute) 230, 233
Shawm 39, 42, 48, 61, 62, 68, 77, 78, 82, 84, 90, 94, 104, 116, 170, 199, 209, 211, 216, 220, 226, 235–238, 248, 266, 267, 269, 272–274, 291, 298, 299, 303, 311
Sheng (mouth harmonica) 215, 216, 219, 220, 226, 229, 234, 236
Shepherd fipple flute 292
Shepherd horn 280, 283, 284
Shepherd trumpet 294
Shofar 41, 42
Shoko (gong) 227, 229
Shruti upangi (bhezana shruti) (bagpipe) 201
Siao (vertical flute) 216
Side-blown (cross, transverse) flute 13, 52, 53, 90, 93, 116, 170, 209, 216, 219, 220, 227, 228, 248, 260
Side drum 13, 79, 195, 196
Silbador (whistle) 248, 253
Sime-daiko (drum) 232
Singing chips 245
Single hand flute 66, 254
Single-headed drum 244, 250, 251, 256
Sistrum (iba rattle, sehem) 36, 38, 40, 52, 61, 265
Skorthom (drum) 235, 239
Skrabalas (bell chimes) 280, 289
Skuducisi (skuduchisi) (flute) 289
Slentem gantung (chimes) 241
Slide trombone 172, 179, 342
Slide trumpet 76, 82, 103
Slit drum 244, 245, 247
Snare drum 13, 195
Snug (metallophone) 266
Sonajas (rattle) 248
Sopel (whistle flute) 283, 284
Sopilka 284
Soprano cornet 179
Soprano lute 106
Soprano recorder 94
Soprano saxophone 166
Sordine 98, 104, 139, 213
Sordine spinet 139
Sordone 81, 84, 87, 88, 116
Sousaphone 181, 182, 191
Sphärophone 330
Spike fiddle 207, 209, 212, 237, 241, 243, 265, 267, 270, 273
Spinet 97, 110, 126, 138, 322
Spinetta (virginal) 110
Sringa (horn) 206
Stamping pit 257
Stamping stick 289
Stamping tubes 245
Stick 80, 195, 196, 207, 227, 237, 245, 247, 250, 273, 310
Stick bow 202
Stick zither 202
Straight trumpet 76, 83
Stråkharpa 278, 280
Subbass tuba 180
Subcontrabassoon 172
Sudrophone 172, 182
Sulino (end-blown flute) 241
Suo-na (shawm) 220, 226
Surnay (shahnai) (double shawm) 198, 201

Sybyzgi (flute) 208
Synthesizer 336–339
Svirel (double flute) 284
Svistilka (whistle) 286
Syrinx (panpipe) 20, 21, 28, 34, 47, 48, 56
Tabla (drum) 203, 205, 207
Table piano 165
Tabor (tambour) 64, 196, 305, 310
Taiko (drum) 229
Taille (pommer) 84
Tála (cymbals) 200
'Talking drums' 222, 263, 264
Tallharpha 278
Tamboril (drum) 305, 311
Tambourine 13, 31, 39, 42, 47, 68, 79, 108, 112, 197, 209, 211–213, 256, 269, 271, 299, 311
Tambura 205, 303
Tam-tam 13, 163
Tanbura 209, 299, 301
Tar (tara, chongur) (lute) 211
Tar (plucked chordophone) 212
Tárogató (shawm) 299
Tartold 87, 90
Tatchang-ku (drum) 223
Tayuc (bowed instrument) 201
Tchun-so (end-blown flute) 234
Temir-komuz (jew's harp) 208
Temur chur (jew's harp) 208
Tenasin (sistrum) 265
Tenor saxophone 166
Tenor trombone 26, 171, 178, 179, 190
Tenor viol 117, 193
Tenor (treble) viola 194
Tenor violin 133, 135, 194
Tenorbass trombone 179
Teponaxtli (slit drum) 247
Terpodion 148, 152
Terzheckelphone 171
Theorbed lute (theorbo) 108, 109, 150
Theorbo 124
Thereminvox 330, 339
Ti (side-blown flute) 216, 219, 220
Tibia 51, 53
Tien-ku (drum) 223
Timbales 13, 196
Tin canh (gong) 238
Tiple (guitar) 249
Tiple (shawm) 311
Tiplipitom 211
Tjango (drum) 230, 234
Tjempelung (dulcimer) 242
Tjurju (trumpet) 277
Tomtom 196
Torupill (bagpipe) 291
Torvi (trumpet) 277
Tournebout 90
Trautonium 330
Treble viol (pardessus de viole) 134, 139, 194
Tres (guitar) 249
Treschotka (cog rattle) 281
Triangle 13, 61, 65, 78, 80, 117, 155, 161
Tricballac (tricca-ballaca) (clappers) 307
Trikitixa (concertina) 311
Trimitas (trumpet) 291
Tro-khmer (fiddle) 238
Tromba clarina (clarina) 69, 116
Trombone 13, 28, 85, 94, 101, 103, 104, 112, 116, 117, 178, 190
Trumpet 13, 26, 34, 38, 39, 41, 42, 49, 51, 54, 55, 60, 67, 68, 76–78, 86, 101, 103, 113, 116, 117, 119, 174, 178, 179, 209, 210, 228, 233, 245, 246, 251, 253, 260, 269, 277, 291, 341
Trumpet marine (tromba marina) 75, 77, 78
Tuba 13, 26, 28, 54, 67, 173, 180, 181
Tubri (tiktiri, jingivi) (clarinet) 200, 201
Tubular bells 13, 164, 341
Tubular flute 246

Tulumi (bagpipe) 273
Tupan (bass drum) 302
Turkish cymbal 162, 200
Txistu (flute) 305, 311
Tympani 13, 68, 111, 196, 184, 343
Tympanon (natulum, cithara) 51, 72
Tyrrhenian trumpet 49
Una (gong chimes) 234
Ubo (lute) 262
'Ud (lute) 213, 269, 270, 273
Ukeke (musical bow) 245
Ukulele (guitar) 245
Unfretted clavichord 110
Upright piano 13
Uranion 148
Valved trombone 179
Valved trumpet 145, 174
Verimbao (jew's harp) 311
Vertical (end-blown) flute 21, 36, 37, 62, 78, 216, 239, 262
Vessel flute 245, 246, 250
Vibraphone 13, 166, 176, 341
Vicitra-vína 202
Vielle (hurdy-gurdy) 310
Vihuela (guitar) 76
Vína 202, 205
Viol 15, 108, 109, 194
Viola 137, 194, 343
Viola alta 194
Viola bastarda (lyra viol) 133, 139
Viola da braccio 104, 109
Viola d'amour (viola da more) 140, 141, 343
Viola da gamba 100, 104, 109, 112, 135, 137, 139, 142, 143
Viola pomposa 134, 139
Violao (guitar) 249, 254
Violetta 141
Violin 9, 11, 94, 104, 106, 108, 112, 121, 122, 127, 131, 133, 135, 137–139, 144, 150, 191, 194, 292, 308, 324, 325, 343
Violin automatophones 325
Violino piccolo (piccolo violin) 133, 135, 137
Violon ténor 194
Violoncello 104, 137, 146, 150, 194
Virginal 96, 97, 110, 126
Wagnerian tuba 182, 342
Waisted drum (binnacle drum, hourglass drum, double goblet drum) 21, 25, 31, 79, 234
Waldteufel (ronker, bourdon, hoo'r) (friction idiophone) 309
Waleko (cai-sinh) (clappers) 237
Walking stick violin 172
Wambi (lute) 262
Whistle 20, 21, 246, 248, 253, 256, 257, 286
Whistle flute 19, 283, 284
Whistling pot 248, 303
White cornett 78, 96, 98, 104
Wind-cap shawm 84, 92, 116
Wind-cap woodwinds 88, 116
Xylophone 13, 156, 167, 217, 233, 235, 236, 238–240, 242, 258, 259, 302, 341
Yamato-goto (wagon) (zither) 227, 230
Yang-ch'in (dulcimer) 219
Yao-ku (drum) 223, 225
Yeh-ch'in (moon guitar) 221, 224
Yelo (palo roncador) (bull-roarers) 253
Yün-luo (gong chimes) 217, 234
Zamr (mizmar) (shawm) 42, 62, 266, 267, 274
Zhaleyka (flute) 284, 286
Zither 161, 191, 207, 213, 219, 221, 227, 229–231, 245, 257, 268, 270, 273, 276, 278, 281, 298, 308, 310
Zukra (bagpipe) 269
Zummarah (double clarinet) 267
Zurla (shawm) 298
Zurna (shawm) 211, 272, 273